Philanthropists & Foundation Globalization

Philanthropists & Foundation Globalization

Joseph C. Kiger

Routledge
Taylor & Francis Group

LONDON AND NEW YORK

First published 2008 by Transaction Publishers

2 Park Square, Milton Park, Abingdon, Oxfordshire OX14 4RN
711 Third Avenue, New York, NY 10017

Routledge is an imprint of the Taylor & Francis Group, an informa business

First issued in paperback 2017

Library of Congress Catalog Number: 2007037643

Library of Congress Cataloging-in-Publication Data

Kiger, Joseph Charles.
    Philanthropists and foundation globalization / Joseph C. Kiger.
        p. cm.
    Includes bibliographical references and index.
    ISBN 978-1-4128-0673-2 (alk. paper)
        1. Philanthropists—United States—Biography.   2.   Charities—United States—History.   3.   Endowments—United States—History.   4.   Globalization.   I. Title.

HV27.K54   2007
361.70973—dc22   2007037643

ISBN 13: 978-1-4128-0673-2 (hbk)
ISBN 13: 978-1-138-51305-1 (pbk)

Contents

Preface

Over the years the American public's perception of philanthropy and the place of foundations in that context has generally been vague and inchoate. A fair Hollywood portrayal of foundations can be seen in the Frank Capra film, *Mr. Deeds Goes to Town*. Gary Cooper plays the role of a shy and learned man who inherits a foundation and is being preyed upon by opportunists. He and his staff, consisting of some dozen men, have been compiling a voluminous linguistic encyclopedia for a considerable number of years as the film begins. The subsequent plot revolves around the introduction of a beautiful, practical, and liberated female, portrayed by Jean Arthur, into this endeavor. Following numerous and amusing episodes the two main characters grow close and declare their love for each other. The film ends with the intimation that all hands will continue the work of the foundation on into the future.

Contributing greatly to such public perception of philanthropy in general, and our foundations in particular, is the relatively sparse serious literature dealing with them, much of that quantitative and statistical in nature. In fact, the publication of *Philanthropy in America, A Comprehensive Historical Encyclopedia,*[1] did not happen until 2004. Little attention has been given to the motives or reasons spurring philanthropists to engage in creating foundations and such motivation needs a historical and comparative analysis. Also, major investigations and studies of them, together with the ancillary national, regional, and international organizations set up in part to facilitate such study, have received little consideration. Finally, which of our major foundations began to cross our national boundaries in their giving and where and when they did so and for what reasons has received even less attention. In short, while some extant literature on these topics is informative, there is not much of it available and it suffers from a lack of interpretation from a historical standpoint. A sampling of literature dealing with American philanthropy abroad and the role of our foundations in such philanthropy provide ample reason for these conclusions.

Historian Merle Curti's *American Philanthropy Abroad* (1963) is a comprehensive historical work on international philanthropy, however it emphasizes individual, governmental, religious and other giving and almost ignores foundations involvement. The book concentrates only thirty pages on foundation giving abroad. Andrew Carnegie's personal and foundation giving abroad is discussed but the Carnegie Corporation of New York does not even appear as an entry in the book's index. Warren Weaver's *U.S. Philanthropic Foundations Their History, Structure, Management, and Record* (1967) deals in a limited way with the international philanthropy of U.S. foundations. Joseph C. Kiger's *Philanthropic Foundations in the Twentieth Century* (2000) allots only its last two chapters to the topic.

Some edited or compiled works consist of articles of differing quality which bear, to a greater or lesser degree, on foundations international activities. Helmut K. Anheier and Stefan Toepler's *Private Funds, Public Purpose: Philanthropic Foundations in International Perspective* (1999), does deal with foundations from an international perspective but presents little on U.S. foundations. Also, in the work, accounts of our foundations are primarily treated on a comparative basis with those located in foreign countries and in other areas of the world. Pablo Eisenberg is a thirty-year gadfly of foundations. He and others of his persuasion ignore the admonition that it is easier to make a million dollars than to give it away wisely. He compiled many of his articles and speeches over that period in his 242-page *Challenges for Nonprofits and Philanthropy. The Courage to Change. Three Decades of Reflections by Pablo Eisenberg* (2005). Only three articles in a section, "Philanthropy's Global Role" pp. 131-138, deal with that role. Also, the major article in the section is a call for the creation of a group, financed by foundations, to study the subject. Brian H. Smith's *More Than Altruism: The Politics of Private Foreign Aid* (1990) in dealing with our private voluntary/nongovernmental organizations providing aid abroad contains only a few brief comments on those of our philanthropic foundations and these are restricted to the Carnegie, Ford, and Rockefeller foundations. *Charity, Philanthropy, and Civility in American History* (2003) by Lawrence J. Friedman and Mark D. McGarvie consists of essays by seventeen authors providing a historical spectrum on American philanthropy, and many of them include discussion and comment on our foundations. Regarding international activities one of the essays is devoted entirely to a comparison of European and American foundations. Still, as Friedman admits: "Even with the space constraints of this volume, the editors and authors could probably have done a good deal more to describe international contexts for American philanthropic traditions" (p. 16).

Some institutional works on foundation philanthropy abroad do deal with it. They deal with individual or a few foundations in their general area of interest and/or with a particular country or countries and regions abroad. Raymond B. Fosdick's, *The Story of the Rockefeller Foundation* (1952) provides a balanced description of domestic and foreign activities of that foundation but, of course, in an institutional setting. Some writers, when it comes to documenting foundation histories, typically devote little or no time at all to a foundation's foreign activities. For example, Ellen Condliffe Lagemann, in her history *The Politics of Knowledge; The Carnegie Corporation, Philanthropy, and Public Policy* (1989), flatly states, "I decided early on not to consider Carnegie Corporation grants outside the United States" (p. 329). Richard Magat's *Ford Foundation at Work: Philanthropic Choices, Methods, and Styles* (1979) includes some description of the Foundation's international activities but as McGeorge Bundy stated in his Foreword to the book it is a "limited essay" and "no full-scale history of the Ford Foundation exists" (p. 17). This statement incidentally is still true. There are a number of autobiographical and biographical works where the history of a foundation or foundations is discussed. Most of these biographical accounts, however, do not concentrate on this aspect of the subject's life. A notable exception is John Ensor Harr and Peter J. Johnson's *The Rockefeller Century* (1987) that centers on the philanthropic history of the Rockefeller family members from 1889 to the 1950s.

Turning to the writings about the motives of those setting up foundations and tying them to the international setting, a persistent theme has been the simplistic view that the Carnegie, Rockefeller, Ford and other large foundations were created in the twentieth century and on into the twenty-first to prevent more benign and just (Marxist/Communist) economic and political measures from being implemented in the United States. Concomitantly, the strategic grants dispensed by these foundations would ensure dominance of a United States exploited by these same philanthropists and their successor trustees and staff, familial or otherwise. In interpreting our foundation activity abroad these same views, as to motive and operations, are advanced. Thus, at their origin and since, such foundations were designed to work hand in glove with corporations and governments, here and abroad, to exploit the downtrodden masses of both worlds. Much of such writing, although sometimes ignoring and sometimes denying, reflects theories advanced by Marxists such as Antonio Gramsci. Edward H. Berman's *The Influence of the Carnegie, Ford, and Rockefeller Foundations on American Foreign Policy, The Ideology of Philanthropy* (1983), is an example of this interpretation.[2] At best, authors of this ilk praise some foundations, usually smaller, whom they label "progressive" and condemn most of the larger ones designated "conservative" for often unacknowledged program failures both here and abroad. For example, journalist Mark Dowie emphasizes the view that the Rockefeller and Ford foundations' sponsorship of the "Green Revolution" agricultural program in foreign countries was a capitalistic response to Communist-inspired insurrections. Even though the program resulted in a tremendous increase in food production, hunger still remained a problem and thus the program was considered a failure.[3] One can only conclude that such authors believe that they could do a much better job of dispensing foundation money if only they were put in charge. Diplomatic historian Akira Iriye questions such interpretations but touches on the international activities of U.S. foundations in his most recent work in a general way.[4]

Philanthropic motives for going international with foundation activity are of particular interest in the contemporary era because such activity has accelerated and vastly increased since World War II. A 2000 study of giving by U.S. foundations by the Foundation Center, in collaboration with the Council on Foundations states, "In 1998, it reached an estimated $1.6 billion, a 66 percent rise over 1994 levels."[5] A follow-up study conducted by the Center/Council in 2004, in drawing much the same growth pattern, concluded:

> International giving by the nation's grantmaking foundations peaked at an estimated $3.3 billion in 2001, and then slipped to $3.2 billion in 2002. Nonetheless, 2002 giving was roughly double the $1.6 billion estimated for 1998. Adjusted for inflation, international giving climbed 79 percent over this period, far exceeding the 42 percent gain in overall giving. International giving in 2003 decreased again in 2003 to $3 billion but can be expected to rebound modestly in 2004.[6]

Such growth has been tellingly reflected in recent popular news journals. In the July 24, 2000 issue of *Time* magazine the cover is entitled "The New Philanthropists" and portrays three contemporary American givers, Bill Gates, George Soros, and Ted Turner. The articles therein dwell on the fact that they then devoted substantial amounts of their money to foreign giving or giving in this country for international purposes or projects established through their foundations. Again, the

April 18, 2005, issue of *Time* is devoted to a discussion of the world's 100 most influential people, among them Bill Gates. A major portion of the article on Gates is devoted to his philanthropy and particularly his international giving. Then the December 26, 2005-January 2, 2006 issue of *Time* has Bill and Melinda Gates on its front cover and devotes an article to their international giving. Yet it appears that only some 500 to 600 of the approximately 10,000 of U.S. larger independent foundations now in existence make grants abroad and most of the funds granted are those made by foundations in the very large asset category such as those of Gates, Soros, and Turner and others included inside this study.

At the outset of this work, brief cogent definitions of the terminology related to American foundations are in order. A foundation is a non-governmental, not-for-profit organization with assets provided by a donor or a group of donors, under the control of an independent board of directors or trustees that dispenses its grants to establish or aid socially useful activities. Within this definition, four major types or classifications of foundations have developed: (1) independent, (2) company, (3) operating, and (4) community. This work is wholly concerned with the first type.

> The independent foundations have usually been set up by an individual or the members of a family and thus have sometimes been referred to or categorized as, "family foundations." Most of the larger and better known foundations in the United States and worldwide have been of the independent type and, when properly set up and organized, have the ability to dispense large or small sums of money to individuals and to organizations such as educational and research institutions, hospitals, libraries, museums, and so on, to enable them to carry out a wide variety of programs and projects enjoying the favor of the donor or their successors.[7]

A distinction between charity and philanthropy must also be made. Charity involves giving to ameliorate social ills caused by wars, earthquakes, famines, floods, disease or hunger. Philanthropy involves giving that attempts to solve the underlying causes of human distress and/or to create new knowledge. Wealthy givers who were the pioneers in the establishment and operation of the larger foundations set up by Americans drew distinctions between charity and philanthropy and generally embraced the latter as the best and most efficient way of giving. Early on, for example, John D. Rockefeller, Sr. stated:

> "The best philanthropy, the help that does the most good and the least harm, the help that nourishes civilization at its very roots, that most widely disseminates health, righteousness, and happiness, is not what is usually called charity."[8]

Andrew Carnegie's and Mrs. Russell Sage's writings reflect the same viewpoint.[9] Here again, however, this distinction has received relatively little attention in intellectual and academic circles and even less among the public at large. Although the foundations they created and our other foundations established later have given substantial amounts for charitable/ameliorative purposes, the major thinking, projects, and activities of many of them at their inception or since have centered on the preventive aspect of philanthropy. This is particularly apparent in recent years. Paradoxically, the charitable aspect of their giving certainly appears to provide additional refutation of the cultural imperialism motive for giving mentioned above. A few of the many examples are the some $22 million in European World War I relief provided by the Rockefeller Foundation following that war.[10] The Ford Foundation similarly aided there following World War II.

It is difficult to define international or foreign giving and differing interpretations, including those presented by others cited in this work, have been provided over the years. Although inclusion or exclusion in some cases would be open to argument, the major criteria utilized for inclusion in this volume as foreign or international activity by our foundations is that the grants made by them are to individuals, organizations, or projects within or outside the United States that are concerned or deal with projects centered or conducted in areas outside the United States. To be more specific, such a criteria would include our foundations' grants to U.S. organizations, universities, academies and think tanks to be used by these grantees for specific international purposes. Foundation grants to such organizations for domestic purposes, i.e., for the direct benefit of U.S. inhabitants, would not meet the international criteria and would not be included.

Covered in this work are some 50 independent foundations meeting the above criteria and entirely or to a considerable extent so engaged, at their founding or somewhat later, in funding international activities. They include a representative group ranging in asset size from those with millions of dollars to those with billions. Their dates of establishment span the years from the 1860s to 1994. Their geographical places of origin range from east-to-west and north-to-south in the United States. The group is also representative of the gender and genealogical diversity of the individuals establishing foundations and the differing methods by which such individuals acquired the wealth to do so. A few exceptions to the international funding criteria have been made, such as the Russell Sage Foundation and George Peabody's Peabody Education Fund, because of their important pioneering role in the history of

U.S. foundations. George Soros' many funds are considered herein as one Open Society Foundation. Parenthetically, some have argued that, strictly speaking, his many philanthropies do not meet the foundation definition. To repeat, domestic programs or projects of the foundations studied are not considered here although some may be mentioned when they are the forerunners of or ancillary to operations centered outside the United States. This work, therefore, studies these philanthropists and their philanthropies and presents, when available, motives and reasons advanced by the founders, successors, or others for setting them up and their engaging in or departing from foreign activities. Descendants or family members of the founders are discussed when they appear to have played a role in the foundation's establishment or activities.

Interspersed at appropriate chronological points in this story are detailed accounts of the major investigations and studies of foundations that have taken place throughout the twentieth century. Their inquiries and speculations form a unique and major concentration and depository of information about our foundations, particularly the larger ones; incidentally providing insight into varying public perceptions or relative lack thereof for the increasing globalization of their activities.

Also provided is identification and a chronological account of our major foundations' activities in Central and Eastern Europe up to and following the collapse of the Communist regimes there in the 1980s. Discussed are their role in that collapse and their part in the encouragement and funding in whole or in part of major non- or semi- governmental organizations in the region since then. Generally, such funding concentrated on and was designed to encourage the establishment/resurrection of "civil society" in Central and Eastern Europe.

In summary, this study encompasses the following three interrelated aspects of foundation history. First, biographical-historical profiles of the founding philanthropists and their heirs engaged in international giving are presented. They are discussed in chronological order from Peabody to Gates, generally based on their establishment of a major foundation. Tied in with this examination are brief presentations of the background and reasons for their development and implementation of programs in, or some cases later out of, the international area. No attempt has been made to present detailed descriptions of such programs over the years but such information can be found in the annual reports and other publications issued by most of them.[11] Second, the major governmental and non-governmental investigations and studies of foundations including domestic ones,[12] and also foreign ones[13] in which U.S. participants played a prominent role, spanning the period 1912 to the present, are chronicled. Third, a chronological study of foundation developments and activities in Central and Eastern Europe at the close of the twentieth century is made. Although duplicative in some cases, it is hoped that this particular study will provide a historical account of some U.S. foundations international activity in a particular region in a specific time period and the accomplishments accruing therefrom. The volume closes with a brief analytical and interpretive conclusion.

Sources on which the work is based include major available autographical and biographical accounts by the foundation founders, their successors, or those in control of the foundations covered. It also includes foundation reports and documents concerning foundations located here and abroad. Governmental and private documents and reports were utilized, particularly the previously mentioned major U.S. and foreign investigations and studies of foundations. Secondary sources utilized were books and articles published both here and abroad about foundations and the recipients of their aid. Extensive use was made of documentary material located at the Foundation Center, New York, New York together with that held at the Philanthropic Studies Archives, Center on Philanthropy, IUPUI; Indianapolis, Indiana.

The author is grateful for the courtesies offered to him at both centers by the staff there. In the case of the Center on Philanthropy, he wishes to thank the officials who granted him a Ruth Lilly Archives Research Award which defrayed most of the costs associated with his travel to and research at the Center.

Various administrative officials at the University of Mississippi were supportive of the author while he was engaged in the research, writing, and publication of this book. In this regard, he is particularly obliged to Chancellor Robert C. Khayat, Vice Chancellor Carolyn E. Staton, and Dean Glenn W. Hopkins. My thanks are due Michael F. Metcalf, Executive Director of the Croft Institute for International Studies, University of Mississippi, who appointed me Senior Research Associate and provided me with office space together with communication access and reproduction facilities at the Institute. I am deeply indebted to Dean and Director of University Libraries Julia M. Rholes and the staff members of the University of Mississippi Library, particularly Reference Librarian Royce Kurtz and Interlibrary Loan Librarian Martha E. Swan, for their aid in bringing the work to completion.

The author is grateful to numerous knowledgeable individuals, including several past and present U.S. foundation officials, who were consulted during the conduct of the study. Special thanks are due President Sara Engelhardt of the Foundation Center who very kindly critically reviewed portions of the manuscript. Her comments and suggestions were invaluable. Finally, my wife Jean read the entire manuscript and I am indebted to her for this and other help too considerable to specify.

Notes

1. Dwight F. Burlingame (ed.), *Philanthropy in America, A Comprehensive Historical Encyclopedia.* ABC-CLIO, Santa Barbara, California, 2004.
2. Other earlier and later examples of the genre presenting this same interpretation are: Horace Coon, *Money to Burn: What the Great American Philanthropic Foundations Do with Their Money,* Longmans, Green and Co., New York, 1938 and Robert F. Arnove (ed.), *Philanthropy and Cultural Imperialism: The Foundations at Home and Abroad* (1980).
3. Mark Dowie, *American Foundations: An Investigative History,* The MIT Press, Cambridge, Massachusetts, 2001, pp. 105-140.
4. Akira Iriye, *Global Community: The Role of International Organizations in the Making of the Contemporary World,* University of California Press, Berkeley, California, 2001. See particularly, pp. 12 and 80.
5. Loren Renz, Josefina Samson-Atienza, et al, *International Grantmaking II: An Update on U.S. Foundation Trends,* Foundation Center, New York, 2000, p.1.
6. Loren Renz, Josefina Atienza, et al, *International Grantmaking III: An Update on U.S. Foundation Trends,* Foundation Center, New York, 2004, p. x.
7. Joseph C. Kiger, *Philanthropic Foundations in the Twentieth Century,* Greenwood Press, Westport, Connecticut, London, 2000, pp. 3. For a recent succinct account of the last three and other differences or distinctions in categorizing foundations, see *Ibid.* pp. 3-5.
8. John D. Rockefeller, *Random Reminiscences of Men and Events*, Doubleday, Page & Company, New York, 1909, pp. 141-142.
9. See, for example, Andrew Carnegie, "Wealth," *The North American Review,* 148, 1889, pp. 653-654 and "The Best Fields of Philanthropy" *Ibid.*, pp. 682-698.
10. Raymond B. Fosdick, *The Story of the Rockefeller Foundation,* Harper &. Brothers, New York, 1952, p. 28.
11. The twentieth century published back annual reports and other material of these and other major foundations are located in the Philanthropic Studies Archives at the Center on Philanthropy, Indiana Purdue University, Indianapolis, Indiana. Since the beginning of the twenty-first century such documents on individual major foundations are usually to be found on the computer internet.
12. These are: the Walsh Commission (1912-1916; Lindemann Study (1936); Harrison and Andrews Study (1946) Buchanan Committee (1950); Cox Committee (1953); Reece Committee (1954); Gaither Committees, (1954-1960); Treasury Committee (1965); Patman Committees (1962-1969); House and Senate Committees (1969), Peterson Commission (1969-1970); Filer Commission (1973-1977); and Foundation Center/Council on Foundation Studies (1997 and 2000).
13. These are Royaumont (1961), Berlin (1964), and Ditchley (1966 and 1972).

Introduction

The modern American foundation, particularly those with the largest assets, as an instrumentality for charitable and philanthropic giving, is in many ways a unique and complex social, economic, and political institution with deep roots in the past. At the start of any degree of civilization consistent patterns of charitable giving and rudimentary forms of foundations begin to emerge. Once enough property or wealth beyond primitive human needs is accumulated some of it begins to be set aside for what the donors of such wealth considered worthwhile purposes. Such wealth was accumulated in China and Egypt and other civilizations of the Near East at an early period in human history.

Chinese documents show that provision for the care of orphans and destitute people was being made around 2000 B.C.[1] Regarding ancient Egypt, it is asserted:

> Fourteen hundred years before the Christian era the Pharaohs of Egypt were thus setting aside funds in perpetuity. Inscriptions show contracts wherein the Pharaoh is the donor of specified kinds and amounts of wealth to a college of priests who, for a designated portion of the income, obligated the order to use the remainder to keep the tomb perpetually protected and the religious ceremonies observed.... The Chaldean civilization had almost identical practices as is shown by a clay tablet, dated 1280 B.C., reciting how King Marouttach bought certain lands from his vassals, built a temple on it, dedicated the whole to the god Marduk, and endowed a college of priests to operate it[2]

From the earliest times the records of the Hebrew people show that they, too, set aside wealth for charitable purposes. "The principle of giving the tithe, or tenth, was firmly established among the Hebrews, beginning with Abram's gift of the tithe to Melchizedek. It was ordinarily a religious offering, paid in kind or money, but sometimes it was a gift to the poor"[3] Many centuries later, the Jewish philosopher Maimonides about 1180 A.D. listed the following precepts for best giving:

There are eight degrees in the giving of charity, one higher than the other.

The highest degree, than which there is nothing higher, is to take hold of a Jew who has been crushed and to give him a gift or a loan, or to enter into a partnership with him, or to find work for him, and thus to put him on his feet so that he will not be dependent on his fellow-men....

Lower in degree to this is the one who gives charity to the poor, but does not know to whom he gives it, nor does the poor man know from whom he receives it.... Related to this degree is the giving to the [public] alms-chest....

Lower in degree to this is when the giver knows to whom he gives, but the poor does not know from whom he receives. An example of this is the great scholars who used to go about in secret and leave their money at the door of the poor....

Lower in degree to this is when the poor knows from whom he receives but the giver does not know to whom he gives.

Lower in degree to this is when one gives even before he is asked.

Lower in degree to this is when one gives after he has been asked.

Lower in degree to this is when one gives less than he should but graciously.

Lower in degree to this is when one gives grudgingly.[4]

Plato's famous Academy received an endowment from him with the proceeds to be used for the benefit of his followers. Established in 347 B.C., the Academy and its operations continued on until its demise about 700 A.D. Prior to the birth of Christ, the Ptolemaic rulers of Egypt provided continuous funding for the operation of the famous Alexandrian Library and Museum which endured down to its ultimate destruction in the eighth century A.D. Rome's rise to power in the ancient world was accompanied by similar benefactions conferred by the wealthy. Not only were gifts and funds set aside for religious purposes and the care of the sick and needy but beneficences were also provided for larger purposes. Thus during the Antonine period of Roman rule, Herodes Atticus, a Greek,

built a water supply system for Troas, endowed a giant stadium at Athens, and restored to its ancient magnificence the theater of Pericles; he provided a temple to Neptune and a theatre at Corinth, a stadium at Delphi, endowed a bath at Thermopylea, and a system of aqueducts at Canusium in Italy. Inscriptions indicate that the people of Epirus, Thessaly, Euboea, Boeotia, and other cities of Greece and Asia Minor gratefully styled Herodes Atticus their benefactor.[5]

The advent of Christianity as a religion marked a singular and important chapter in the history of charity/philanthropy and the emergence of foundations. As one specialist on philanthropy and foundations flatly stated, "The teachings of Jesus set up a new and lofty personal ethic for givers, which became the most important single influence on the philanthropy of the Western world."[6] An equally important chapter in that history was the spread of this teaching throughout Western Europe through the aegis of the Roman Catholic Church. From the first decades of its existence the Church had set aside funds to be used for charitable purposes. A pivotal moment in its early expansion was the Roman Emperor Constantine's reign from 324-337 A.D. which was marked by his tolerance of Christianity and his issuance of decrees which were favorable to Christians and the Christian Church. The most important, from the charity/philanthropic standpoint, were those which legally recognized the Church as a philanthropic foundation and that forbade the shifting of funds provided it for purposes other than the good ones envisaged by Constantine and other donors of such funds. From that time forward various measures to see that the Church made proper use of the funds entrusted to it actually served to strengthen it as the essentially sole organized means of doing well. For example, in the sixth century A.D. Emperor Justinian's *Corpus Juris Civilis* (the Justinian Code) established certain legal safeguards regarding the dispensing of funds and the operation of bequests under Church supervision. Thus these charitable funds entrusted to the Roman Catholic Church grew at an increasing rate and eventually the burgeoning medieval Church became the supreme charitable and philanthropic institution of Western Europe.

In Eastern Europe the history of the Greek Orthodox Church paralleled, to a considerable degree, that of the Roman Catholic Church in its emergence as the preeminent charitable/philanthropic institution there. Only a few organizations bearing some elements of secular foundations or trusts, however, were set up there by the nineteenth century. The chaos and turmoil associated with World War I in Central and Eastern European countries was capped by the establishment of a Communist government in Russia. World War II also saw the establishment of similar governments. For ideological and fiscal reasons, these Communist governments, to a large degree, stripped both the Roman Catholic Church and the Greek Orthodox Church of much of their previous wealth and charitable functions and almost completely eliminated secular foundations and trusts under such regimes.

The emergence of Islam in the Near East in the seventh century A.D. saw the spread of a religion and civilization throughout much of the Mediterranean area and beyond that was in many respects unlike that of Europe. However, its founder Mohammed early on advocated the establishment by believers of *vaqf* (a word derived from Arabic meaning "to stand still"), entities created in perpetuity upon which wealth was to be settled. The income derived from such entities was to be given and used for purposes considered good and praiseworthy by the Islamic religion.

Grades of goodness, although not as detailed as those spelled out for Judaism by Maimonides, were recognized. First and most important, was the donor's remembering of, and benevolence to, members of his own family. Second, was wealth to be provided for the support and promulgation of the Islamic religion. Third, were moneys set aside for the sick and the poor plus other programs aiding and helping the general populace. From the seventh century onward to the present day, despite periodic efforts by governing authorities to control or eliminate them, wherever Islam has spread, Mohammedans have established them in great numbers. A recent work[7] by a Turkish historian shows that they presently hold and control great wealth in such modern-day countries as Turkey, India, Pakistan, Saudi Arabia, Malaysia, the Philippines, and Iran. In the last country, for example, the largest *vaqf* there was created, following the revolution of 1963, from the assets confiscated from the deposed Pahlawi family. This same work, moreover, advances the claim that: "Having lost all contact with the ancient wold [*sic.*] Medieval Europe had to become acquainted with philanthropic endowments through the Islamic waqf system" and that "the origins of the English trusts can almost certainly be traced back to the Islamic waqf system."[8] Regardless of perceived origins of foundations, these earlier-described philanthropic developments in the Near Eastern and Mediterranean areas were superseded in historical importance by those in Western Europe, particularly North Western Europe, toward the close of the medieval period.

Returning to Western Europe, one of the prevailing threads in the history of the Western European medieval period, roughly the time from the sixth to sixteenth centuries A.D., was the struggle between the Church and secular governments, particularly the emerging nation states toward the last centuries of this period. Usually viewed from a political, religious, economic, or military standpoint, this struggle took place also in the charitable and philanthropic area.

The charitable motives and purposes for which medieval wealth was to be distributed were a subtle mixture of the spiritual and secular. The medieval Church was, at least fundamentally, a spiritual organization, and in its fostering and operation of funds entrusted to it, the Church naturally tended to emphasize the former rather than the latter. While the medieval union of Church, state, royalty, nobility, and peasants, in its inter-relationships usually designated the feudal system, held together there are few instances of charitable gifts made by the wealthy to institutions and groups which can be viewed as completely outside Church control.

Nevertheless, as the relative power and wealth of the emerging nation states and its rulers in Western Europe grew, the Church's philanthropic role was correspondingly diminished. Of equal importance was the gradual emergence toward the close of the medieval period of a group we today call the middle class, centering in the then diminutive but slowly growing towns. Tied in with this emergence was the creation of guilds and companies in these towns that gradually engaged in philanthropic activity falling outside the control of the Church.

Out of this evolving and complicated situation several major shifts in philanthropic thinking and action began to occur. First, there was a change in giving emphasis from the spiritual to the secular, i.e., rather than concentrating on the next life, increasing attention was devoted to the amelioration of suffering in this one. Second, there was an accompanying diminution of the Church's virtual monopoly on charitable getting and giving. Third, a relatively new and independent institution, much more clearly defined than those previously described, the trust or foundation, comes into being largely to implement these shifts. These three changes first took place in England. The first two spread later to the rest of Western Europe, but the third only in a fragmentary manner and, as has been related, often truncated by reversals. Therefore, the really tangible history of the emergence and development of the large modern American foundation initially centers on England.

The Roman Catholic Church, with its emphasis upon the spiritual model or mode of charity and philanthropy practiced in the rest of Western Europe, prevailed there before the Norman conquest of England in 1066. After the conquest, the newly established nobility gradually rejected the idea that charitable holdings and giving were the prime concerns of the Church and outside the purview and even control of the state, i.e., their authority. Closely tied in with this change was a slowly growing shift in emphasis in the creation of bequests and the dispensing of wealth for charitable and philanthropic purposes. Some donors, particularly among the emerging artisan, merchant, and commercial classes, began to devote some of their accumulated wealth for good works in this world rather than using such wealth to attempt to ensure their salvation or that of others in the next. This shift can be detected in William Langland's fourteenth-century poem *The Vision of Piers the Plowman,* which approved of secular good works. In the poem, benefactors seeking to do good with their wealth were advised to:

> (…) build hospitals, helping the sick,
> Or roads that are rotten full rightly repair,
> Or bridges, when broken, to build up anew,
> Well marry poor maidens, or make them nuns,
> Poor people and pris'ners with food to provide,
> Set scholars to school, or some other crafts,
> And relieve the religious, enhancing their rents.[9]

By the 1530s these shifts in thought are among the factors leading to King Henry VIII's break with the Roman Catholic Church and the confiscation by the crown of that Church's wealth—which has been estimated as high as one-half of the total wealth of England at the time. Much of that confiscated property was diverted from the charitable purposes carried on by the Church and served to enrich Henry and succeeding monarchs, together with much of the English nobility and gentry. Still, considerable portions of this wealth were eventually used to establish trusts and foundations for beneficent purposes by the crown, nobility, and gentry. These changes in thought and action are clearly revealed in the passage in 1601 of the Elizabethan Statute of Charitable Uses. The Statute provided that foundations could be set up for the following purposes:

> Some for relief of aged, impotent and poor people, some for maintenance of sick and maimed soldiers and mariners, schools of learning, free schools, and scholars in universities, some for repair of bridges, ports, havens, causeways, churches, sea-banks and highways, some for education and preferment of orphans, some for or towards relief, stock or maintenance for houses of correction, some for marriages of poor maids, some for supportation, aid and help of young tradesmen, handicraftsmen and persons decayed, and others for relief or redemption of prisoners or captives, and for aid or ease of any poor inhabitants concerning payment of … taxes.[10]

This Statute, authorized and promulgated by the state, not the Church, in addition to spelling out those primarily secular charitable and philanthropic uses considered good, also provided for the legal safeguarding of gifts and bequests to foundations created for carrying them out. It is for these reasons that the Statute of Charitable Uses is universally referred to as the cornerstone of English law concerning foundations and trusts.[11]

In the centuries that followed, Englishmen, particularly the rising middle classes, devoted an increasing amount of their wealth to charitable and philanthropic purposes; more and more through the foundations they set up. Thus, historians of English philanthropy state that as early as the seventeenth century: "the failure of a London merchant to settle some substantial and conspicuous charitable trust or gift was generally regarded as little short of shocking unless there had been a grievous wasting of the estate because of age, ill-health or commercial misfortune."[12]

Also, by the 1770s "English charity had already taken on the dignity of a national tradition."[13] Furthermore, in England, relatively few legal restrictions were then or subsequently enacted by the state to hamper the creation of such foundations or to restrict their operation. In contrast, in France, particularly after the French Revolution, the accompanying disestablishment of the Roman Catholic Church and the almost simultaneous adoption of the Napoleonic legal system saw the creation and operation of foundations subject to mandatory governmental authorization and controls which, in large measure, account for the paucity of foundations there.[14] The statutes and legislation affecting foundations in other states of Western Europe have fallen somewhere between these two diverging governmental attitudes towards foundations. Other areas of the world, such as the Asia Pacific nations, have generally followed the more restrictive policy regarding foundations. In Japan, for example, although post-World War II U.S. influences brought some liberalizing modifications, the fields of activity of Japanese foundations still suffer from restrictive legal statutes. The author of a brief history of the Toyota Foundation, for example, noted the "disadvantages" accruing to that foundation when it decided to provide major support for the humanities and social sciences rather than concentrating its grantmaking in the natural sciences and technology areas.[15]

The centuries from the 1500s onward were marked by the expansion of Europeans all over the globe and the ensuing establishment of colonies in many areas. They brought with them differing governmental, legal, economic, and social structures and approaches, which in large measure were woven into and made a part of these colonies. Understandably, this was true when it came to philanthropy and is the key explanation for the differing approach and structure of philanthropy and attitudes towards foundations that eventually emerged in these colonies and carried over after most achieved their independence. Regions colonized by Europeans have tended to follow the English or the Napoleonic legal approaches in their establishment and operation. Thus former English colonies, such as Canada, the United States, Australia, and India, copied the freedom of founding and action afforded foundations in the colonizing mother country. The reverse is true in the former colonies of France and to a somewhat lesser degree of other Western European countries, particularly Spain and Portugal. Such Napoleonic legal influence is quite noticeable in the legislation affecting foundations in present-day Latin American countries such as Brazil, Mexico, and Argentina.

By the 1770s the population of the thirteen colonies of what was to become the United States of America consisted primarily of native Indians, imported Africans, and immigrants from England and various other European countries. By that time, however, a majority of the white colonial population was English in origin, and the thirteen colonies generally copied the political, legal, and social structures of England, including the legality and status of philanthropy and philanthropic giving through foundations. During the American Revolution there was a bias against all things British, including its legal system. But, as one scholar observes:

> On the other hand, English law was admittedly the foundation of American legal thinking. American lawyers, however intense their patriotism, could not escape their legal past. They found it necessary to retain the framework of English jurisprudence, cleansed of what they considered to be its most undesirable elements.[16]

Consequently, although there was some dissension, by 1844 the tolerant English attitude toward philanthropy and foundations had become the "dominant" legal position.[17]

During the colonial period the colonists were generally the recipients of aid from the mother country rather than the reverse. In England, for example, Thomas Bray led in the establishment of the Society for the Promotion of Christian Knowledge and Society for the Propagation of the Gospel in Foreign Parts. During the years from 1695 to 1785 he and the Society were responsible for the founding of:

> seventy libraries on the North American continent almost single-handedly. The libraries stretched from Newfoundland in the North to the Carolinas in the South. In addition, he provided libraries in the West Indies, on the coast of Africa, established sixty-one libraries in England and Wales, ten on the Isle of Man, and several in the highlands of Scotland.[18]

From the colonial period through independence and down to the American Civil War, there were only a few noteworthy trusts and foundations established here. Benjamin Franklin established a number of them during the 1700s. For example, he founded the American Philosophical Society in 1743, which has since acquired a substantial endowment and devotes much of its income to grants for scholarly research and can be viewed as a foundation. Still, it is now more properly renowned and designated a learned membership society. The Magdalen Society was founded in 1800 to care for non-virtuous females and is probably the first true foundation established in the United States. The Smithsonian Institution was established in 1846 as the result of a bequest to the

United States by an Englishman, James Smithson, and then and since, although having close financial and political ties to our government, has to a considerable degree functioned as a foundation.

During this period there were also a few notable examples of American philanthropic giving abroad. One of the earliest was that of Benjamin Thompson. Born and reared in New England, Thompson, a Tory, sought refuge in Europe following the American Revolution and in 1784 became a Bavarian official bearing the title of Count Rumford. His philanthropy extended to the Old World as well as to the New in the form of his setting up of a Rumford prize to be awarded by the Royal Society of Great Britain and a similar one to be awarded by the American Academy of Arts and Sciences located in Boston. Also, Thompson's will called for the establishment of a Rumford professorship at Harvard. Another New England Tory, Francis Green, moved to England following the American Revolution and, in large measure because his son was a deaf mute, led in the establishment of a school for teaching the deaf there and a similar one in the United States following his return to Massachusetts in 1803. William Maclure, a Scottish-born naturalist known for his geological work in the United States, bought land in Spain in 1819 with the view of establishing a school for needy people in that country; a project which ultimately failed. A somewhat similar attempt by Maclure to provide educational aid for Mexican Indians suffered the same fate.

With such individual exceptions, giving abroad during the U.S. pre-Civil War period centered on relief provided to foreigners as the result of various catastrophes abroad such as political revolutions, earthquakes, floods, famine or disease. Notable examples included aid provided to the refugees from the Santo Domingo revolution of the 1790s, the victims of earthquakes in Venezuela in 1812, and the starving people of Ireland caused by their potato famines of the 1840s. The financial means in furtherance of such giving was largely provided through the solicitation of funds, by newspaper appeals and meetings from individuals, churches, and other organizations. Such aid was supplemented by appropriations from our city and state governments. In the case of Santo Domingo and Venezuela, despite some congressional opposition arguing that national aid for such purposes to these countries was unconstitutional, the U.S. government appropriated moneys to aid them. Similar appeals at the national level for aid to Ireland, Canada, and other countries, however, failed as the result of political party differences and other reasons.[19] These cases of individual and collective foreign aid were made through means other than a trust or foundation. It remained for the American Civil War to usher in the first significant national and foreign aid being rendered through the establishment and use of such trusts or foundations.

During the 1700s and on into the 1800s various American wars were fought prior to our Civil War—the Revolutionary War, the War of 1812, and the Mexican War. It has also been previously noted that there were few foundations established in the period during which these earlier wars were fought. Those established, furthermore, were overwhelmingly founded for and engaged in domestic rather than foreign activity. In contrast, from the standpoint of the history of larger U.S. foundations and their activity abroad, the Civil War marks the industrial transformation of the United States, the beginnings of the growth of such foundations, and the eventual surge in our international philanthropy through them. This change is a relatively overlooked watermark aspect of our Civil War history. Not until the prosecution and aftermath of that war do we see the creation of the large American foundations with their burgeoning interest and activity in the provision of aid not only at home but also abroad. The rapid accumulations of great wealth in the United States as the result of the tremendous economic expansion during and after the Civil War provided the moneys for the ability to establish large foundations for national as well as international purposes. For the major catalytic agents in this change, however, we must look to the thinking and actions of human beings and in their forefront was a New Englander named George Peabody.

Notes

1.   *The Li. Ki.* A Collection of Treatises on the Rules of Propriety or Ceremonial Usages, Trans. James Legge, in *The Sacred Books of the East,* F. Max Muller (ed.), vol. 27, Clarendon Press, Oxford, England, 1885, pp. 243-244.

2.   Ernest V. Hollis, "Evolution of the Philanthropic Foundation," *Educational Record,* vol.20, October, 1939, pp. 575-576.

3.   F. Emerson Andrews, *Philanthropic Giving.* Russell Sage Foundation, New York, 1950, p. 33.

4.   Jacob R. Marcus, *The Jew in the Medieval World.* Sinai Press, Cincinnati, 1938, pp. 364-365.

5.   Hollis, p. 578.

6.   Andrews, *Philanthropic Giving,* p. 34.

7.   Murat Cizakca, *A History of Philanthropic Foundations: The Islamic World from the Seventh Century to the Present.* Bogazici University Press, Istanbul, Turkey, 2000. See also: F. Emerson Andrews, "On the Nature of the *Vaqf,*" *Foundation News,* vol. 5, September, pp.6-7; Yediyildiz Bahaeddin, *Institution du Vaqf au XVIIIe siecle en Turquie: Etude socio-historique,* Societe d'Historie Turque, Ankara, Turkey, 1985 ; and Joseph C. Kiger, ed., « Vehbi Koc Foundation» »,

International Encyclopedia of Foundations, Greenwood Press, Westport, Connecticut, 1990, pp. 233-238.

8. Murat Cizakca, *A History of Philanthropic Foundations: The Islamic World from the Seventh Century to the Present,* pp. 8, 12.

9. William Langland, *The Vision of Piers the Plowman,* Translated into modern English by W. W. Skeat, Chatto and Windus, London, 1931, p.114.

10. Danby Pickering, *The Statutes at Large* from the Thirty-ninth of Q. Elizabeth to the Twelfth of K. Charles II, inclusive, Printed at Cambridge University, 1763, vol. 7, p. 43.

11. For a succinct discussion of the background for, enactment of, and important impact of the passage of the Statute on the philanthropic history of England and the United States see W K. Jordan, *Philanthropy in England, 1480-1660: A Study of the Changing Pattern of English Social Aspirations,* Russell Sage Foundation, New York, 1959, pp. 109-117.

12. Jordan, *Philanthropy in England,* p. 153.

13. David Owen, *English Philanthropy, 1660-1960,* Belknap Press of Harvard University Press, Cambridge, Massachusetts, 1964, p. 2.

14. For a discussion of this difference, see M. Michel Pomey, "Fondations," *Encyclopedia Universalis,* vol.7, 1971, pp. 134-138. See also Klaus Neuhoff and Uwe Pavel (eds.), *Trusts and Foundations in Europe, A Comparative Survey,* Bedford Square Press, London, England, 1971. Pomey, who also wrote the article on France in the Neuhoff-Pavel work, states therein: "Traditionally, foundations in France have always been regarded with a certain amount of suspicion by Government.... The result is that the charitable, or philanthropic sector (i.e. including the foundations) has never really developed very much," p. 191.

15. Rebecca M. Davis, "Toyota Foundation" in Joseph C. Kiger (ed.), *International Encyclopedia of Foundations,* Greenwood Press, Westport, Connecticut, 1990, p.158. See also, Tadashi Yamamoto, *Survey Reports. Research Institutions, NGOs, and Philanthropy in Asia Pacific,* Japan Center for International Exchange, Tokyo, Japan, 1994.

16. Howard S. Miller, *The Legal Foundations of American Philanthropy, 1776-1844,* The State Historical Society of Wisconsin, Madison, Wisconsin, 1961, p. xi.

17. Ibid., p. 50.

18. Charles T. Laugher, *Thomas Bray's Grand Design, Libraries of the Church of England in America, 1695-1785,* American Library Association, Chicago, Illinois, 1973, p. 77.

19. For a discussion of this period and aspect of American giving abroad, see Merle Curti, *American Philanthropy Abroad: A History,* Rutgers University Press, New Brunswick, New Jersey, 1963, pp. 11-64.

1

Peabody, Sage, Carnegie, and Rockefeller

Peabody

George Peabody rose from a poor background beginning with his birth on February 18, 1795 in South Danvers, Massachusetts. His hometown was later renamed Peabody in his honor in 1868. He started with little formal education and turned into a merchant-financial prince of international stature. In 1814 Peabody moved to Georgetown, in Washington D.C. and entered into a partnership with Elisha Riggs in a dry-goods business. A year later, the firm of Riggs and Peabody relocated to Baltimore, Maryland and Peabody started traveling on the firm's behalf to Europe during the 1820s and 1830s. By then he had taken up permanent residence in London, although he later made six visits to the United States, and retained his U.S. citizenship throughout the rest of his life. During the 1830s he established George Peabody and Company, a very lucrative and successful enterprise dealing in foreign exchange and American securities. He was able to sell abroad the bonds of Maryland and other states at a considerable profit to himself. Thus, he gradually made the transition from merchant to banker during the years between 1837 and 1845, laid the foundation of his fortune, and from that time forward became the leading financial agent between the United States and England. In 1854 another New Englander, Junius Spencer Morgan, became a junior partner in the Peabody Company and made significant contributions to the financial success of the firm. His more famous son, J. Pierpont Morgan, began his banking career as the New York agent for the Company. This eventually led to the formation of New York's J.P. Morgan Company and Morgan's emergence as the dominant financial figure in the United States at the turn of the century.[1] Thus, by the 1860s, Peabody had amassed a great fortune for that time running into the millions of dollars.

A key factor in Peabody's financial success was his acknowledged integrity and honesty in his business dealings; another was the ease with which he moved into and established himself in the top circles of British society. In this same connection, he became a go-between in bringing prominent Americans coming to England into contact with these circles. Much of this was accomplished through lavish receptions and dinners he gave and his Fourth-of-July dinners that developed into a legendary feature of the social season in London.[2] When he was in his forties, Peabody made a proposal of marriage to an American woman that was eventually rejected. After that, Peabody never again expressed any interest in getting married.[3] His permanent bachelorhood, however, appears to have enhanced rather than detracted from his social dealings. Although throughout his life Peabody provided significant sums benefiting his relatives in the United States, his lack of direct familial ties, coupled with his financial and social activities, undoubtedly contributed to Peabody's growing interest in devoting portions of his wealth to worthy causes. In the 1850s and 1860s he gave money for a variety of educational and scientific causes in the United States. The major ones included moneys for the establishment of Peabody Institutes in Baltimore, Maryland, and Peabody and Salem, Massachusetts, with amounts totaling $1,400,000; $217,600; and $100,000 respectively; and Peabody Museums at Harvard and Yale Universities, and Salem, Massachusetts, with funds totaling $150,000; $150,000; and $140,000 respectively. In addition, benefactions were provided for hospitals, churches, libraries, historical societies and other worthy causes in England, Europe, and the United States. It was the coming of and the aftermath of the American Civil War, however, that saw the emergence of Peabody as the founder of modern foundation philanthropy and, particularly so, in the international area. The awarding of this title to him was clinched by his setting up of the Peabody Donation Fund in 1862 and the Peabody Education Fund in 1867.

It should be emphasized at this point that, although a New Englander, Peabody's previously mentioned financial and social activities had always crossed the increasingly sectional divide between the inhabitants of the northern and southern states of the United States. Peabody's position *vis-à-vis* the coming of and the prosecution of the American Civil War has been aptly summarized as follows:

> Peabody, who had, by temperament, an aversion to extremes of any kind, tried to keep aloof from the feverish partisanship expressed by the people about him, especially by his fellow Americans. He made an effort not to align himself with the abolitionists, though he privately accepted their humanitarian ideals, nor with the states'-rights group. As a result, he was often called a "traitor" by Northerners.

Personally he suffered greatly when hostilities began, and his mental conflict was very painful. As the war progressed, he supported the North, but he could never forget his many Southern friends nor fail to see their point of view....

The Civil War was particularly distressing for Peabody because, rightly or wrongly, he was convinced that the conflict should have been avoided.[4]

Peabody Donation Fund

For some time, prior to the beginning of the Civil War, Peabody had been considering making some gift for the betterment of the inhabitants of London where he had so long resided and prospered. He looked into an elaborate scheme to set up a water purification plant to pipe pure drinking water for Londoners to fountains located at various places in the city but eventually rejected that idea. A plan to provide educational aid for poor London children was also eventually rejected in favor of what was then considered a more pressing need: the building of improved housing for poor Londoners to replace some of the existing slums. The formal outcome of this plan in 1862 bore the title Peabody Donation Fund wherein Peabody named a small group of American and English friends as self perpetuating trustees, none of whom were then or since family members or related to him, and eventually the Fund consisted of a corpus of $2,500,000 provided by Peabody. The establishment of the Fund came at the time of the Trent Affair, a naval altercation between the United States, Britain, and the Confederate States of America and did much to soften a then hostile official and public attitude in England towards the United States.

The British Charity Commission arranged for the legal acceptance of Peabody's gift that has been lauded by a student of English philanthropy as:

perhaps the most dramatic event in the history of Victorian housing. It originated in an act of individual philanthropy unparalleled in its time, and the donor attached almost no strings to his benefaction.... His purpose, as his letter to his trustees stated, was "to ameliorate the condition and augment the comforts of the poor" of London … this can still be regarded as one of the more original and productive philanthropies of a century that, with all of its humanitarian and charitable concern, was not conspicuously inventive in its philanthropy.[5]

At the time Peabody's liberality was universally acclaimed in England and the press was one in acclaiming his action. For example, the London *Times* commented:

Many have bequeathed fortunes to charity posthumously, leaving behind what cannot be taken to the grave. But this man gives while he lives to those who can make no return. He gives a fortune so that one part of this vast, ill-built, ill-kept city, which the rich never see, will be more comfortable and respectable for the poor. He does this in a country not his own, in a city he may leave any day for his native land. Such an act is rare in the annals of benevolence.[6]

Queen Victoria offered him a baronetcy or the Grand Cross of the Bath which he declined but Oxford University awarded him an honorary D.C.L. and the City of London gave him many honors including the erection of a still existing imposing statue of him prominently located next to the Royal Exchange. Peabody had planned well and his Donation Fund was an initial and continuing success through the wise administration of his first and succeeding trustees. By 1882 the fund owned and administered some 3,500 homes; by 1914, 6,400; by 1939, 8,000; and, despite the ravages of World War II, they still stand as monuments to Peabody.

Peabody Education Fund

The Peabody Donation Fund was obviously motivated by his desire to help the poor inhabitants of the foreign city where he had resided and prospered for so many years and it was certainly international in character. His other major foundation, the Peabody Education Fund, established in 1867-1869 to aid the devastated post-Civil War Southern states, technically cannot be considered so. Yet such aid provided by him, while certainly falling within the war motive posited above, could also be viewed as a foreign activity. The Confederate States of America had operated as a separate country from 1861 to 1865.[7] The philanthropic aid provided to the former German Democratic Republic by West German foundations beginning as early as 1989-1990 could be viewed as a contemporary analogue.[8] In any case, because of its trailblazing character and influence on succeeding U.S. philanthropists, a description of the motive for, founding, method of operation, perception of, and effect of the Peabody Education Fund is provided here.

Following the establishment of the Peabody Donation Fund and prior to a visit to the United States in 1866, it appears that Peabody contemplated providing some similar form of aid for the same purpose for the poor of New York City. After arrival and conversations and correspondence acquainting him with the misery and poverty prevalent in the defeated Confederacy, however, Peabody decided that his aid was much more needed there. He also became convinced that such aid for education would be the best long-range solution for the South's problems and, probably of equal importance to him, that such aid would contribute to sectional reconciliation following the Civil War and lead to a more reunified United States. His initial endowment of $1 million in 1867 established the Fund, coupled with an additional $1 million two years later, named sixteen distinguished Northerners and Southerners to a board of trustees to carry out its purpose. The Fund's work was to be conducted through programs which eventually resulted in the setting up and operation of public and normal schools previously lacking in the Southern states. Prior to the Fund's dissolution in 1914, its activities were capped in 1908 by the establishment in Nashville, Tennessee of the George Peabody College for Teachers. From that time down to the College's merger with Vanderbilt University in 1979, the College was probably the preeminent institution of its type in the South.

When Peabody died in England in 1869, his death was universally mourned there and in the United States, particularly in the Southern States. As an early biographer of him noted: "The death was most sincerely lamented in all the Southern States, and called forth from the Press, from public authorities, from schools, from individuals, the tenderest expressions of gratitude and love."[9] Although burial in Westminster Abbey had been offered for Peabody's remains by the Dean and Chapter of the Abbey and endorsed by Queen Victoria, his will specified that he was to be buried in Salem, Massachusetts. Consequently, a memorial service in the Abbey was held in his honor and Queen Victoria expressed a desire that Peabody's coffin be transported to the United States by Britain's newest and mightiest warship, the *Monarch*. There was some U.S. opposition to the proposal because it came at the same time as the diplomatic controversy over American claims for reparations as the result of depredations of the British-built Confederate warship, the *Alabama*. U.S. President Ulysses S. Grant eventually agreed to the Queen's proposal, with the understanding, however, that the *Monarch* be accompanied by an American warship to the United States.

Peabody during his life had only a few detractors in England and the United States regarding his philanthropy: Benjamin Moran, Assistant Secretary of the American Legation in London, and William Lloyd Garrison, the prominent abolitionist New Englander. Moran appears to have been jealous of Peabody's social and economic success and his easy access to successive ambassadors from the United States to England. He kept a secret diary in which he viewed Peabody as: "heartless, and has never given a farthing in charity that he did not expect three fold return. All his benevolence is based on future personal gain." Moran opined regarding the Peabody Donation Fund that "The appropriation of this Fund, arose from a selfish vanity solely, unattended by a shade of benevolence, and which will never benefit those for whose use it was so pompously announced to be intended."[10] Garrison, in an article following Peabody's death and significantly entitled "Honored Beyond His Deserts," stated that vanity was Peabody's primary motive in giving, offered no praise for the creation of the Peabody Education Fund, and asserted:

> During his long years in England he never once aided popular liberty or spoke against slavery. His sympathies were with the pro-slave South right to the outbreak of the rebellion. His patriotic record cannot be examined with any pride or pleasure.... He did not want the Union dissolved; neither did he want the South conquered. He wanted peace which would satisfy the South, leaving slavery intact.[11]

As has been remarked above, however, such critiques were miniscule in comparison to the overwhelmingly laudatory ones about Peabody.[12] What then was the motive or motives for Peabody's benefactions through the two foundations he created? The evidence seems overwhelming, from his own writings and that of his close associates, that it was a sincere desire to help those in need. A major and probably the best proof of this conclusion is to be found in Peabody's letters of gift setting up the Peabody Donation Fund and the Peabody Education Fund. In the first instance, Peabody wrote:

> Early in my commercial life I resolved that if my labors were blessed with success I would devote a portion of my property to promote the intellectual, moral, and physical welfare of my fellowmen wherever their need was greatest....
>
> Twenty-five years ago I came to London to live and to engage in business. I did not feel myself a stranger in a strange land long. For in all my dealings with British friends I received courtesy, kindness, and confidence.
>
> With a sense of gratitude for the blessings of a kind Providence, and in keeping with my early resolve, I have confided to personal friends a desire to make a donation to the poor of London.

Following this statement, Peabody asked that a few "principles" be observed and "suggested that the fund be applied to construct improved dwelling for the poor of London."[13]

In his letter of gift for the establishment of the Peabody Education Fund, Peabody referred to "the educational needs of those persons of our beloved and common country which have suffered from the destructive ravages, and the not less disastrous consequences of civil war." He then went on to say:

> I feel most deeply, therefore, that it is the duty and privilege of the more wealthy and favored portions of our nation to assist those who are less fortunate; and with the wish to discharge so far as I may be able my own responsibility in this matter,

as well as to my desire to aid those to whom I am bound by so many ties of attachment and regard, I give to you, gentlemen, most of whom have been my personal and especial friends, the sum of one million dollars, to be by you and your successors held in trust, and the income thereof used and applied in your discretion for the promotion and encouragement of intellectual, moral, or industrial education among the young of the more destitute portions of the Southern and Southwestern States of our Union; my purpose being that the benefits intended shall be distributed among the entire population, without other distinction than their needs and the opportunities of usefulness to them.[14]

Putting contemporary pros and cons concerning Peabody and conjecture as to his motive for giving to one side and viewing Peabody from the perspective of history, however, there is no naysaying the great significance of the following innovative contributions he made to the philanthropic and foundation record. First, there were no sectarian or religious restrictions in his benefactions. Second, great discretion in the operation of his foundations was provided his original and succeeding trustees. Such discretion included provisions for their ability to terminate his benefices. Third, full disclosure to the public of foundation operations was specified and made. Fourth, much of his aid was international in character. Fifth, and perhaps of equal or more importance, Peabody's thoughts on and method of giving greatly influenced others in the United States and abroad in the establishment and operation of succeeding foundations and other institutions. Initially, there were the John F. Slater Fund for the Education of Freedmen, Johns Hopkins and Tulane Universities and, somewhat later, as will be related, the philanthropies of Mrs. Russell Sage, Andrew Carnegie, and John D. Rockefeller. Although now a rather neglected figure in the history of American philanthropy and foundations, never the less, in 1907 Daniel Coit Gilman, the first president of Johns Hopkins University, credited Peabody with influencing the formation and operating principles of later U.S. foundations and labeled him "pioneer of National beneficence."[15] A February 9, 1917 article in the *Christian Science Monitor* concluded: "In a sense the Peabody Fund was not the only monument to George Peabody, for the example he set has been followed by a host of other Americans." Too, in 1964, an official of the Rockefeller Foundation marked the establishment by Peabody of the Peabody Education Fund "to aid the stricken South in 1867 as the beginning of the foundation as we know it"[16]

Sage

An even more neglected figure in the history of American foundations is Margaret Olivia Slocum Sage. A brief autobiographical article,[17] brief biographical[18] and genealogical articles,[19] plus obituary notices,[20] form the chief published sources of information about her. A book-length biography of this foundation pioneer has yet to be published. A 1971 biographer of hers noted that, "Mrs. Sage's personal papers are at the Russell Sage Foundation, unorganized and largely unused."[21] A two-volume history of the Sage Foundation was published in 1947 which contains some information about her. [22]

Mrs. Sage was born in Syracuse, New York, on September 18, 1828. She was the daughter of Joseph and Margaret Pierson (Jermain) Slocum, of English/Quaker descent. Her father was a prosperous Syracuse merchant, and Olivia, as she was known, lived a genteel life and attended local schools until 1846. In that year she embarked for Mount Holyoke College but a combination of illness and the urging of an uncle located in Troy, New York, led to her enrollment in the Troy Female Seminary, now Russell Sage College, where she graduated in 1847. Financial reverses of her father at that time turned her to teaching in Philadelphia and other schools for the next two decades.

In 1869, at the age of forty-one, she became the second wife of Russell Sage, a widower whose first wife had developed a close friendship with Olivia while they attended the Troy Seminary. By the time of their wedding Sage had risen from a prosperous merchant and prominent political figure in Troy, New York, to a commanding presence in the financial and banking world of New York City. Although he and his second wife lived a comfortable life, throughout his life Russell Sage was noted for his frugality, and the few philanthropies in which he engaged have been credited to the urging of this wife. Thus, by the time he died on July 26, 1906[23] at their Long Island home, he had acquired a fortune estimated at $70 million which he willed in its entirety to his wife.

Mrs. Sage began immediately to give away this fortune for a wide array of philanthropic and charitable purposes: education, hospitals, and social and relief agencies. Robert W. de Forest, her attorney and friend, noted however, that "She was overwhelmed with applications for both individual and institutional aid from all over the world." He added that "During the two years following her husband's death, she received over 50,000 applications by letter, and personal applications without number."[24] In partial response to this situation, it was de Forest who was largely instrumental in convincing Mrs. Sage to incorporate the Russell Sage Foundation in New York in 1907[25] with an original corpus of $10 million from which the income only was to be expended for charitable purposes and it eventually received about a third of all of Mrs. Sage's gifts and bequests. Public and private response to its creation was over-whelmingly favorable.[26] Although later dwarfed by the foundations es-tablished by Carnegie and Rockefeller, the Sage Foundation was heralded at the time as "the largest single gift to philanthropy in the history of the world."[27] A notable exception to such commendation was Franklin H. Giddings, professor of Sociology at Columbia University. Giddings stated that the Sage and other large foundations "afforded good examples of the general excellence of the objects for which the benefactions are made." He nevertheless objected to the fact that they were set up as perpetuities and that their income would and could go to "a fluctuating, somewhat indefinite, body of beneficiaries."[28] Looking to the future he warned that foundations in general, and the Russell Sage foundation in particular, might be used for purposes other than what their originators declared. He then opined:

> Experience, however, does not warrant the expectation that great trust funds will ever be diverted to the promotion of any kind of moral or social radicalism. The dangers that lie in them are rather in the temptations that they offer to designing persons to control them in the interests of either speculative enterprises or of established privilege. So far as they are controlled in the interest of privilege their influence is ultra-conservative, tending always to become obstructionist. [29]

The stated purpose of the Russell Sage Foundation was "the improve-ment of social and living conditions in the United States of America." and its charter gave the greatest latitude to its trustees in carrying out this purpose. Until her death in 1918 at the age of 90, Mrs. Sage was the president of the board of trustees and played a dominant role in shaping and conducting the Foundation's varied programs. The other eight mem-bers of the board were personal friends of hers but included no family members.[30] A 1970s biographer noted:

> The wellsprings of Mrs. Sage's charity were her childlessness, a desire to improve her husband's reputation, a passion for memorializing her family (but not herself), a commitment to Christian stewardship, and a sense of class obligation—*richesse oblige*. Places, institutions, and causes with which she and her family had been intimately associated enjoyed special favor…. Her interest in practical education and uplift reflected her belief that what the poor needed most was instruction in self-help and moral responsibility. Though she talked much of equality, her conception of servants as erring and naughty children, her strictures on the "moral filth" of the poor, and her insistence on the need for missionary work among them betrayed a strong class bias.[31]

Class bias or no, Mrs. Sage steadily and judiciously, but not capri-ciously, distributed her wealth in the last twelve years of her life. One writer noted as an example of this approach that her husband's nephew once wired her from college: "Please send money. Am one jump ahead of the sheriff." Instead of a check, she sent back the advice, "Keep jumping."[32] She, and those few involved with her in this formative period, charted the course for the future of the Foundation. It was to alleviate bad social conditions rather than relieve individual poverty. Foundation aid was not to be provided for individuals or families in need. The foundation thereupon launched studies and programs, bewildering in their variety and scope, but generally falling under what today would be called social work or betterment. A historian summarized that "the foundation became the pioneer research institute, grant maker, and coordinator of research, experiment, and reform legislation in the fields of social work, urban planning, and industrial relations. It has then and since used ... "its own staff and facilities to carry out most of its activities."[33] Although the Foundation's charter restricted its activities to the United States, numerous studies conducted abroad and international congresses on various subjects were financed by the foundation in an effort to cast light upon the best avenues of change for the United States to follow. Following the death of Mrs. Sage in 1918, her will provided an additional $5 million bequest to the Foundation and it continued pretty much on the course originally charted until the advent of World War II.

The conduct of the Foundation during this period between the two World Wars was to a large extent directed by John M. Glenn. The latter was a leader in the Charity Organization Societies of Baltimore and New York City and was one of the small group instrumental in the setting up of the Foundation and a member of its original board of trustees. He occupied various positions in the Foundation from its inception, including trustee, director, and secretary, and maintained a position of leadership there until his death in 1950. In 1948, Donald R. Young, a sociologist, was appointed president of the Foundation. He has been followed by a succession of social scientists, economists, and political scientists, in positions of leadership. Since the 1950s it has used the income from its endowment, presently valued at about $200 million, to finance and publish studies in basic and applied social research. Noteworthy in this area has been the leadership role it has played in the study of philanthropy. Such role is tellingly illustrated by the fact that its longstanding program of data collection, studies, and publications on foundations and charities became the literary nucleus in the setting up of an independent Foundation Library Center (later Foundation Center) in 1956.

Carnegie

George Peabody's foundations, together with the Russell Sage Foundation, marked the beginnings of the foundation as we know it. The foundations established by Andrew Carnegie and John D. Rockefeller were also pioneers, and these two dominated U.S. foundation giving in the period between the Civil War and World War I. Their advent and operation on the foundation scene, however, was marked by a subsequent substantial increase in the scope, number, and assets of other foundations established, and the number and size of the grants made by them.

Andrew Carnegie was born on November 25, 1835 in Dunfermline, Scotland to a family with a skilled working-class background of weaving and shoemaking. Carnegie was the son of political and social reformers from both sides of his family. Industrialization in Scotland and resultant hard times for skilled hand craftsmen caused the Carnegie family to emigrate to the United States in 1848 and settle in Pennsylvania. Andrew Carnegie at the age of thirteen began work there in that year as a bobbin boy in a cotton factory. With little formal education, Carnegie relied on books borrowed from a local personal library to underpin his subsequent meteoric rise from telegraph messenger boy to superintendent of the Western Division of the Pennsylvania Railroad at the age of twenty-four. From that point on he moved into a wide variety of business and manufacturing ventures centering on railroads, rails, railroad cars, and bridges. In 1873 he set up the first of his steel manufacturing enterprises. He prospered mightily and, by the time he sold out his steel manufacturing Carnegie Company to J. Pierpont Morgan in 1901, he sat atop a fortune valued in excess of $400 million making him one of the wealthiest men—if not the wealthiest—in the United States. This feat was even more impressive at that time, particularly when gauged as readily available funds at his disposal.[34]

Early in his business career Carnegie was evidently well acquainted with and apparently approved of Peabody's business career and his philanthropies. For example, upon Peabody's death, there had been some opposition to bringing his remains home for burial in the United States in Britain's newest warship. The young Carnegie made his views known as to the means to be used in an 1869 telegram which he sent to John Bright, a statesman in the British Cabinet at that time. Carnegie urged: "First and best service possible for Monarch, bringing home body Peabody."[35] There are other indications, at various points in his life, of his attitude toward business and philanthropy. In 1868 he had written a remarkable letter to himself, when he had already amassed a fortune of about $400,000, as to a planned future although it was never carried out. It is quoted verbatim in its entirety here because it is so revealing of the philanthropic motive animating this man. A motive that was to continue to actuate him after he had acquired much, much more money:

Dec. '68
St.Nicholas Hotel
N. York

Thirty Three and an income of 50,000$ per annum
By this time two years I can so arrange all my business as to
secure at least 50,000 per annum. Beyond this never earn-
make no effort to increase fortune, but spend the surplus each
year for benevoelent purposes. Cast aside business forever
except for others.
    Settle in Oxford & get a thorough education making the ac-
quaintance of literary men- this will take three years active
work- pay especial attention to speaking in public.
Settle then in London & purchase a controlling interest in
some newspaper or live review & give the general management of it attention, taking a part in public matters especially
those connected with education & improvement of the poorer
classes.
    Man must have an idol- The amassing of wealth is one of
The worst species of idolitary. No idol more debasing than
the worship of money. Whatever I engage in I must push inor-
dinately therefore should I be careful to choose that life which
will be the most elevating in its character. To continue much
longer overwhelmed by business cares and with most of my
thoughts wholly upon the way to make more money in the
shortest time, must degrade me beyond hope of permanent re-
covery.
    I will resign business at Thirty five, but during the ensuing
two years, I wish to spend the afternoons in securing instruc-
tion, and in reading systematically.[36]

Regardless of his avowed business and career intentions at this early age, Carnegie had begun to devote funds for charitable and philanthropic purposes around the same time. His first effort internationally centered on Scotland and his birthplace, Dunfermline. Thus, his first considerable gifts were for the construction of swimming baths there beginning in 1875. In 1887 Carnegie married Louise Whitfield after a long courtship. His and her commitment and determination to devote his ever increasing fortune to philanthropic purposes is revealed in another remarkable document, their nuptial agreement, which stated in part: "Andrew Carnegie desires and intends to devote the bulk of his estate to charitable and educational purposes and said Louise Whitfield sympathizes and agrees with him in said desire."[37]

In addition to these personal statements of intent and many acts of charitable giving by this time, the very articulate Carnegie, through his speeches and writing, laid the basis for what may be called the ideological underpinnings and rationale for the creation by him and eventually others of a host of large foundations for national and international purposes. Such efforts culminated in the publication in 1886 of his *Triumphant Democracy* and *The Gospel of Wealth* in 1889.

> The basic premise of these two works was that the prevailing socio-politico-economic system was good in that it furnished a greater and greater number of people with the good things in life. This process was accompanied, however, by a corresponding increase in the amounts of surplus wealth held by a few individuals. Carnegie felt that these extremely wealthy men could do one of three things with their wealth. Leave it to heirs. Leave it for charitable purposes at death. Give it away for charitable purposes in their own lifetime. The first two he rejected as having been tried and found wanting. He concluded that the third alone affords the men of great wealth a means for its wise disposition.[38]

Carnegie, putting action to words, had thus begun the task of giving away his money for useful purposes long before he retired from business in 1901; much of it was devoted to such purposes abroad. For example, he had given funds for the construction of about 1,000 public library buildings, including one in Dunfermline in 1881, all over the world. Also, between 1873 and 1919 he had donated over 7,000 church organs in thirteen countries all around the globe. Inaugurated long before the time when he began the setting up of his multitudinous foundations, such beneficences were continued by Carnegie after those foundations began operation, in some cases through them, and continued to the time of his death. Such beneficences, however, were what might be called retail giving and made but a slight dent in his capital. Thus, when he retired in 1901, Carnegie's total giving appears to have totaled less than $30 million. This at a time when his fortune stood at some $400 million in liquid assets as the result of the sale of his steel and other interests to J.P. Morgan and with a resultant income amounting to over $15 million annually. It was at this juncture that he turned to the creation of foundations to in large part carry out his "Gospel of Wealth."

Great Britain and Ireland

Although the setting up of the Carnegie Institute of Pittsburgh preceded it by a few years, the establishment of the Carnegie Trust for the
Universities of Scotland was inspired by essentially the same motive: a
desire to provide educational aid for the city where he had made his fortune on the one hand and the country of his birth on the other. The Trust
was the first of the international philanthropic foundations established
by Carnegie and it grew out of his numerous sojourns to Scotland from
the 1870s where he became acquainted with its educational structure.
Carnegie learned that, while elementary and preparatory education was
within the reach of worthy and able Scottish youths, the fees charged
by the then four universities of Scotland made it impossible for those of
modest means to aspire to higher education. On a visit to Scotland in
1901 he determined to remedy the situation by placing $10 million into
a foundation for that purpose. Carnegie's deed of trust to the foundation
called for two major programs. The sum of $5 million was set aside and
the income from it was to be used for the payment of university fees for
those Scots unable to pay them. The income from the other $5 million
was to be used by the existing four Scottish universities—St. Andrews,
Glasgow, Aberdeen, and Edinburgh—for their improvement. There
was some opposition in Scotland to the proposed gift on the grounds
that admission of such impecunious youths might result in a lowering
of the academic standards of the universities and that it might place the
universities control in the hands of an autocratic and dictatorial Carnegie
or subject them to similar control by the successor trustees of the Trust.
The prospect of obtaining such moneys—the combined assets of the
four universities at that time was about 72,000 pounds—overcame such
qualms. The foundation was thus incorporated in 1902 by Royal Charter
and designated twenty-four distinguished Britons as trustees and the legal
instruments creating the Trust provided for great freedom to the trustees
in its administration. Up until World War I some criticism of the Trust
still remained and turned on the expressed belief that its operations had
indeed resulted in a lowering of the academic standards of the universities and that its remission of fees restriction to Scots only was an undue
discrimination. Since that time such criticism has been largely stilled
due to the fact that the trustees have made wise and just adjustments
regarding the academic standards charge plus the extension, since the
1960s, of the benefits of the Trust, to four newly established Scottish
universities: Strathclyde, Heriot-Watt, Dundee, and Stirling. The offices

of the Trust are located in the Merchant's Hall in Edinburgh and carry out its disbursements from there.[39]

The second foundation established by Carnegie for international philanthropic purposes in Scotland was the Carnegie Dunfermline Trust. Prior to its establishment, he had already given much, including the first Carnegie library, to this place of his birth and his home until age 12. Carnegie had determined to do much more. Spurred by his affection for the "Auld Gray Toun," Carnegie in 1902 had purchased Pittencrief Glen and Park, a historic 70-acre site close by his birthplace. He then presented the Glen and Park as a gift to the town. Later, in writing of these events, Carnegie revealingly and unabashedly avowed "Pittencrief Glen is the most soul-satisfying public gift I ever made, or ever can make."[40] Such sentiments were probably spurred by the fact that as a child he had been denied entrance there. In the following year, 1903, the Trust was established in the United Kingdom with an eventual endowment of $3,750,000. It was originally administered by twenty-five Scottish trustees with successors named by them since then. Its office is located in Abbey Park House, Dunfermline and the income from the endowment has since been used for a wide variety of social, educational, and recreational purposes, in and around the Glen and Park, benefiting the people of Carnegie's native town.

Carnegie established the Carnegie United Kingdom Trust in Britain in 1913 with an endowment of $10 million. The Trust deed specified that the original trustees named and their elected successors had to be residents of the United Kingdom. Carnegie intended and spelled out in the deed that the income from it should be used for the library building and church organ needs of Great Britain and Ireland. Although its earlier program continued this provision of funds for such purposes in the United Kingdom. Carnegie, with the exception noted below, gave the trustees great latitude in the future operation of this endowment. He stated that its income shall:

> be applied by them [trustees] for the improvement of the well-being of the masses of the people of Great Britain and Ireland, by such means as are embraced within the meaning of the word "charitable," according to Scotch or English law, and which the Trustees may from time to time select as best fitted from age to age for securing these purposes, remembering that new needs are constantly arising as the masses advance.[41]

Tied in with Carnegie's continuous crusade for the outlawing of war and drive for world peace, however, he "specially" provided that:

> Trustees shall apply no part of the income towards research designed to promote the development of implements or munitions of war, and I expressly prohibit any part of the Trust funds from being used in any way which could lend countenance to war or to warlike preparations.[42]

Over the years since its founding, the Trust's income has been dispensed to support voluntary groups in the areas of education, the arts, and museums with the general purpose of improving the quality of life in neighborhoods of the United Kingdom. Since 1927 the offices of the Trust have been located in Comely Park House, Dunfermline where a secretary and small staff dispense aid for the above purposes in amounts of about 500,000 pounds annually.

Achievement of Peace and Prevention of War

The previously described foundations were established largely from a desire by Carnegie to benefit the land of his birth. By 1913, as can be seen in the clause inserted in the instrument creating the foundation domiciled in Britain and described above, however, his concern for the achievement of peace and the prevention of war had become a full blown philanthropic motive.

An earlier international foundation effort for this purpose was an outgrowth of the Hague Peace Conference of 1899 that called for the creation of a Permanent Court of Arbitration. Carnegie provided $1,500,000 in 1903 for the establishment of a foundation in the Netherlands that oversaw the construction in 1907-1913 of a Peace Palace at The Hague to house the Court together with a library of international law. An International Court of Justice, created in 1946, has since been housed there.[43]

At about the same time Carnegie provided an endowment of $5 million for setting up of the first of his hero foundations in the United States. His motive for the creation of the first Carnegie Hero Fund Commission, restricted to the United States, Canada, and Newfoundland, was his desire to eliminate war. It was another and central part of his continuous creation of international entities designed to do so. A biographer notes, for example: "To Carnegie, however, the Simplified Spelling Board, established in 1903, [mentioned below] and the Hero Fund, first set up in the United States in 1904, were not tangential but central to the cause of world peace."[44] Too long, Carnegie maintained, had warriors been acclaimed as heroes for killing others but now, as he stated in the opening paragraph of the deed of trust setting up his first hero fund foundation: "We live in an heroic age. Not seldom are we thrilled by deeds of heroism where men or women are injured or lose their lives in attempting to preserve or rescue their fellows; such the heroes of civilization. The heroes of barbarism maimed or killed theirs."[45]   Although there was some disapproval, alleging that he was bribing people to risk their lives, Carnegie was so satisfied with the operation, and resultant public approval and acclaim of this first hero fund, that he decided to extend it further internationally. He endowed the Carnegie Hero Fund Trust for Great Britain and Ireland with the sum of $1,250,000 in 1908 and, during the years 1909-1911, followed it with gifts totaling $4,290,000 for the creation of similar foundations abroad for the same purpose in nine other western European countries. Most of these funds have maintained operational offices in their respective countries, with national trustees and staff, and have continued to make awards to the present.

At the same time that Carnegie was funding these foundations in the cause of peace, he was being urged by many leaders in the cause, such as Baron d' Estournelles de Constant of France, head of the Association for International Conciliation and Nicholas Murray Butler, president of Columbia University, to fund a larger and more comprehensive one for that purpose. Eventually they convinced him that political and economic leaders, particularly those in the United States, Britain, and Germany, could eliminate war through education and recourse to arbitration in disputes between nations.

The outcome was the establishment in 1910 of the Carnegie Endowment for International Peace with an endowment of $10 million. With twenty-eight leaders from American business and public life designated as trustees, Carnegie gave them the widest latitude as to current and future operations of the Endowment. Using the simplified spelling he championed, he optimistically charged them:

> When … war is discarded as disgraceful to civilized man, as personal war (duelling) and man selling and buying (slavery) hav been discarded within the wide boundaries of our English-speaking race, the Trustees will pleas then consider what is the next most degrading evil or evils whose banishment – or what new elevating element or elements if introduced or fosterd, or both combined- would most advance the progress, elevation and happiness of man, and so on from century to century without end, my Trustees of each age shall determin how they can best aid man in his upward march to higher and higher stages of development unceasingly; for now we know that man was created, not with an instinct for his own degradation, but imbued with the desire and the power for improvement to which, perchance, there may be no limit short of perfection even here in this life upon erth.[46]

Carnegie's last major endowment in the cause of peace, the Church Peace Union was established in 1913. In view of his previous lack of support for religious institutions, it appears that his wife, Louise Whitfield

Carnegie, was the agent in getting him to fund it. The Union also appears to attest to Carnegie's willingness to embrace any possibly effective means in his drive for peace. The ecumenical board of trustees of the Union received the same optimistic charge from Carnegie provided in the Endowment and in practically the same language and was endowed with $2 million through a grant from the Carnegie Corporation of New York established by Carnegie two years earlier. The Endowment and Union (the Union was renamed the Carnegie Council on Ethics and International Affairs in 1986) have continued in operation down to the present; primarily through publications, notably the Endowment's publication of *Foreign Affairs,* research forums, conferences, and education and, in the case of the Union/Council, aid for refugees displaced by war or other disasters.

By 1911, Carnegie's funding of his international philanthropies plus even more for domestic purposes totaled about $150 million. Despite the size of such giving, his fortune still stood at more than double that sum and at age seventy-six he decided to transfer the bulk of it to a general purpose perpetual philanthropy to dispose of it. He thereupon set up the Carnegie Corporation of New York in that year with an endowment of $125 million, the largest single foundation established up to that time. The Corporation's stated purpose was:

> to promote the advancement and diffusion of knowledge and understanding among the people of the United States, by aiding technical schools, institutions of higher lerning, libraries, scientific research, hero funds, useful publications, and by such other agencies and means as shall from time to time be found appropriate therefore.[47]

Soon after, in January 1912, Carnegie added a small endowment, since fixed at 7.4 percent of the total, to be set aside and used for similar philanthropic purposes in Canada and what were then British colonies; subsequently modified to include countries that are or have been members of the overseas British Commonwealth. Such modifications and others in the Corporation's operations were made easily possible by the broad freedom of action afforded it in Carnegie's letter of gift endowing it. In a separate paragraph, again pursuing his cherished simplified spelling, he specified:

> Conditions upon the erth inevitably change; hence no wise man will bind Trustees forever to certain paths, causes or institutions. I disclaim any intention of doing so. On the contrary, I giv my Trustees full authority to change policy or causes hitherto aided, from time to time, when this, in their opinion, has become necessary or desirable. They shall best conform to my wishes by using their own judgment.[48]

The trustees that Carnegie named for the Corporation in 1911 included him as president and a few of his close friends, employees and heads of foundations previously set up by him in the United States. From that date until his death in 1919, the grants made by the Corporation, unless not legally possible,[49] followed his wishes in its domestic and international pattern of giving. In his biography of Carnegie, Burton J. Hendrick simply states: "The new agency [Carnegie Corporation of New York] might well have been called Andrew Carnegie, Inc." [50] Carnegie's wife, Mrs. Louise Whitfield Carnegie, who passed away in 1946, was elected to the board on his death and served to 1929. The Carnegie's only child, Mrs. Margaret Carnegie Miller, died in 1990 at the age of 93 and was survived by one of her four children, thirteen grandchildren; twenty-six great-grandchildren; and two great-great-grandchildren. She was elected to the board of trustees of the Carnegie Corporation in 1934 and served therein until 1973. From that year until her death she was designated an honorary life trustee. In the case of both mother and daughter, regardless of designation, their tenures were honorary and apparently they never participated actively in the conduct and direction of the foundation.[51] Indeed, a recent Carnegie biographer noted: "There was too much hypocrisy for her [daughter]; she wanted nothing to do with his philanthropic work, along with its pomp and circumstance, which rang so hollow to her."[52]

Immediately following Carnegie's death, there was a short period of transition, under the presidencies of James R. Angell, 1920-1921 and Henry S. Pritchett, 1921-1923. This was followed by the election of Frederick P. Keppel as president in 1923. His tenure, 1923-1941, ushered in the professionally managed foundation with a much more diverse board of trustees and staff. The present president Vartan Gregorian and the staff have since guided the Corporation's programs and projects.

Rockefeller

John Davison Rockefeller was an American contemporary of Andrew Carnegie, born about the same time on July 8, 1839 in Richford, New York. He was the eldest of three sons and the second of six children born to William Avery Rockefeller and Eliza Davison Rockefeller. John's father was an adventurous, spirited, and roving individual, often away from home pursuing mysterious and lucrative business endeavors. A nondrinker, he undoubtedly engaged in a number of extramarital sexual affairs. In his autobiography, John D. Rockefeller repeatedly acknowledges a debt to his father in developing his business acumen and no derogatory remarks concerning him are to be found there.[53] His mother was a study in contrast: ascetic, straight-laced, and very religious; the acknowledged disciplinarian in the family. Their son was deeply influenced, although in different but related ways, by these dissimilar parents. Indeed, John D. Rockefeller's latest biographer puzzles that:

> The religious and acquisitive sides of his nature were intimately related.... and that he ... was such an implausible blend of sin and sanctity. Further, seldom has history produced such a contradictory figure. We are almost forced to posit, in helpless confusion, at least two Rockefellers: the good, religious man and the renegade businessman, driven by baser motives. Complicating this puzzle is the fact that Rockefeller experienced no sense of discontinuity as he passed from being the brains of Standard Oil to being the monarch of a charitable empire... He [Rockefeller] was always insistent that his massive philanthropy paled in importance besides the good he had done in creating jobs and furnishing affordable kerosene at Standard Oil.[54]

A move from New York in 1853 by the Rockefeller family to the environs of Cleveland, Ohio saw John D. attending the Cleveland High School for two years followed by a three-month stint in a commercial business school. By the age of sixteen, the youth had acquired an excellent academic education together with considerable knowledge of bookkeeping and commercial practices. It was at that time that he launched his business career with a commission merchant firm at a weekly salary of $3.50. Following three-and-a-half years of experience there, where he gained the respect and confidence of numerous Cleveland businessmen, Rockefeller formed a mercantile partnership, Clark & Rockefeller. In its first year of operation, 1859-1860, the firm made a profit of $4,000 and it continued to prosper during the economic boom accompanying the Civil War.

By 1865 Rockefeller discontinued his commission business to concentrate on the rapidly developing oil-refining business. Buying out several previous partners and enlisting his brother William, together with such men as Samuel Andrews, Henry M. Flagler, Stephen Harkness, and other investors, resulted in 1870 in the formation of the Standard Oil Company of Ohio with Rockefeller as president. Rockefeller continued his previous policy of obtaining the best transportation rates for the transit of his oil; building the most efficient refineries for its processing; leading in the developing of new products; all of this accompanied by meticulous cost cutting. Plowing his own profits back into the business and adeptness in securing outside capital enabled him and the "Standard" to swallow up practically all of their competitors. Thus, by 1880 the Company and its subsidiaries exercised a virtual monopoly in the transportation, refining, and sale of American petroleum products. In the next decade, the Standard Oil Company extended its operations abroad and eventually became one of if not the preeminent worldwide merchant of oil and a bewildering variety of oil products. The creation of this gigantic business, however, was accompanied by a swelling tide of public and political opposition to this and similar monopolies in railroads and other businesses and the passage of the Sherman Anti-Trust Act of 1890.

John D. Rockefeller's acquisition of this economic empire was accompanied by and in tandem with activities reflecting the other side of an upbringing deeply influenced by his mother that reinforced his own innate outlook and nature. Outside his business activities his early life largely centered on his family and church and the beneficences and charities associated with it. While still in his twenties, he became a leading figure in a Cleveland Baptist Church and about this same age began keeping his famous "Ledger A." This account booklet carefully listed, down to the last cent, his gifts for charitable purposes; significantly including an entry of ten cents for "Foreign Mission."[55] His marriage in 1864 to Laura Celestia Spelman, daughter of a Cleveland businessman, with a religious and social outlook quite similar to his own, reinforced the religious/beneficent segment of his makeup. By the 1880s the offspring of this marriage included three daughters and one son, John D. Rockefeller, Jr. By this time, too, he had accumulated a fortune in the millions of dollars and, in line with his earlier giving, by the early 1890s his annual beneficences also ran in the millions, much of it for international purposes.

Perhaps the best illustration of Rockefeller's own views on this getting and giving of wealth is the statement attributed to him:

> I believe the power to make money is a gift from God—just as are the instincts for art, music, literature, the doctor's talent, the nurse's, yours—to be developed and used to the best of our ability for the good of mankind. Having been endowed with the gift I possess, I believe it is my duty to make money and still more money, and to use the money I make for the good of my fellow man according to the dictates of my conscience.[56]

Carrying out this belief in giving without foundering, however, was another matter. As word of his growing wealth and accompanying beneficences spread, one biographer described the postal appeals for aid that deluged him and the dilemma that confronted him:

> The volume of mail defied the imagination. One steamer alone brought five thousand begging letters from Europe. After the announcement of one large educational gift, Rockefeller received fifteen thousand letters during the first week and fifty thousand by the end of the month. He needed a staff just to sift through these appeals. His

overtaxed subordinates opened each envelope and tried to identify genuine cases of need, but they could gratify only a tiny fraction of such hopefuls. Many requests were frankly selfish, as Rockefeller [himself] tartly noted, [57] "Four-fifths of these letters are, however, requests of money for personal use with no other title to consideration than the writer would be gratified to have it."[58]

Frederick T. Gates, a Baptist minister who eventually became a chief architect in alleviating this situation, observed: "Mr. Rockefeller was constantly hunted, stalked and hounded almost like a wild animal. Neither in the privacy of his home nor at his table, nor in the aisles of his church, nor during his business hours, nor anywhere else, was Mr. Rockefeller secure from insistent appeal."[59]

By this time Rockefeller had been influenced by the thinking and examples of Peabody and Carnegie as to the duty and wisdom of creating a philanthropic structure for the effective distribution of his wealth.[60] It was at this juncture that he turned to Gates, the Baptist minister, with whom he had become acquainted during his initial gift in 1891 leading to the founding of the University of Chicago. In that year Gates came to New York and became the leading financial adviser and philanthropic planner to Rockefeller, together with John D. Rockefeller, Jr., until Gates' retirement in 1923. The first philanthropic organization launched on Gates' watch in 1901 was the Rockefeller Institute for Medical Research, in 1965 re-named Rockefeller University, to be closely followed by the General Education Board in 1902. Developing out of somewhat the same concerns for the post-Civil War South that had motivated George Peabody, the GEB concentrated its major efforts there. Its educational aid programs in the region worked closely with the Peabody Education Fund and other foundations active there until its termination in 1964 by which time it had expended about $325 million.[61] Closely aligned with the work of the GEB was the Rockefeller Sanitary Commission, a separately funded and organized entity that, from 1910 to 1914, labored to alleviate health problems, particularly hookworm, endemic at that time in the South.

Spurred on by the success of these initial philanthropies and reflecting the fact that from its very beginnings an ever increasing amount of Rockefeller business was done abroad, Gates convinced the elder Rockefeller of the need to create a larger and more far ranging foundation to carry out beneficial programs in not only the United States but internationally. Attempts in 1910, 1911, and 1912 to obtain a federal charter for such purposes were rebuffed by the U.S. Congress and, as a result, the Rockefeller Foundation, with the mandate: "To promote the well-being of mankind throughout the world," was incorporated by a 1913 act of the New York State Legislature. Since much of the Rockefeller earlier philanthropies centered in the health and medical areas it was natural that the earliest foreign activities of the Rockefeller Foundation did the same. In 1913 an International Health Commission was created under Foundation auspices[62] to deal with health and medical problems worldwide. Similarly, in 1915 the China Medical Board was established to deal with these problems in China alone. An International Education Board was set up in 1923 to carry on overseas programs similar to those carried on domestically under the General Education Board. While the other boards were eventually absorbed into and became divisional programs of the Rockefeller Foundation, the China Medical Board was incorporated as a separate foundation in 1928 and has continued its existence to the present day with current assets of more than $200 million.[63]

From the time of its incorporation in 1913 the Rockefeller Foundation's control and direction largely rested in the hands of Gates and John D. Rockefeller, Jr., until Gates' retirement in 1927. JDR, Sr., however, was invariably consulted for counsel and advice until his death in 1937. Following the death of JDR, Jr., in 1960, leadership passed to John D. Rockefeller III where it remained until his death in 1978. Since then, although members of the Rockefeller family have served on the board of trustees, a succession of professional officials, presently headed by President Judith Rodin, has been largely responsible for the conduct and operation of the foundation.

Notes

1. For a detailed discussion of Peabody's earlier mercantile and financial career see, Muriel Emmie Hidy, "George Peabody, Merchant and Financier, 1829-1954," Unpublished Ph.D. Dissertation, Radcliffe College, 1939. See also, Vincent P. Carosso with the assistance of Rose C. Carosso, *The Morgans: Private International Bankers, 1854-1913.* Harvard University Press, Cambridge, 1987.

2. See Franklin Parker, *George Peabody: A Biography.* Vanderbilt University Press, Nashville, 1971, particularly pp. 60-65. This work contains an extensive bibliography and is largely based on Parker's dissertation, "George Peabody, Founder of Modern Philanthropy," 3 vols. George Peabody College for Teachers, 1956.

3. Ibid. In this connection, Parker makes reference to rumors of an illegitimate daughter of Peabody and a 1940 statement by John Pierpont Morgan, Jr., attesting to such an offspring. Parker dismisses the rumors and the statement as "not proved to be true by any but circumstantial evidence." p. 29-33, 152.

4. Ibid., p. 114.

5. David Owen, *English Philanthropy, 1660-1960,* pp. 380-381.

6. *The Times,* London, March 26, 1862.

7.   This view of the Southern States "as a foreign nation" within the United States was widely held at the time. For example, George Trollope, the English novelist, in his account of a visit to the United States in the midst of the Civil War, advanced the erroneous belief that, regardless of the outcome of the war, two separate countries would emerge as a result. See Anthony Trollope, *North America, Vol. II.* The Trollope Society, London, 2001, pp. 452-454.

8.   See Rupert Graf Strachwitz, "Foundations in Germany and Their Revival in East Germany after 1989," in Anheier and Toepler, (eds.), *Private Funds. Public Purpose, Philanthropic Foundations in International Perspective*, pp. 227-231.

9.   J.L.M. Curry, *A Brief Sketch of George Peabody and a History of The Peabody Education Fund Through Thirty Years.* University Press, Cambridge, 1898, p. 54. See also, Franklin Parker, *George Peabody: A Biography,* pp. 180-187.

10. Franklin Parker, *George Peabody: A Biography,* pp. 64, 136.

11. William Lloyd Garrison, "Honored Beyond His Deserts," *The Independent,* New York, February 10, 1870, p. 1.

12. See the exhaustive Part I. Comprehensive Bibliography of Documents Mentioning George Peabody, 1795-1969 compiled in vol. 3, 1094-1219 of Franklin Parker's dissertation, "George Peabody, Founder of Modern Philanthropy."

13. *The Times,* London, March 26, 1862, p. 9.

14. J. L. M. Curry, *A Brief Sketch of George Peabody,* pp. 19-20.

15. Daniel C. Gilman, "Five Great Gifts," *The Outlook,* No. 13, July 27, 1907, pp. 648-656.

16. Robert S. Morison, "Foundations and Universities," *Daedalus,* Fall, 1964, p. 1111.

17. Margaret Olivia Sage, "Opportunities and Responsibilities of Leisured Women," *North American Review,* vol. CLXXXI, November, 1905, pp. 712-721.

18. See Arthur Huntington Gleason, "Mrs. Russell Sage and Her Interests," *World's Work,* vol. XIII, no. 1, November, 1906, pp. 8182-8216 and Robert W. de Forest, "Margaret Olivia Sage, Philanthropist," *Survey,* vol. XLI, November 9, 1918, p. 151.

19. Charles E. Slocum, *A Short History of the Slocums, Slocumbs, and Sclocombs of America,* vol.1, 1882 and Henry Whittemore, *History of the Sage and Slocum Family,* 1908.

20. *New York Times,* November 4, 5, and 14, 1918 and *New York Tribune,* November 5, 1918.

21. Irvin G. Wyllie, "Margaret Olivia Slocum Sage" *Notable American Women.* Belknap Press of Harvard University Press, Cambridge, vol. 3, pp. 222-223.

22. John M. Glenn, Lilian Brandt, F. Emerson Andrews, *Russell Sage Foundation, 1907-1946.* 2 vol., Russell Sage Foundation, New York, 1947.

23. Sage's death was noted on the front page of the *New York Times.*

24. *Survey,* p. 151.

25. See *Russell Sage Foundation, 1907-1946,* vol. 1., pp. 3-12, for the role of de Forest in the genesis of the Foundation.

26. Ibid., pp. 13-17.

27. Irvin G. Wyllie, "Margaret Olivia Slocum Sage," *Dictionary of American Biography,* Charles Scribner's Sons, New York, vol. VIII, p. 291.

28. Franklin H. Giddings, "The Danger in Charitable Trusts," *Van Norden Magazine.* Vol. II, no. 3, June, 1907. p. 43.

29. Ibid., p. 47.

30. See *Russell Sage Foundation, 1907-1946,* vol. I, p. 9 for the names and backgrounds of these members.

31. *Notable American Women,* p. 223.
32. Bess Heitner, "One Woman's Vision," *Reporting from the Russell Sage Foundation,* No. 11, March, 1989, p. 3.
33. David C. Hammack, "Russell Sage Foundation," Harold M. Keele and Joseph C. Kiger (eds.) *Foundations.* Greenwood Press, Westport, Connecticut, 1984, pp. 374.
34. For two full length biographies of Carnegie, see Joseph Frazier Wall, *Andrew Carnegie.* Oxford University Press, New York, 1970 and Burton J. Hendrick, *The Life of Andrew Carnegie.* 2 Vol., Doubleday, Doran Co., New York, 1932.
35. Andrew Carnegie, *Autobiography of Andrew Carnegie.* Houghton, Mifflin Co., New York, 1920, p., 282. In 1928, Mrs. Carnegie endowed the Andrew Carnegie Birthplace Memorial and turned it over to the Carnegie Dunfermline Trust for administration. The income from the Memorial is used to maintain the cottage where Carnegie was born, and an adjoining building and a playground for children.
36. Copy on deposit in New York Public Library.
37. *Carnegie Reporter,* Vol.1 No.2, Carnegie Corporation of New York, New York, 2001, back page 42.
38. Joseph C. Kiger, *Operating Principles of the Larger Foundations.* Russell Sage Foundation, New York, 1954, p. 22.
39. See Wall, *Andrew Carnegie,* pp. 836-845 and Sara L. Engelhardt, (ed,) *The Carnegie Trusts and Institutions.* Carnegie Corporation of New York, New York, pp. 10-12.
40. Andrew Carnegie, *Autobiography of Andrew Carnegie,* p. 291. For Carnegie's "story" of his gift and the setting up of the Trust see pp. 287-291.
41. Robert M. Lester, *Forty Years of Carnegie Giving.* Charles Scribner's Sons, New York, 1941, p. 174.
42. Ibid., p. 174.
43. In his efforts for the promotion of peace Carnegie also made the following direct grants for the construction of buildings for two other agencies also involved in the cause of peace: $850,000 in 1907-1911 for the Pan American Union Building, now the Organization of American States in Washington, D.C.; and $200,000 in 1908-1910 for the Central American Court of Justice in San Jose, Costa Rica.

    Also to be noted and springing from this same motive was Carnegie's embracing of and usage of simplified spelling of English words. The upshot was the provision of funds, initially amounting to $170,000 and later $110,000, for the creation in New York in 1906-1907 of a Simplified Spelling Board.
44. Wall, *Andrew Carnegie,* p. 891.
45. Lester, *Forty Years of Carnegie Giving,* p.143.
46. Ibid., p. 162.
47. Ibid., p. 166.
48. Ibid., p. 166.
49. In the establishment in 1913 of the Carnegie United Kingdom Trust discussed above, for example, Carnegie was forced to use some of his own remaining moneys because the charter of the Corporation ruled out appropriations by it for use in the United Kingdom.
50. Hendrick, *The Life of Andrew Carnegie,* Vol. 2. p. 352.
51. In her history of the Corporation, Ellen Condliffe Lagemann's *The Politics of Knowledge. The Carnegie Corporation, Philanthropy, and Public Policy.* Wesleyan University Press, Middletown, Connecticut, 1989, there are only three passing references to Mrs. Louise Whitfield Carnegie and none to Mrs. Margaret Carnegie Miller.

52. Peter Krass, *Carnegie*. John Wiley and Sons., Hoboken, New Jersey, 2002, p. 536.
53. John D. Rockefeller, *Random Reminiscences of Men and Events*. Doubleday, Doran & Company, Inc., Garden City, New York, 1933.
54. Ron Chernow, *Titan, The Life of John D. Rockefeller, Sr.* Random House, New York, 1998, p. *xv,* 468, see also, pp. *xii-xiv*, 3-44; 56-61; and 458-465. For additional discussion of these two dissimilar characters and their bifurcated influence on Rockefeller, see also: Allan Nevins, *Study in Power: John D. Rockefeller, Industrialist and Philanthropist.* Charles Scribner's Sons, New York, 1953, 2 vols., particularly Vol.I. pp. 1-12, 30, 336-337 and Vol., II, pp. 88, 343; David Freeman Hawke, *John D. The Founding Father of the Rockefellers.* Harper & Row Publishers, New York, 1980, pp. 1-19 *; and* John Ensor Harr and Peter J. Johnson, *The Rockefeller Century,* Charles Scribner's Sons, New York, 1988, p. 16.
55. Allen Nevins, *Study in Power,* Vol. I, pp. 16-17.
56. John T. Flynn, *God's Gold: The Story of Rockefeller and His Times.* Harcourt, Brace and Company, New York, 1932, p. 401.
57. Ron Chernow, *Titan, The Life of John D. Rockefeller, Sr.,* p. 300.
58. John D. Rockefeller, *Random Reminiscences of Men and Events,* p. 109.
59. Frederick T. Gates, *Chapters in My Life.* The Free Press, New York, 1977, pp., 299-300.
60. See Allen Nevins, *Study in Power,* Vol. II, pp. 92-93.
61. For the history of the GEB, see Raymond B. Fosdick, with Henry F. Pringle and Katherine Douglas Pringle, *The Story of the General Education Board.* Harper& Row, New York, 1962.
62. Later called the International Health Board and finally, in 1927, the International Health Division.
63. For a brief history of the Board see, "China Medical Board," Harold M. Keele and Joseph C. Kiger (eds.) *Foundations.* Greenwood Press, Westport, Connecticut, 1984, pp. 76-77. See also, *Annual Report, 1977-1978,* of the Board which reviews the Board's programs for the period 1928-1978.

2

Harkness, Guggenheim, Mott, Markle, Kellogg, Mellon, Luce, and Ford

World War I (1914-1918) was followed by the economic boom of the 1920s, the Depression of the 1930s, and the onset of World War II. Despite the varying economic conditions during the passage of these decades, by 1939 it can be estimated that some 200 to 400 foundations of some size and scope had been established.[1] In that year, however, in addition to the philanthropists discussed in Chapter 1, only eleven others established during these decades were major actors on the foreign activity scene. They were the Commonwealth Fund and Pilgrim Trust established by the Harkness family; John Simon Guggenheim Memorial Foundation; Charles Stewart Mott Foundation; John and Mary R. Markle Foundation, W.K. Kellogg Foundation; Henry Luce Foundation; Bollingen Foundation, Old Dominion Foundation, and Andrew W. Mellon Foundation established by the Mellon family, and Ford Foundation.

Harkness

The ancestors of Edward S. Harkness emigrated from Scotland to Massachusetts in 1710. The family moved westward in the early eighteenth century to New York state and Stephen V. Harkness, the father of Edward S. Harkness, was born there in 1818. Orphaned at the age of seven, Stephen had little formal education and was apprenticed in his youth as a harness–maker. Sensing greater opportunities farther west, in 1840 he moved to the state of Ohio where he gradually shifted from harness-making to highly successful and lucrative livestock, grain, and other commercial enterprises. By 1870 Stephen V. Harkness had acquired enough wealth to invest in and become one of the six original and major stockholders of John D. Rockefeller's Standard Oil Company. He continuously augmented his spectacular returns from this investment in Standard Oil with other highly profitable business ventures. Harkness had bequeathed his second wife (nee Anna M. Richardson) one of the great fortunes of American history by the time of his death in 1888. Reflecting this wealth, their second son, Edward S. Harkness, born in Cleveland, Ohio in 1874, was educated in New England at St. Paul's School and graduated from Yale University in 1897. In 1904 Edward married Mary E. Stillman, the daughter of a well-to-do New York lawyer. The couple had no children. The family fortune continued to grow under the watchful eyes of Stephen Harkness' widow, those of an older son Charles, who died in 1916, and Edward.

Commonwealth Fund

In the meantime, members of the Harkness family made numerous and sizeable gifts to various religious, educational, medical, and civic institutions. As word of their wealth circulated, Mrs. Harkness was inundated with appeals for aid and assistance which proved impossible to handle personally and effectively. "After much thought on these problems, and after many discussions with Edward, Mrs. Stephen V. Harkness decided to establish a charitable foundation as a means whereby a portion of her benefactions might be carried out with greater efficiency and purpose than was possible on a personal, individual basis."[2] The foundation was incorporated in 1916 in New York as the Commonwealth Fund with an initial endowment by Mrs. Harkness of $10 million and with subsequent gifts by Edward S. Harkness and his wife of some $78 million. The original five-member board of directors (trustees) of the Fund, with Edward S. Harkness serving as president until his death in 1940, consisted of him and four friends. Following his death his wife served as honorary president until her death in 1950. Malcolm P. Aldrich followed Edward Harkness as president of the Fund and was succeeded by Quigg Newton, Carleton B. Chapman, Margaret E. Mahoney, and the incumbent Karen Davis.

The Fund was given complete freedom to chart its own course under the broad mandate "to do something for the welfare of mankind."[3] The initial activities of the foundation centered on providing relief for war torn Europe; particularly grants for food and medical relief. Over $2 million for these purposes were expended by 1923 together with a considerable amount of it devoted to the relief of impoverished intellectuals in central Europe. At the close of this period the Fund turned its giving to the domestic scene, first in the educational sector and then increasingly and permanently in the health area. As the historian of the Commonwealth Fund succinctly stated, "Since its founding, the Commonwealth Fund has directed its attention and resources primarily to the development of ideas, talents, institutions, and arrangements promising to strengthen the extent and quality of medical care in American society."[4]

In the 1920s, however, largely because of Edward S, Harkness' interest in fostering close ties with the English speaking nations, the Fund inaugurated a fellowship program to help students from Britain and several Commonwealth countries to come to U.S. universities for graduate study. Following World War II, the range of recipients of such fellowships has been expanded to include those from various European countries. At that time the name of the fellowships was changed from "Commonwealth Fellowships" to "Harkness Fellowships of the Commonwealth Fund."[5] Thus from its beginnings and down to the present the Fund has continued to support foreign fellows for study in the United States.

Harkness House at One East Fifty-Seventh Street in New York City was built as a wedding gift from Anna Harkness to her son and daughter-in-law. They moved into the mansion in 1908 and it was their home until the death of Edward's wife in 1950. As the Harknesses had no children, the house was left to the Commonwealth Fund and since 1952 its offices have been located there. The understated grandeur and beauty of the house was noted at the time of its construction and since. In 1988, for example, an architectural critic noted:

> One East Seventh-fifth Street has not only escaped the sad fate of demolition that has overtaken so many of its neighbors on Fifth Avenue—it has never, in a sense, left the Harkness family. It remains in the hands of the family's foundation, which continues to maintain it with care and respect—recognizing that the preservation of one of New York City's most distinguished houses can, in and of itself, be a philanthropic gesture that enriches the quality of life for the entire city.[6]

Pilgrim Trust

The establishment by Edward S. Harkness through the Commonwealth Fund of the international fellowships discussed above was in a large degree a reflection of his admiration and warm feelings for Britain, his ancestral home. He traveled there frequently and developed numerous and influential friendships. In due course he became thoroughly conversant with and esteemed many things British. Imitation can be said to be the sincerest expression of such feelings and this was certainly true of Edward S. Harkness' views of British education at the secondary and university level. His admiration of their structure and system led to his provision of funds directly to St. Paul's School, which he had attended, and Phillips Exeter that greatly contributed toward these U.S. preparatory schools' replication to a considerable degree of the methods followed at Eton and other notable British public schools. Similarly, his gifts to Harvard and Yale universities made it possible for them to introduce the "residential" or "house" plan which was designed to emulate the "college" system at Oxford and Cambridge universities. It is against this background, following World War I and the trying years for Britain following peace, that Edward S. Harkness decided to provide help there then and on into the future. Initially, he thought that his aid might be funneled through the Commonwealth Fund. However, Sir James Irvine, one of the handfuls of Britons he consulted with on the matter, explained that this idea was rejected by him on the grounds that, to be effective, an organization of that kind must work in the country it is designed to assist. Moreover, he believed that British problems should be

> solved by British people and that, in such matters, there must be "no reference to a New York headquarters." Stage by stage the discussion moved inexorably to the conclusion that a British Trust should be formed with complete independence; in short, what he contemplated was "a free gift to our nation."[7]

Thus the Pilgrim Trust, a name suggested by Mrs. Harkness as reflecting its purpose and origin, was established in 1930. With an initial endowment of about $10 million, the Trust was chartered in the United Kingdom without any restrictions and its income was and has been administered solely by Britons. In the 1930s some of its funds were devoted to the alleviation of the vicissitudes associated with the depression, the welfare of the armed forces during World War II, and since then, solving some of the weaknesses in the emergent Welfare State.

> From the start they [trustees] felt, however, that Harkness ... would wish them to devote attention to preserving what may be termed the national heritage—the heritage of historic architecture, works of art, historical records, human learning, and the beauty of countryside and coast.... Pari passu with their help to ecclesiastical buildings and their contents, the trustees have contributed to the preservation of secular buildings, including many in historic towns such as Oxford, Cambridge, Lincoln, Bristol, and York, always provided they are not in private ownership. The National Trusts, in both England and Scotland, have been helped to acquire a number of historic houses, as well as stretches of the sea coast and countryside.[8]

In addition and over the years, the Pilgrim Trust has aided many museums, galleries, and libraries, as well as learned bodies such as the Royal Society and the Royal Academy.

Guggenheim

The grandparents of Simon Guggenheim, Simon and Rachel Guggenheim, emigrated to the United States from Europe in 1847. He and his son Meyer began life in the New World as peddlers in Pennsylvania. By the time Meyer died in 1907 he had become a wealthy man, particularly by investing in and developing mining and mineral interests in the western States. Building on this base, Meyer's son Simon, born in 1867, and his six older brothers had each acquired substantial fortunes, particularly in the copper industry. A U.S. Senator from Colorado from 1907 to 1913, Simon and his wife had only two children, sons, the youngest a ne'er-do-well who eventually committed suicide. The elder, John Simon, a contrast in promise and on the point of entering Harvard as an undergraduate in 1922, was struck down with a fatal illness and died in that year.

John Simon Guggenheim Memorial Foundation

During the period of pain and sorrow immediately following John Simon's death the concept of establishing a foundation in his memory took shape in the minds of Simon Guggenheim and his wife. They initially leaned towards the establishment of a fellowship program similar to the Rhodes scholarships. Instrumental to a great degree in leading them in this direction were two men, each of whom had previously been Rhodes Scholars, attorney Carroll A. Wilson and college president Frank Aydelotte. Discussions and further consideration among them in 1923 and 1924, however, led in 1925 to a much broader undertaking with the chartering in that year in New York of the John Simon Guggenheim Memorial Foundation. Guggenheim's initial letter of gift of $3 million to the Foundation spelled out these broader purposes in terms which provided great freedom and latitude for its future operation. Thus the foundation established in memory of and bearing the name of their son would: "promote the advancement and diffusion of knowledge and understanding, and the appreciation of beauty, by aiding without distinction on account of race, color or creed, scholars, scientists and artists of either sex in the prosecution of their labors." The Fellowships thus envisioned would be awarded "to provide opportunities for both men and women to carry on advanced study in any field of knowledge, or in any of the fine arts, including music … under the freest possible conditions." It was hoped that they would operate both "to add to the educational, literary, artistic and scientific power of this country, and also to provide for the cause of better international understanding."[9]

Playing an important role in the fashioning of this now free and flexible mandate for the future direction of the Fellowships was another Rhodes Scholar, Henry Allen Moe. Then thirty years old and newly returned from England, Moe had been engaged by Aydelotte at Wilson's suggestion in August of 1924. He was actively involved in the deliberations and planning which culminated in the broader role and scope of the Foundation which was established in February of 1925. At that time Moe was employed by the Foundation and, as one chronicler observed:

> for thirty-nine years he ran it, serving in various official capacities. He served first as secretary, 1925-1938; as secretary-general 1938-1954; and still later as secretary-general and vice-president. In 1945, he became a member of the board of trustees, and from 1961-1963, he served as its president, resigning in 1964 to conduct a study for the National Science Foundation. In 1970, Moe was made president emeritus of the board and continued in that capacity until his death in 1975.[10]

The great freedom and latitude of operation afforded the Guggenheim from its inception is strikingly illustrated by the gradual geographical expansion of its areas of operation. Originally, the Guggenheim awards were restricted to U.S. citizens and permanent residents, including its territories and some possessions. In the 1930s several South American countries were added to its purview; in the 1940s Canada and Newfoundland were included; and since the 1950s fellowships were being awarded to all of the countries in the western hemisphere together with the Philippines, the latter originally falling in the possessions category and kept open for awards after its independence had been achieved. The beginnings of this foreign expansion of the foundation had been launched by a second gift of a million dollars to the foundation by the Guggenheims in 1929. The primary motive for this move was succinctly stated in a letter from Guggenheim accompanying the gift: "My brothers and I have long been engaged in commerce with many of the republics to the south of the United States, and we know that there are no longer any important factors of economic isolation separating us. But a similar commerce of things of the mind, of spiritual values, is yet to be accomplished."[11] By the 1950s, however, out of annual income amounting to about $1 million only some $90,000 was being spent for foreign grants. In 1978 with about $2.6 million in grants awarded annually only about $380,000 fell to grantees outside the United States and Canada. The proportion has remained about the same since that time.

All accounts of the John Simon Guggenheim Memorial Foundation aver that Simon Guggenheim, and only to slightly lesser extent his wife, had a deep interest in the conduct of the foundation after its establishment. He served as its president from 1925, at its beginning, to his death in 1941. He was succeeded in that office by Mrs. Guggenheim who served until she resigned in 1961 but remained president emeritus until her death in 1970 when the Foundation received a $40 million bequest from her. Throughout these years, however, the actual administration and operation of the Foundation had fallen upon Henry Allen Moe. Upon his retirement in 1963, he was succeeded by Joel Connaroe who remained chief executive until 2003 when he was followed by Edward Hirsch.

Mott

Charles Stewart Mott (1875-1973), the son of John Coon Mott and Isabella Stewart Mott was born in Newark, New Jersey. His father was of English and his mother of Irish descent. At that time his father operated a successful cider and vinegar business. Following graduation from high school, the younger Mott was slated by him to enter that business. Mott was otherwise inclined and began studying to be an engineer at the Stevens Institute of Technology in Hoboken, New Jersey. In a vain effort to dissuade him from an engineering career the father dispatched him to Europe for a year to examine fermentation processes in use there that might be used for the benefit of the family business. Upon his return Mott completed his engineering studies and by 1894 he had organized a company which engaged in the production of carbonation equipment. In 1900, following a stint as a gunner's mate in the U.S. Navy during the Spanish-American War, Mott became the manager of Weston-Mott Company, a bicycle wheel factory, acquired earlier by his father and uncle. Sensing the future of the automobile, Mott steered the company into concentrating on the production of automotive wire wheels. By 1906, at the encouragement of the legendary automotive tycoon William C. Durant, then engaged in the founding of the General Motors Corporation headquartered in Flint, Michigan, Mott agreed to open a plant there. While continuing control of his manufacturing operations, Mott oversaw its merging with GM through his acceptance of stock in the firm. From the 1920s on he had become a director and official on its board and was and continued to be one of its largest stockholders. In tandem with his business activities, Mott was heavily involved in civic and political affairs at the local level; serving as mayor of Flint in 1912, 1913, and 1918. His General Motors holdings together with banking and other business interests resulted in his eventually becoming one of the richest men in the United States by the time of his death in 1973 at the age of 97.[12]

At the inception of his business career, Mott married Ethel Culbert Harding in 1900. Prior to her death in a tragic accident in 1924, she bore him three children: a son, Charles Stewart Harding Mott, called Harding Mott, and two daughters Aimee and Elsa. Two succeeding marriages followed; one ending in the death of the wife in 1928 followed by a divorce of a second in 1929. In 1934, Mott married a younger cousin, Ruth Mott Rawlings and they had three children: a son, Stewart Rawlings Mott and two daughters, Susan and Maryanne.

Charles Stewart Mott Foundation

From the beginning of his life and career in 1900, Mott's charitable impulses centered on people and causes associated with Flint, Michigan. He provided money for hospitals, parks, and a variety of youth-oriented programs. Prior to 1926, these were carried out personally. In that year, however, with the creation of the Charles Stewart Mott Foundation, it became the major vehicle for his giving. The catalysts in its creation were the complexities he encountered in settling his father's estate, tax considerations, and "a way of organizing his help to the community and making it businesslike—taking as much care in the spending of his money as he had devoted to earning it."[13] Foundation giving followed this same path, from 1926 until 1935, when Mott came under the influence of Frank J. Manley, then the physical education supervisor for the Flint public schools. Their association culminated in a program of aid for all of the city's schools. In addition to providing schooling, it enabled the schools to become civic centers for all ages. By the 1960s some 80 percent of foundation giving was devoted to this purpose. Such foundation aid surpassed $100 million by the 1980s and the program eventually became a national and international model of its type.

With the death of Mott and a tremendous increase in its assets from his estate in the 1970s, there was a major change in the foundation's orientation.[14] Although continuing to give significant support to the Flint schools to this day, the foundation launched programs devoted to urban, racial, environmental and other problems nationally and eventually internationally.

The board of trustees of the Mott Foundation for several decades after its creation consisted of Chairman Charles Stewart Mott, several family members, including his son (C.S.) Harding Mott, and close friends of the elder Mott. Following the latter's death in 1973, the board was enlarged and reconstituted to provide a majority of non-family members. C.S. Harding Mott then became the chairman of the foundation's board of trustees and his son-in-law William S. White, became and remains its president to the present day. Still, as of 1999, "Thirty-two trustees have served the foundation during its lifetime; of those thirteen have been Mott family members."[15] The geographical spread of foundation grants by 1982 showed

> the Mott Foundation made 361 grants totaling $26,096,455 to organizations in 46 states, Australia, Canada, Colombia, and England … in 1982 Flint and Genesee County received 48 percent of the 54 percent that was distributed in Michigan. Except for one-half of one percent that went to international grantees, the remaining 45 percent went to other states.[16]

In 1989, President White noted the death of C.S. Harding Mott the previous year and announced:

> Appointed to the board was Rushworth Kidder, senior columnist for the *Christian Science Monitor*. A native New Englander, he is the author of "An Agenda for the 21st Century" and "Reinventing the Future: Global Goals for the 21st Century." With his work on global issues, Rush brings to the board experience in many areas and interests that coincide with our future direction.[17]

Thus, the 1990s witnessed the inauguration of a considerable increase in the foundation's international programs in various world areas, accompanied by a significant increase in foundation staff. In 1994 a new three-year grants program was launched that included Central and Eastern Europe, Russia and the Republics, and South Africa. Regarding the first two areas, it was announced:

> The goal of grantmaking in this program area was to help emerging civil societies in Central / Eastern Europe, Russia and the Republics, in their transition to open, democratic and pluralistic societies and strong market economies by strengthening the nonprofit sector and providing technical assistance and training to the public and private sectors…. Also, the foundation established a field office in Prague, Czech Republic, in 1994. This program area will evolve as the field office expands in 1995-96.[18]

Regarding South Africa:

> The goal of grantmaking in this program area was to strengthen civil society in South Africa during the transition from apartheid toward a democratic, nonracial, nonsexist society by encouraging formerly disenfranchised populations to participate at the local, regional and national levels in decision making that affects their communities.[19]

By 1997, following the establishment of a foundation field office in Johannesburg, South Africa, President White announced: "Out of 461 grants we made last year, 100 were to grantees located outside the United States, and 49 were expenditure responsibility, meaning the Foundation undertook additional tax-reporting requirements to ensure that the grants were expended properly."[20] All of the foregoing grant activities were done in partnership with many other United States and foreign foundations, such as the Ford Foundation and Rockefeller Brothers Fund.[21] With these changes, accompanied by a considerable increase in foundation staff, since the 1990s the foundation has continued to conduct an extensive international program on into the twenty-first century; particularly in Central and Eastern Europe despite the withdrawal of some other foundations from foreign activities there.[22]

Markle

John Markle was born in 1858 and grew up in Hazleton, Pennsylvania. He was the son of George B. Markle, a coalminer, who had established a company engaged in the mining industry. John Markle entered the mining industry in the firm his father had founded after acquiring a degree in mining engineering in 1880. He became one of the most successful and wealthiest coal mining executives in the country and achieved national recognition for his engineering prowess in the field.

Markle's early philanthropy consisted of personal and palliative giving to individuals and causes. With ever increasing wealth, he and his wife, the former Mary E. Robinson, in 1902 moved to New York in order to better manage his burgeoning business interests. Eventually, directly influenced by his friend J. Pierpont Morgan, and indirectly by the examples of John D. Rockefeller and Andrew Carnegie, Markle turned to the foundation as the best organizational means to carry on his philanthropy. Another significant factor in this decision was the fact that the Markles had no children

John and Mary R. Markle Foundation

In 1927 John Markle set up the John and Mary R. Markle Foundation with an initial endowment of $3 million. His wife had little to do with the operation of the foundation and only served on the foundation's board of trustees for the first year of its existence. Until his death in 1933, John Markle operated the Markle Foundation as a personal gift-giving device for grants to designated worthy individuals or causes that he had previously supported. Each year until his death he would supplement foundation giving allocations with monies from his own income. Such benefactions were carried out under a very detailed charter but one which left it with the widest latitude in what it could do then and in the future. The charter specifically stated that its purpose was:

> To promote the advancement and diffusion of knowledge among the people of the United States and to promote the general good of mankind; to aid preparatory, vocational and technical schools, institutions of higher learning, libraries, scientific and medical research; to provide shelter, the necessaries of life and financial and medical assistance to such persons as the directors shall select among those in want, poverty and destitute circumstances; to establish and maintain charitable, benevolent, educational, vocational, industrial, recreational, and welfare activities, agencies and institutions engaged in the discovery , treatment, and cure of diseases and in medical research work…. The operations of the corporation may be carried on within the state of New York and elsewhere throughout the United States and in foreign countries.[23]

Following John Markle's death in 1933, the foundation received additional sums from his estate which left it with a total endowment of about $15 million and a board of directors in a dilemma as to how the foundation's money was to be spent. Its two programs, which evolved since then, have generally reflected the decisions of the board of directors at the time and the interests of its chief executives. The first program extending from 1937 to 1969 generally concentrated on giving in the physical and medical sciences. From 1947 through 1969, with John Russel as its president during that period, the best known and principal foundation program in this area was the assistance provided for Markle Scholars in Academic Medicine.[24] The second program was inaugurated in 1969 with the election of Lloyd N. Morrisett as foundation president and, upon his retirement in 1998, continues under the present president, Zoë Baird. As Morrisett succinctly stated: "in 1969, the [foundation] program was dramatically changed. The Foundation's attention shifted from academic medicine and medical interests to mass communications. It was the Markle Foundation's flexible tradition of public trust that made this possible."[25] Throughout its existence, with no geographical restrictions in its charter on its operation, the Markle Foundation has made foreign as well as domestic grants.

Kellogg

A son was born to John Prescott Kellogg, a struggling broom manufacturer, and his wife Ann Janette Kellogg in Battle Creek, Michigan in 1860. The baby was named Willie Keith Kellogg at birth but "Always hating the name 'Willie' and not liking 'William' much better, Mr. Kellogg waited until he was thirty-eight years old before having his name changed by court order to "Will Keith Kellogg." [26] This long delay in a name change coincides with the equally long delay in his establishment of a great American corporation, his enormous pecuniary success, and his noteworthy achievements in philanthropy. With little in the way of education, the boy became a traveling broom salesman for his father at an early age and then went to work in 1879 for his older brother Dr. John Harvey Kellogg who, following medical training in New York City, had founded what was to eventually become the national and world famous Battle Creek Sanitarium. A key feature in its development was Dr. Kellogg's espousal of a primarily vegetarian diet for the thousands of patients and visitors that eventually came to the "San" for rest and treatment of ill-health and diseases. Growing out of Dr. Kellogg's belief were continuous experiments by him and his brother to make grains and nuts more appealing to patients as food, particularly when it came to breakfast food. These experiments were so successful that many individuals on leaving the San sent back for supplies of the "breakfast foods" they had enjoyed there.

During the twenty-five years of his association with the San, the younger Kellogg "was bookkeeper, manager, and janitor of the world famous hospital. In fact, virtually any task outside of medicine that needed doing fell to him."[27] Thus, Will Keith Kellogg was overshadowed during this period by his increasingly famous physician-brother. Eventually, however, the brothers came to a parting of the ways when the younger Kellogg, realizing the financial potential in the creation of a mass market for the wheat and corn flake and other breakfast foods they had developed, in 1906 set up his own Battle Creek Toasted Corn Flake Company. Although beset from the start by rivals, some forty other cereal companies began operations in the period 1900 to 1905, W.K. Kellogg's neverending toil and business acumen outstripped them all. As he himself noted he often put in 120 hours a week on the job and never learned to play. In the ensuing decades the company went on to become the world's largest manufacturer of a full line of ready-to-eat cereals, with plants in the United States and all over the world, with annual sales in the billions of dollars, and with millions of dollars in profits flowing to Kellogg.

W.K. Kellogg's personal life was not as propitious or successful as his business career. He was married in 1880 to Ella Davis, the daughter of a grocer and part-time clock repairer, who was not in good health in her later years and who died in 1912. There followed a second marriage for Kellogg in 1918 which led to estrangement a few years later. Although his first marriage had resulted in five children, three died while still young. Also, attempts by Kellogg to groom a surviving son and eventually a grandson as successors at the helm of the company were unsuccessful.

W.K. Kellogg Foundation

"Kellogg had a strange distaste for the words 'philanthropy' and 'philanthropists,' once writing to Paul de Krief that "a philanthropist is one who would do good for the love of his fellowmen. I love to do things for children because I get a kick out of it. Therefore, I am a selfish person and no philanthropist."[28] In any case, as Kellogg prospered he made many charitable gifts as an individual. By 1925, furthermore, he set up the Fellowship Corporation as a more efficient method of dispensing his benefactions and in the next five years about $1 million was channeled through this organization. During this period most of such aid was primarily of a local or regional character. Then in 1930 the W.K. Kellogg Foundation was organized with the initial purpose of "receiving and administering funds for the promotion of the welfare, comfort, health, care, education, feeding, clothing, sheltering, and safeguarding of children and youth, directly or indirectly, without regard to sex, race, creed or nationality, in whatever manner the Board of Trustees may decide."[29] In a history published by the Foundation, it is noted that, at Kellogg's suggestion, this wording was changed and broadened:

> "by redefining the beneficiaries to be ... mankind, but principally children and youth." Subsequently, he recommended a deletion of this latter portion of the new definition so that the amended purpose of the organization was stated to be "for the promotion of the health, education and welfare of mankind." Eventually, the purpose of the Foundation was further broadened and today reads "to receive and administer funds for educational or charitable purposes." These important alterations provided the trustees and officers the opportunity greatly to expand the scope of the Foundation's activities in ensuing years. [30]

Kellogg named six friends and associates as trustees and eventually provided the foundation with approximately $50 million. At the same time Kellogg provided substantial separate trusts for his children and grandchildren. W.K. Kellogg served as chairman of the foundation board of trustees from 1934 until his death in 1951 at age 91. A grandson, John L. Kellogg, Jr., briefly served there from 1930-1933.

By the 1940s W.K. Kellogg had become totally blind and, during these last years of his life, his attention turned increasingly to philanthropy in general and the Kellogg Foundation in particular. Despite disclaimers on his part, it appears that Kellogg played an active role in planning and launching the programs of the foundation. Initially, the Kellogg Foundation concentrated its programming on education and health, with special attention to children and youth. During World War II it added agriculture to its areas of interest. It was about this time, too, that projects in these areas began to be funded abroad, with W.K. Kellogg's full approbation and approval, and eventually included Canada, Latin America, Australia, New Zealand, and various European countries. At the present time, foreign activities of the Kellogg Foundation are concentrated in the Caribbean, Latin America, and five African countries. The foundation also supports an international fellowship program in its areas of interest in these and other foreign countries. In the 1950s, with total annual grants amounting to approximately $4 million, foreign grants were about $400,000 annually. Today, with annual grants totaling about $300 million, the foundation makes foreign grants in about the same proportion. Since the 1950s, when the board of trustees numbered about ten members, the board of trustees was gradually enlarged with a diverse membership now totaling about twenty people

Mellon

Thomas Mellon, the founder of the Mellon fortune in the United States, was born in Northern Ireland in 1813, the son of a farming family. In 1818, following the sale of the family farm, the family emigrated to the United States and purchased a farm of about 160 acres in Western Pennsylvania near what is now present-day Pittsburgh. Although his parents prospered, acquired other farms, and eventually offered Thomas a farm of his own, he early on decided that he wanted to pursue another career path. The catalyst in this projected change he attributed to a reading of Benjamin Franklin's autobiography at the age of fourteen. While he kept on intermittently working on the family's farms, from that point on his continued readings and subsequent education at the secondary and collegiate level resulted in his admission to the bar and his opening of a law office in Pittsburgh in 1839. Thomas Mellon continually placed his money in lucrative real estate and other investments after prospering in his legal practice and becoming a judge from 1859-1869. In the 1860s and 1870s he loaned money to Andrew Carnegie and Henry Clay Frick. During this period he courted and married Sarah Jane Negley and the couple had six sons and two daughters. After leaving the bench in 1869, he established a private bank, T. Mellon and Sons, in Pittsburgh in the same year and by 1882 had transferred ownership of the bank to his twenty-seven-year-old son Andrew W. Mellon. In the 1880s, while the elder Mellon continued to maintain an office at the bank and remain active in financial affairs, he took time to make an extended trip to Ireland. A major reason for the journey was to visit the ancestral cottage from which he had departed so many years earlier and for which he had fond memories. Despite such memories, it remained for his descendants to provide funds for the cottage's renovation in the 1960s. For, in the words of the editor of the second edition of his autobiography, although he provided monetary aid to needy family members and friends, "Thomas Mellon was never interested in public philanthropy."[31] In a Foreword to this autobiography, the noted biographer David McCullough aptly characterizes this work as a "remarkable autobiography" (p. vii), and "The story he unfolds is amazing" (p. viii). The present writer has based much of his account of the life of Thomas Mellon on this autobiography and completely shares McCullough's strong endorsement.

In addition to holding and expressing the above view on philanthropy, Mellon advanced his ideas on an amazing varieties of topics, including war, education, crime, religion, and others. Regarding war, for example, he stated:

> There may be occasions justifying war and making it the duty of every citizen to engage in it, but in the present state of civilization such occasions can seldom occur; and there is always a disproportionately large class of men fitted by nature for a service which requires so little brain work as the common soldier, and who are more valuable to their country and themselves as soldiers at such a time than in any other capacity.... On this account the parents and friends of young men of promise should use all their influence to guard them from the temptations brought to bear on them in times of military excitement.[32]

Mellon expounded these views at length to his own sons and successfully persuaded them not to engage in military activity to any great degree during the Civil War. He expressed and held a low opinion of Catholic Irish and Mormons. Regarding socialism/communism, he feared that "Nothing has appeared in my time which threatens more serious consequences than socialism."[33] As to its proponents, he avers:

> At first he becomes possessed of the idea that the present system is not as it should be and does not suit him, that he does not get his full share of the good things of the world. He never looks for the cause of this in himself; men are never inclined to do this. He never thinks of reforming his own conduct to suit society, but forthwith concludes that society must be reformed to suit him.

Mellon concludes, however, that "Society is not likely to lose its sense entirely, and devote itself to destruction. The real danger to our liberties is from the aggressive element, the socialism of the state—the insidious encroachments of legislation on the domain of personal liberty and private enterprise."[34] Despite the fact that he had played a leading role in the social and economic transformation of the United States, he deplored its effect on laborers:

> Formerly workingmen were individualized in character and condition. They were distributed throughout the country and associated with other classes, and better influences surrounded them than now ... the crowding of men and families of the same occupation together has a demoralizing effect; it dwarfs individuality, reduces all to a common level in a monotonous condition, and creates a caste feeling and discontent with their lot. The stimulus to improvement by the moral effect of associating with others of different occupations and of other conditions is removed. The employees and their families in the larger manufacturing and mining establishments are often designated each by his number, and live in numbered tenements, and are all subjected to the same routine, and treated alike: too much like the soldiers of an army or the inmates of a prison.[35]

In any case, by the time of his death in 1908, Thomas Mellon had amassed a fortune of some $2 to $4 million, which he had largely transferred to his children.

Mellon's two daughters lived only a few years after birth; one son died prematurely at age nine; two died late in the nineteenth century. Three sons lived on into the 1930s and it is primarily around two of the latter, Andrew W. Mellon, Richard B. Mellon, and their descendants that a foundation story unfolds. Richard B. Mellon left his very large fortune to his son Richard King Mellon on his death in 1933. The latter, who augmented his inheritance through judicious business investments, founded the Richard King Mellon Foundation in 1947. This foundation lies outside the scope of this study because the terms of its charter specified no grants outside the United States, and was destined to become one of the larger U.S. foundations with present-day assets in excess of $1.5 billion dollars, Judge Mellon's two sons built their sizeable fortunes in the late nineteenth and early twentieth centuries by making early investments in and later taking control of what would become some of the behemoths of American industry; to name but a few, Aluminum Company of America, Carborundum Company, Gulf Oil Corporation, and New York Shipbuilding Company. These do not include their core holdings in the Mellon Bank, a great and continuing financial power in the United States. A biographer states that Andrew W. Mellon was "at one time a director or officer of more than sixty corporations"[36] and it is this Mellon and his descendants that figure prominently in the foreign activities of their foundations.

A.W. Mellon Educational and Charitable Trust

Up until 1900 Andrew Mellon remained a bachelor, living at his parent's home. On a voyage to Europe in 1898, however, he had been introduced to a beautiful and vivacious twenty-year-old Irish girl. He fell in love with her and, initially rebuffed, eventually persuaded her to marry him. The couple had a daughter and a son, Ailsa and Paul. The marriage, however, was an unhappy and scandalous one and eventually resulted in a divorce in 1912. Following World War I, Mellon served as Secretary of the Treasury in the Harding, Coolidge, and Hoover presidential administrations[37] and towards the close of his life was appointed American Ambassador to Great Britain. Meanwhile, Andrew Mellon had become increasingly involved in philanthropy, initially centered on gifts and grants in the Pittsburgh area. At the same time, in the course of frequent and lengthy trips to England and Europe, he was amassing what was to become one of the largest private collections of fine arts masterpieces in the world. He established the A.W Mellon Educational and Charitable Trust in 1930, primarily for funding the construction, completed in 1941, and endowment of the National Gallery of Art, Washington, D.C. and the subsequent transfer of his art collection to the Gallery. Upon his death in 1937, his remaining considerable wealth in large measure was transferred to his son and daughter. In 1940 Ailsa Mellon Bruce established the Avalon Foundation which made grants for a variety of purposes and primarily in the New York area.

Her brother, Paul Mellon, founded the Old Dominion Foundation a year later. It made grants for a wide variety of purposes with some concentration in the state of Virginia. The foreign activities of the foundation grew out of three interrelated aspects of Paul Mellon's life and career. First, the traumatic effect on him and his sister as the result of the turmoil and stress in their childhood associated with the separation and eventual divorce of their parents.[38] Second, his long sojourns in England during his childhood and youth, particularly in summers, with his mother then living there; in his twenties, studies at Clare College, Cambridge University; during World War II his service in OSS and based in England; finally, his developing and continuous interest in all things English, art, and foxhunting. Third, he ultimately became an avid art collector, like his father, early on concentrating almost solely on British art works and later, largely under the influence of his second wife, collecting French impressionistic art works.

Although Paul Mellon continued to make other large benefices personally as the result of the three above influences, seriatim examples of his major foreign activities and grants through the Old Dominion Foundation were the following. In 1943 he established and funded the Bollingen Foundation through the earlier one as the direct result of his and his first wife's reliance on the psychiatric counseling of Carl G. Jung, much of it taking place at the Bellagio, Italy home of Jung. The Bollingen Foundation made grants to individuals here and abroad in the arts and humanities and provided moneys for the publication of Jung's writings. Also, from 1973 through 1983 grants were made to the Anna Freud Foundation, London, a psychiatric organization. Funds were provided from 1964 to 1969 for the establishment and operation of the Paul Mellon Foundation for British Art located in London. During the period 1952 through 1990, it covered the costs of an interchange of fellows between Clare College, Cambridge University and Mellon's alma mater Yale University.

In 1969 the Avalon Foundation and the Old Dominion Foundation were merged into the Andrew W. Mellon Foundation. In that same year Ailsa Mellon Bruce died and the newly formed foundation received more than $400 million from her estate. Since then, a succession of ex college presidents, Nathan Pusey, Harvard; John E. Sawyer, Williams; and William G. Bowen, Princeton, have served as chief executives of the foundation. The program of the foundation gradually shifted during those decades to support for the needs of higher educational institutions, particularly the prestigious ones. Conservation and environmental projects have also figured largely in its agenda. Paul Mellon served as a trustee of the foundation from 1969 to 1985 and honorary trustee until his death in 1999. He had a son and daughter by his first marriage and their son Timothy continues to serve as a trustee of the foundation.

Luce

The father of Henry R. Luce was Henry Winters Luce (1868-1941), who was the seventh-generation descendent of an Englishman who emigrated to the New World in 1643. His mother was from Pennsylvania of English and German descent. The father, following his education in preparatory school, graduated from Yale in 1892. An ardent Presbyterian, he engaged in further study and then attended and graduated from the Princeton Theological Seminary in 1896. He was ordained to the ministry in 1897 and in the spring of that year, he married Elizabeth Middleton Root of Pennsylvania and, in the fall, the couple moved to China to be missionaries and educators.

Each of their four children, including their oldest son Henry Robinson Luce, was born in China. Henry "Harry" R. Luce, who learned Chinese before he learned English, developed an admiration and liking for the Chinese people and culture early on that stayed with him for the rest of his life. Throughout his life Luce displayed continuous reverence and veneration for his father. Following secondary school in the United States and collegiate education at Yale, he worked on several newspapers. In 1922 he and a classmate at Yale, Briton Hadden, borrowed $86,000 to establish a corporation which began the publication of a magazine called *Time*. By 1927 it had achieved enough circulation to show a profit, and following the death of Hadden in 1929, control of the corporation passed to Luce. The subsequent founding and publication of *Life*, *Fortune*, and other magazines made Luce a very wealthy man by 1935. Luce married his first wife in 1923 and the couple had two sons, Henry Luce III and Peter Paul Luce. The marriage ended in divorce in 1935, however, and shortly thereafter he married Clare Boothe Brokaw. Reportedly, she had a great influence on her husband's publishing and other business interests as well as pursuing a notable career of her own in theatrical as well as political and diplomatic areas.

Henry Luce Foundation

In a fifty-year history of the Henry Luce Foundation, written by a close associate and employee of Henry Luce for over thirty years, the author states that Luce made sizeable personal charity donations before and after its establishment in 1936. For example, the year before Luce funded the foundation he gave $50,000 to Yenching University in Peking, China as an endowment to specifically honor his father. The author then comments at length on the major possible motives and reason for its founding: qualms over his riches, foundation administration and handling of the many requests of those applying for some of it; foresight as to taxation; and deep interest in the Presbyterian Church. The author concludes, however:

> Finally, slowly over the years, there emerged what was to become the most important reason of all for Luce's ever more generous contribution to the foundation and for the large endowment he willed it when he died. The reason, seldom mentioned in earlier years, evidently grew steadily in Luce's mind and has been given appropriate prominence by Henry Luce III: to dedicate the foundation as a tribute to Henry Winters Luce and Elizabeth Root Luce, Henry R. Luce's parents.[39]

The first five-member board of directors of the foundation consisted of Luce, his wife, Clare Boothe Luce, his sister, and two close business associates of Luce. Its beginning endowment consisted of 38 shares of publishing stock held by Luce that in two years carried a market value of about $56,000. Its first grants were small ones in the hundreds of dollars and almost wholly for missionary and educational purposes, particularly in China. As Luce prospered, however, his giving to the foundation grew and by 1949 its assets stood at about $800,000. With the Communist takeover of China in 1949 and their drive to expel every thing American and particularly missionaries and educators, the Luce foundation moved its granting abroad to the East Asian areas peripheral to China.

The death of Luce in 1967 saw a vast expansion in the assets and the grant making of the foundation. His fortune had grown to over $100 million by that time and the major beneficiary of his estate was the Henry Luce Foundation. By 1981 assets amounted to about $120 million and annual grants were between $2 million and $3 million. These assets were further augmented with a bequest of about $60 million from Mrs. Clare Boothe Luce upon her death in 1987. Today the foundation's assets are about $700 million and grants amount to about $27 million annually. The program and projects of the Luce Foundation, while thus augmented, have engaged in a number of new areas over the years. For example, the Clare Boothe Luce Fund provides grants to enhance the careers of women in selected fields. Still, the foundation has maintained a remarkably similar pattern to that from its beginnings. In passing judgment on the foundation record, the foundation's historian also aptly summarizes its activities thus:

> Especially, the judgments should be made about the Luce Foundation's activities in academia (Luce professors), in East Asia (a plethora of programs), in art (an encouragement to museum scholarship), in theology (improvement of faculties in theological seminaries and divinity schools, and in public affairs (especially leadership among minority groups).[40]

Four generations of the Luce family have played a significant role in its history. They have included Henry R. Luce's sister, Mrs. Elizabeth Moore, who continuously served as a member of the foundation's board of directors from its origin to her death in 2002 at the age of 98. Similarly, Henry Luce III became the foundation's president and chief executive officer in 1958 and acted in that capacity until he assumed emeritus status in 2002. Since that time, Margaret Boles Fitzgerald and Michael Gilligan have acted as chairman and president respectively. In another generation of the Luce family, H. (Henry) Christopher Luce, is a member of the board of directors and is also an active staff member of the foundation.

Ford

Henry Ford's grandfather, John Ford, was descended from seventeenth-century English Protestant freeholders in Ireland following English occupation and colonization there. In 1847 John Ford emigrated to the United States from Ireland accompanied by his wife and seven children, including his oldest son William, and settled on a farm near present-day Dearborn. In 1861 William, who had also taken up farming in the area, met there and married Mary Litogot, who apparently was of Dutch or Belgian descent. Henry Ford, the second son of eight children sired by the couple, was born in a farmhouse near present day Dearborn, Michigan on July 30, 1863.

Working on the family farm into his teens, Henry Ford was deeply imprinted with the individualistic outlook and values of nineteenth-century rural America. This outlook was reinforced by the curriculum and schoolbooks, particularly the McGuffey readers, of the rural schools in the Dearborn area he attended from 1871 to 1879. In this same period, perhaps because of these factors, the youth became increasingly fascinated by machines and mechanization; which included becoming a skilled watch and clock repairer. This bent, accompanied by the 1876 death of a mother who had been a profound influence on him, saw his departure from the farm in 1879 to employment as a handyman in a machine shop in nearby Detroit, Michigan. Although acquiring ever increasing mechanical lore at the shop, a weekly salary of $2.50 forced Ford to work in a jewelry shop at night repairing watches and clocks in order to make ends meet. The next year saw him move to a shipbuilding firm where he worked on various engines utilized there. In 1882 he moved to another firm where he became a roving consultant and serviceman on the engines on steam tractors increasingly used by farmers in southern Michigan. In later years Ford reminisced that: "From the beginning I never could work up much interest in the labor of farming. I wanted to have something to do with machinery."[41] He states that this early outlook and experience was a key factor in imbuing him with an intense interest in the substitution of engines for men and animals in all manner of work and activities, culminating in the concept of a horseless carriage for transportation of materials and people. From that year on into the remainder of the 1880s, Ford alternated between farming and working on engines at home plus occasional employment stints in factories in Detroit. It was also during this period that he met and married (in 1888) Clara Bryant, the daughter of a neighboring farmer. Despite material and verbal encouragement from his father that he abandon his love affair with engines and concentrate on farming, Henry did not do so. Instead, in a shop which he constructed next to the couple's farm home, he spent most of his time constructing and experimenting with engines of various types.

By the late 1880s and early 1890s, automotive pioneers, such as George B. Selden and Charles E. and J. Frank Duryea in the United States and Gottlieb Daimler and Karl Benz abroad, were successfully designing, building, and selling operable internal combustion automobiles. News and information about these early achievements spurred Ford's determination to center his interest in and enter the field. Abandoning the farm altogether, the Fords moved to Detroit in 1891 where, by 1893, he had become a chief engineer for the Edison Illuminating Company, the local electrical company. In that year, their only child, Edsel Bryant Ford, was born.

Utilizing his spare time from 1893 to 1899 working in the shed attached to his home, while remaining in full time employment with the electrical company, by the latter year Ford had produced an operable automobile which established his reputation as a pioneer in the field. In 1899, with the financial support of the mayor of Detroit and other influential citizens, Ford led in the setting up of the Detroit Automobile Company, the first such to be organized in the city. That year on to 1903, although the Detroit Automobile Company and several successors failed, saw Ford moving full time into the automobile business. During this period, too, he made successful forays into automobile racing, which provided a great deal of favorable publicity for him and his automobiles. Ultimately the Ford Motor Car Company was incorporated in 1903 with twelve stockholders and an influx of needed new capital. Henry Ford became a major stockholder and general manager in the company and in 1903 the first Ford automobile, the Model A, was produced and sold by the company. From that time on to 1906 the company prospered as other different models were produced and sold which were more expensive than the Model A. By this time a split had developed within the stockholders of the company as to whether it should concentrate its efforts on the production of the more expensive autos or not. Ford led in the belief that the future lay in bringing to market a relatively inexpensive but dependable automobile designed for the use of the masses rather than expensive ones which would be available only to those of considerable means. Ford won out and, in the process, wound up with the outright ownership of almost sixty percent, i.e. controlling interest, of the outstanding stock. No longer hampered by this internal dissension, Ford led in the introduction of the famous Model T in 1908, which has been viewed as "the greatest single vehicle in the history of world transportation."[42] This car which had a standardized chassis and used interchangeable parts was accompanied by Ford's introduction of the moving assembly line in his plants. Also, for practical and humanitarian reasons, early in 1914 Ford introduced the "Five Dollar Day" a daily basic wage plan for his workers which was far in excess of sums being paid by his competitors and overnight made Ford a folk hero to American workers. By 1915, the automobile industry, practically non existent twenty years earlier,

> had created a wholly new type of transportation. Some two and a half million Americans now possessed automobiles, and the life of the nation was changing because of this fact; for the motor vehicle was the first free-ranging form of inland transportation, not tied like locomotives to rails, or steamboats to piers. Remotely situated farmers, miners, or shop owners were no longer isolated economically because they were far from rail-road stations or ports.[43]
>
> In this growing industry the Ford Motor Company towered above its associates[other automobile companies] like a mammoth skyscraper soaring upward from a village, to contain almost as many people and as much activity as the rest of the community combined. Of the 880,000 motor vehicles produced in 1915, Ford made 308,000, or thirty-five percent.[44]

The dominant position reached by the Ford company in the automotive industry during this period was achieved despite the long (1903-1911) but successful court battle over alleged violation by Ford of the patent rights of George B. Selden. The period 1915-1920 witnessed further controversy between Ford and the remaining minority stockholders in the company which resulted in their complete buyout by Ford in 1920. The newly organized Ford Motor Company resulted in the following division of Company shares within the Ford family: Henry (55.2%); Clara (3.1%); and Edsel (41.7%). Thus, the Company was wholly owned by them with no other shareholders to share in the profits of the Company.

This rise of the Fords, with Henry Ford having a controlling interest, as the complete owners of the tremendously successful Ford Motor Company saw them eventually acquiring millions of dollars per year in profits from its operation. By 1921 Ford's Model T automobile accounted for over fifty percent of those sold in the United States. By 1926 Ford could boast: "With the Ford Motor Company of Canada, there are now a total of eighty-eight plants, of which sixty are in the United States and twenty-eight in foreign countries."[45]

This national and foreign expansion and amassment of wealth was accompanied by Henry Ford's formulation and articulation orally and in print of his views on many controversial topics and issues. The following, selected among many social, political and economic topics elaborated on by Ford, form a bewildering meld: Recreation, Education, History, Dancing, Diet and Health, Crime and Criminals, Jews, Poverty, Government, Democracy, Farming, Urbanization, Natural Resources, Poverty, Machines and Power, Banks, Lawyers, Unions, Wages, Stock Market and Dividends, Charity and Philanthropy, and War. They are touched on to a greater or lesser extent in the four books Ford authored (see endnote 41) from 1923 to 1931. The following excerpts are provided as illustrative of the foregoing observation. Regarding banks and bankers, Ford opined:

> I determined absolutely that never would I join a company in which finance came before the work or in which bankers or financiers had a part. And further that, if there were no way to get started in the kind of business that I thought could be managed in the interest of the public, then I would simply not get started at all.... I regard a bank principally as a place in which it is safe and convenient to keep money.... I would not say that a man in business needs to know nothing at all about finance, but he is better off knowing too little than too much.... Manufacturing is not to be confused with banking, and I think there is a tendency for too many business men to mix up in banking and far too many bankers to mix up in business.[46]

Ford endorsed governmental prohibition of liquor and adamantly opposed its consumption, particularly by those engaged in manufacturing or business. He stated:

> My experience has been that there can be no temporizing whatsoever with liquor. We must have men who can and will use the brains they possess. Therefore, since the very beginning, we have in our industries enforced the rule of absolute, total abstinence, both in and out of the shop and offices.... The nearer we approach national total abstinence, the more brains and initiative we shall have at command. Brains and initiative are dulled by even the occasional use of alcohol. They are made permanently dull by even the most moderate habitual use, and they vanish altogether in the steady, heavy drinker.... Brains and booze will not mix.[47]

Ford's views on Jews and War undoubtedly involved him in the most controversy. Regarding Jews, he held that they were an alien race and religion attempting to change a Christian United States. Thus, according to Ford,

> There has been observed in this country certain streams of influence which were causing a marked deterioration in our literature, amusements, and social conduct; business was departing from its old-time substantial soundness; a general letting down of standards was felt everywhere.... The fact that these influences are all traceable to

one racial source is a fact to be reckoned with, not by us only, but by the intelligent people of the race in question.... Time will also show that we are better friends to the Jews' best interests than are those who praise them to their faces and criticize them behind their backs.[48]

Ford was adamantly opposed to war, particularly to U.S. participation in World War I and later World War II. Following the outbreak of World War I in 1914, he engaged in and gave financial support to a pacifist organization calling for an end to hostilities. This culminated in his chartering of a "Peace Ship" which sailed to Europe in the fall of 1915, with the peace advocates and Ford aboard and with his announced intention of getting "the boys out of the trenches before Christmas." The failure of such efforts, costing Ford an estimated $465,000, and the eventual entry of the United States into the war, saw Ford reversing course and devoting all-out efforts to the U.S. and Allied cause. After World War I his previous efforts for peace embroiled him in an acrimonious court battle with the *Chicago Tribune* in which he sued the paper for libel. A nominal victory verdict for him in 1919 emerged but with an award of six cents in damages. Ford's attempt to be elected as an independent candidate for the U.S. Senate in 1918 saw him fail by a few thousand votes. His expressed antipathy for Jews, on broad grounds quoted above, coalesced to foster the belief on his part that they were all part of a banker/Jewish conspiracy against him and led to his founding and support of the *Dearborn Independent*; a journal which carried on a relentless anti-Semitic campaign from 1920 to its demise in 1927 at a cost to Ford of almost $5 million.

Charity and Philanthropy

Henry Ford's acquisition of millions of dollars was accompanied by the same avalanche of appeals for aid that had inundated others acquiring similar great wealth. Letters appealing for aid from him were sent from every part of the United States and Canada, as well as from many other countries in the civilized world. They came by ordinary, registered and special delivery mail and were hauled to Ford's office in bundles, bales, and crates.... In 1915 these letters were pouring in at the rate of two hundred a day, and Ford's personal secretary, Ernest G. Liebold, was compelled to hire three assistants to open, sort, and process the avalanche of appeals. By 1924 Ford was receiving ten thousand letters a week—more than 500,000 a year—from persons who thought him a likely benefactor.[49]

His reaction and blunt responsive opinions on Charity and Philanthropy, however, form a piece with his outspoken and differing views on other topics. In his brief testimony before the 1914 Walsh Commission, he stated that he had "little use for charity or philanthropy as such." and declined to express an opinion on the efficacy of philanthropic foundations. His later writings amplified and clarified his views on the matter and, interestingly, "smack of much of the present day foundation principle of the venture capital function in the use of foundation funds."[50] In 1923 and again in 1930, for example, in books with chapters titled respectively "Why Charity," and "Toward Abolishing Poverty." Ford presents paragraphs:

> It is easy to give; it is harder to make giving unnecessary. To make the giving unnecessary we must look beyond the individual to the cause of his misery—not hesitating, of course, to relieve him in the meantime, but not stopping with mere temporary relief. The difficulty seems to be in getting to look beyond to the causes. More people can be moved to help a poor family than can be moved to give their minds toward the removal of poverty altogether.[51]

> Human sympathy is a great motive power, and no cool, calculating attitude will take the place of it. All great advances are due to human sympathy. But we have been using this great motive force for too small ends. If human sympathy prompts us to feed the hungry, why should it not give a much greater prompting toward making hunger impossible? If we have sympathy enough for people to help them in their trouble, surely we ought to have feeling enough to help them out of their trouble. It is a curious fact that more people can be got to help relieve poverty than can be got to devote their energies to removing poverty altogether.[52]

Accompanying such advanced views on giving, however, was Ford's continuing and outspoken resistance to the ideas of Carnegie and Rockefeller that called for the creation of organizations, particularly philanthropic foundations, to carry them out. In response to a 1927 inquiry as to Ford's setting up a foundation or similar institution, he stated: "Endowment is an opiate to imagination, a drug to initiative.... One of the greatest curses to the country today is the practice of endowing this and endowing that ... No, inertia, smug satisfaction, always follows endowments."[53] Henry Ford

> "held an almost inflexible prejudice against community chests. As a rule, such contributions were made by Clara and Edsel Ford, who gave generously to the Detroit Community Fund, the predecessor of the United Foundation."

Very rarely, and only late in his life, however, did Ford soften such opposition. Typical of his attitude was the remark he made to a committee of the Detroit Community Fund that called on him to ask for a contribution: "There is only one lower thing in the world than you have done in asking me to give to charity and that would be for me to do what you ask." He refused to give a penny. In that same year, however, Clara and Edsel Ford together donated $100,000 to the fund.[54]

Holding such views, it comes as no surprise that Henry Ford, during his lifetime (1863-1947), gave an estimated $37.5 million on a primarily individualistic basis for philanthropic and charitable purposes compared to an estimated $600 million by John D. Rockefeller and $325 million by Andrew Carnegie in their lifetimes.[55]

Ford Foundation

The Ford Foundation was not established until 1936 with an initial corpus of $25,000 provided by Edsel Ford and with the stated purpose of "advancing human welfare." He and two officials of the Ford Motor Company comprised its initial board of trustees. The primary motive for setting it up was undoubtedly the high federal income and inheritance tax laws passed by the Roosevelt administration in 1935. The response of Henry, Clara, and Edsel Ford was (1) their drawing up of wills to become effective upon their deaths and (2) the creation of the Ford Foundation.

> The effects of these steps would be to enrich the Foundation with a ninety-five percent equity in the Ford Motor Company, but to leave the management of the corporation entirely in the Ford family. Henry had made sure his heirs would keep authority, and that the government would reap only a minor tax harvest. He had also made sure that that the Americans would soon witness the birth of the richest philanthropic organization on the globe. [56]

Also, as has been pointed out, Clara and Edsel Ford did not share many of the aforementioned views of Henry Ford regarding philanthropy and they visualized it at the time as an administrative vehicle to centralize the community and other philanthropic giving being carried on by them. At its founding, "The foundation will take care of the various charitable, educational, and research activities that I don't care to do personally," said Edsel. "It will be on a small scale and I have no intention of making it larger."[57]

From that time to the end of World War II, although the foundation grew in assets and grants made, it essentially fulfilled this stated purpose. Edsel Ford's untimely death in 1943; Henry Ford's death in 1947; and Clara Ford's death in 1950, however, dramatically changed things. Their deaths came in the middle of and shortly following the end of a war in which U.S involvement was adamantly opposed by Henry Ford but which saw huge profits accruing from it to the Ford Motor Company and the Ford family. Also, following Henry Ford's death, a power struggle developed for control of the company which eventually resulted in Henry Ford II emerging as the victor. The eldest son of two other sons and a daughter of Edsel Ford, "Young Henry," as he was called, was then faced with the daunting task of running the company and simultaneously facing the impact of the terms of the wills left by his grandparents and father. Under these terms, the Ford Foundation acquired some ninety percent of the non-voting stock of the Ford Motor Company. What to do with this accretion that would make the corpus of the foundation far in excess of that of the Rockefeller and Carnegie philanthropies? The answer was the 1948 naming of a study committee, headed by a San Francisco lawyer, H. Rowan Gaither Jr., which conducted an exhaustive and expensive inquiry including consultation with a considerable number of persons associated with other existing foundations. In 1949 the committee presented a report to the foundation's now seven member board of trustees, charting its future course, which was unanimously adopted by the board and its chairman Henry Ford II.

The report recommended that the foundation concentrate its giving in five broad program areas: The Establishment of Peace; The Strengthening of Democracy; The Strengthening of the Economy; Education in a Free Society; and Individual Behavior and Human Relations. In the introductory chapter of the report, followed by a chapter by chapter detailed discussion of the five program areas, the statement is made that "The Committee and its advisers agree unanimously that the most important problem confronting the world today is to avoid world war—without sacrifice of our values or principles—and to press steadily toward the achievement of an enduring peace."[58] Consequently, beginning in the 1950s:

> Gradually, the foundation's international interests expanded to virtually every region of the globe. At one point, the foundation maintained more than twenty field offices in the developing countries, each with resident staffs and an array of project specialists. Indeed, in many places the foundation was the major, if not exclusive, aid-giving agency. Among the foundation's special interests abroad were agriculture, education, strengthening government institutions, rural development, and language problems.[59]

Henry Ford II served as president of the Ford Foundation from 1943 to 1950; chairman of its board of trustees from 1950 to 1956; and remained as a member of the board until his resignation in 1977. His younger brother, Benson Ford, served as a member of the board during this same period; resigning also in 1977. Although there were intimations that the

Fords did not always agree with some of the domestic and international projects launched by the foundation board of trustees and staff, it appears that they did not actively interfere with their adoption or execution.[60] Apparently such differences had reached an impasse, however, under the leadership of the-then president, McGeorge Bundy, which resulted in the 1977 resignation of the Ford brothers from the board of the foundation. Henry Ford II's terse letter of resignation alluded to his pride in the accomplishments of the Ford Foundation and the role he had played in its operation. He added, however, that he was not as enthusiastic as he had once been in this regard. A major criticism of the board and staff followed:

> The foundation exists and thrives on the fruits of our economic system. The dividends of competitive enterprise make it all possible. A significant portion of the abundance created by U.S. business enables the foundation and like institutions to carry on their work. In effect, the foundation is a creature of capitalism—a statement that, I'm sure would be shocking to many professional staff people in the field of philanthropy. It is hard to discern recognition of this fact in anything the foundation does. It is even more difficult to find an understanding of this in many of the institutions, particularly the universities, that are the beneficiaries of the foundation's grant programs.[61]

The letter warned of the dangers of omniscience. "I detect this to some degree in the foundation, particularly among staff people. It's a danger sign. The "not invented here" attitude robs an organization of the benefits of new thinking and should be fought at every turn." A concluding paragraph averred: "Although my formal role with the foundation now comes to an end, my interest in its progress will continue for a long time to come. If I can ever at any time be of any help, I am at the service of the trustees."[62]

McGeorge Bundy, in an annual report, praised Henry Ford's service with the operation of the foundation and particularly his decision to enlarge and diversify the board of trustees. He added, however, that "there had been a steady and growing understanding that the Board, as a Board, is the ultimate responsible governing body of the Foundation." Nevertheless, Bundy opined that; "The questions he [Ford] raised are good ones: Are we spread too thin? Do we guard against ingrown judgment? Are we sufficiently innovative? Should we pay more attention to the economic health of our free society?"[63] There was no mention, however, of utilization in the future of the help offered by Ford. Since that time the executive direction of the foundation has fallen to Bundy's successors; Franklin Thomas, (1979-1995) and Susan V. Berresford (1995 to the present).

Notes

1.   Prior to 1960, the statistical material and information, number, assets, grants, etc. is incomplete and conjectural. The best sources for such information prior to that date are: pamphlet bibliographies, Russell Sage Foundation, New York, 1915, 1920, 1922, 1924, and 1926; *American Foundations for Social Welfare,* Russell Sage Foundation, New York, 1930, 1938; Shelby M. Harrison and F. Emerson Andrews, *American Foundations for Social Welfare,* Russell Sage Foundation, New York, 1946; *American Foundations and Their Fields.* Twentieth Century Fund, New York, 1931, 1932, and 1935; *American Foundations and Their Fields,* vol.4. Raymond Rich Associates, New York, 1939 and vol. 5, 1942; Wilmer Shields Rich and Neva R. Deardorff (eds.) *American Foundations and Their Fields,* vol. 6. Raymond Rich Associates, New York, 1948; and Wilmer Shields Rich, *American Foundations and Their Fields,* American Foundations Information Service, New York, 7ᵗʰ ed., 1955.

       For complete and accurate information since 1960 see *The Foundation Directory.* Editions 1 through 27. Foundation Center, New York, 1960-2005.
2.   James W. Wooster, *Edward Stephen Harkness, 1874-1940.* Commonwealth Fund, New York, 1949, p. 43. This brief biography, an even briefer one in the *Dictionary of American Biography* by the same author, and numerous obituary notices, are among the few published materials dealing with this philanthropist.
3.   *The Commonwealth Fund: Historical Sketch, 1918-1962.* The Commonwealth Fund, New York, 1963, p. 4.
4.   A. McGehee Harvey, "The Commonwealth Fund" in Harold M Keele and Joseph C. Kiger (eds.), *Foundations.* Greenwood Press, Westport, Connecticut, 1984, p.89. For a detailed history of the Fund see A. McGehee Harvey and Susan L. Abrams, *"For the Welfare of Mankind" The Commonwealth Fund and American Medicine.* Johns Hopkins University Press, Baltimore, Maryland, 1986.
5.   See "International Fellowships," *The Commonwealth Fund: Historical Sketch, 1918-1962,* pp. 80-90.
6.   Paul Goldberger, *Harkness House,* The Commonwealth Fund, New York, p. 42.
7.   James Edward Wooster, *Edward Stephen Harkness, 1874-1940,* p. 131.
8.   Alastair Hoyer Millar, "Pilgrim Trust" in Joseph C. Kiger (ed.) *International Encyclopedia of Foundations.* Greenwood Press, Westport, Connecticut, 1990, pp. 287-288.
9.   Gordon N. Ray, "Report of the President," John Simon Guggenheim Memorial Foundation, New York, 1978, pp. xx-xxi.
10.   Harriet Chappell Owsley, "John Simon Guggenheim Memorial Foundation" in Harold M. Keele and Joseph C. Kiger (eds.), *Foundations.* Greenwood Press, Westport, Connecticut, 1984, p. 223.
11.   Milton Lomask, *Seed Money: The Guggenheim Story.* Farrar, Straus and Co., New York, 1964, p. 258. This work tells the story of the five foundations established by members of the Guggenheim family and concludes with a chapter on the John Simon Guggenheim Memorial Foundation. In addition to a biographical sketch of Simon Guggenheim, of particular interest is a detailed description of the selection process followed by the Foundation staff in the selection of Guggenheim Fellows.
12.   See *In Memoriam, Charles Stewart Mott,* 1975 which contains a number of insightful photographs of Mott.
13.   Clarence H. Young and William A. Quinn, *Foundation for Living: The Story of Charles Stewart Mott and Flint.* McGraw-Hill Book Company, Inc., New York, 1963, p. 97.

14. See "A Long, Fruitful Relationship" a paper published by the foundation outlining this change.

15. Charles Stewart Mott Foundation, *Annual Report,* 1999, p. 5.

16. Charles Stewart Mott Foundation, *Annual Report,* 1982, p. 9.

17. Charles Stewart Mott Foundation, *Annual Report,* 1989, p. 9.

18. Charles Stewart Mott Foundation, *Annual Report,* 1994, p. 44.

19. Ibid., pp. 44-45.

20. Charles Stewart Mott Foundation, *Annual Report,* 1997, p. 8.

21. Charles Stewart Mott Foundation, *Annual Report,* 1998, pp. 6, 15.

22. See Charles Stewart Mott Foundation, *Annual Report,* 2002. This report is entitled "Staying the Course" and provides justification for such continued support.

23. David C. Lamb, "John and Mary R. Markle Foundation" in Harold M. Keele and Joseph C. Kiger (eds.), *Foundations,* Greenwood Press, Westport, Connecticut, 1984, p. 209.

24. For a history of the program, see Stephen P. Strickland, *The Markle Scholars: A Brief History,* John and Mary R. Markle Foundation, New York, 1976.

25. Lloyd N. Morrisett, "The John and Mary R. Markle Foundation" in *The Art of Giving: Four Views on American Philanthropy- Proceedings of the Third Rockefeller Archive Center Conference, October 14, 1977,* Rockefeller Archive Center, New York, 1977, p. This article describes the background of and rationale for these changes in the programs and operation of the foundation.

26. Horace B Powell, *The Original Has This Signature-W. K. Kellogg* Prentice-Hall, Inc., Englewood Cliffs, New Jersey, 1956, p. 23.

27. Robert E. Hencey, "W.K. Kellogg Foundation" in Harold M. Keele and Joseph C. Kiger (eds.) in *Foundations,* Greenwood Press, Westport, Connecticut, 1984, pp. 446-447.

28. Horace B. Powell, *The Original Has This Signature-W.K. Kellogg,* p. 287.

29. *Ibid.,* p.306.

30. *The First Twenty-Five Years: The Story of a Foundation,* 1955, p. 10-11.

31. Mellon, Thomas, *Thomas Mellon and His Times.* University of Pittsburgh Press, Pittsburgh, Pennsylvania, 2nd ed., 1995. Mary Louise Briscoe, (ed.), p.391.

32. *Ibid.,* p. 239-240.

33. *Ibid.,* p. 361.

34. *Ibid.,* pp. 364-365.

35. *Ibid.* pp. 346-347.

36. Allan Nevins, "Andrew William Mellon," *Dictionary of American Biography,* Vol. XI, Supplement 2, Charles Scribner's Sons, New York, 1940, p. 447.

37. His success in the reduction of the federal deficit incurred during our involvement in that war and the simultaneous elimination or reduction of wartime taxes is tersely and cogently told in Andrew W. Mellon, *Taxation: The People's Business,* The Macmillan Company, New York, 1924.

38. A balanced description of the course of this ill fated match and a touching description of its effect upon him and his sister is provided in Paul Mellon's autobiography, *Reflections in a Silver Spoon, A Memoir,* William Morrow & Company, New York, 1992.

39. Walter Guzzardi, Jr., *The Henry R. Luce Foundation: a History, 1936-1986,* University of North Carolina Press, Chapel Hill, North Carolina, 1988, pp., 18-10.This history of the foundation is the major source of information about its founding and operation since most biographical and other accounts of Luce devote little or no attention to his philanthropy or the foundation. See, for example, Robert E. Herzstein, *Henry R. Luce, Time, and the American Crusade in Asia.* Cambridge University Press, Cambridge, 2005.

40. Ibid., p. 194.
41. Henry Ford , in collaboration with Samuel Crowther, *My Life and Work,* Double-day, Page & Company, Garden City, New York, 1922, p. 24. This autobiography was one of four volumes which he authored, all in collaboration with Samuel Crowther. The others were: *Today and Tomorrow,* Productivity Press, Cambridge, Massachusetts, 1926; *Edison as I Knew Him,* Cosmopolitan Book Corporation, New York, 1930; and *Moving Forward,* Doubleday, Doran & Company, Garden City, New York 1931. They provide valuable insight into the method of thinking, ideas, and the formulation of these ideas by Ford on a bewildering variety of top-ics.
42. Allan Nevins and Frank Ernest Hill, *Ford, Expansion and Challenge, 1915-1933* , vol. II, Charles Scribner's Sons, New York, 1957, p. 377.
43. *Ibid.,* p. 5.
44. *Ibid.,* p. 9.
45. Henry Ford, in collaboration with Samuel Crowther, *Today and Tomorrow,* p. 41.
46. Henry Ford, in collaboration with Samuel Crowther, *My Life and Work,* pp. 40, 136.
47. Henry Ford, in collaboration with Samuel Crowther, *Moving Forward,* pp. 284-285. In the 1950's several high Ford Company officials told this writer that no liquor was ever served at any receptions or parties held in the home of Henry and Clara Ford. They added, however, that after "Old Henry" and his wife retired from such affairs, usually at an early hour, liquors of various types were introduced and consumed.
48. Henry Ford, in collaboration with Samuel Crowther, *My Life and Work,* pp. 250-253.
49. William Greenleaf, *From These Beginnings; The Early Philanthropies of Henry and Edsel Ford, 1911-1936,* Wayne State University Press, Detroit, Michigan, 1964, p. 5.
50. For a discussion of the history of this principle see, Joseph C. Kiger, *Operating Principles of the Larger Foundations.* Russell Sage Foundation, New York, 1954, pp. 49-66, 91, 110, 111, 112, 119.
51. Henry Ford, in collaboration with Samuel Crowther, *My Life and Work,* p. 296.
52. Henry Ford, in collaboration with Samuel Crowther, *Moving Forward,* pp. 118-119.
53. William Greenleaf, *From These Beginnings; The Early Philanthropies of Henry and Edsel Ford,* p. 5.
54. *Ibid.,* p. 18.
55. *Ibid.,* p. 7.
56. Allan Nevins and Frank Ernest Hill, *Ford, Decline and Rebirth,* vol. III, Charles Scribner's Sons, New York, 1963, pp. 411-412.
57. William Greenleaf, *From These Beginnings; The Early Philanthropies of Henry and Edsel Ford,* p. 188.
58. *Report of the Study for the Ford Foundation on Policy and Program.* Ford Founda-tion, Detroit, Michigan, November, 1949, p. 25.
59. Oona Sullivan, "Ford Foundation" in Harold M. Keele and Joseph C. Kiger (eds.) in *Foundations.* Greenwood Press, Westport, Connecticut, 1984, p. 129.
60. For example, see comments in Richard Magat, *The Ford Foundation at Work: Philanthropic Choices, Methods, and Styles.* Plenum Press, New York, 1979, p. 32.

61.   Henry Ford II, "Henry Ford II: Text of Letter to Alexander Heard," *Foundation News,* March/April, 1977, pp. 6, 40.
62.   Ibid., p. 40.
63.   Ford Foundation, *Annual Report*, 1976, "The President's Review," p. vi.

3

Investigations and Studies

Prior to World War II

George Peabody and Mrs. Russell Sage had encountered little or no opposition in the setting up of their foundations. By the turn of the century Andrew Carnegie, John D. Rockefeller, and other individuals in the forefront of the country's industrialization had accumulated vast wealth far overshadowing that acquired by Peabody and inherited by Mrs. Sage. This wealth was viewed by many as having been acquired by dubious moral and legal business methods and being held by them in their newly created corporations and trusts. Such individual wealth was juxtaposed against what reformers viewed as the relatively meager wages paid the masses of workers, many of them newly arrived immigrants in the mines, factories, and railroads owned by these so-called "Robber Barons," rulers and owners of the new economy. Such wages were accompanied by long working hours, often in a physically dangerous workplace, with poor housing, medical and educational facilities available to workers and their families. Many felt that these conditions were traceable to and exacerbated by the setting up and operation of the aforementioned trusts. Consequently, national and state legislative efforts at that time to remedy this situation centered on the regulation of the corporate trusts and culminated in the passage of the Sherman Anti-Trust Act in 1890. Industrial unrest among workers, however, continued unabated on into the twentieth century.

Two early foundations of Carnegie had encountered little or no opposition in their creation and had been chartered by acts of the U.S. Congress in 1904 and 1906. Towards the close of the nineteenth century, however, a distinct change in attitude toward them on the part of the increasing number in the Congress and in significant segments of public opinion was taking place. This change was spurred by the aforementioned working conditions, resulting industrial unrest, and the growth in the size and number of the corporate trusts. Foundations or charitable trusts, it was argued, were nothing more than counterparts or adjuncts of the hated corporate trusts. It appears that this attitude was to a large degree responsible for the failure in 1911 of the U.S. Congress to act on legislation purporting to incorporate the Carnegie Endowment for International Peace and it was only a couple of decades later that the Endowment was incorporated in the State of New York. In the same year, 1911, Carnegie simply bypassed the U.S. Congress as to incorporation of his Carnegie Corporation of New York and went directly to the State to successfully incorporate the Corporation. Similarly, Rockefeller encountered little opposition in establishing his earlier benefactions.[1] It was quite to the contrary in the case of his later setting up of the Rockefeller Foundation. His failed attempts from 1910-1913 to incorporate the Rockefeller Foundation by an act of the U.S. Congress led him also, in 1913, to successfully turn to the New York State legislature for incorporation. It is against the background of these decades of industrial unrest and the creation of these foundations that a Congressional Commission on Industrial Relations was brought into existence in 1912, running on to 1916, and commonly called the Walsh Commission for its chairman, attorney Frank P. Walsh. The Commission lasted four years, producing a report of eleven, finely-printed volumes.[2] Some twenty-eight individuals testified in the hearings, including such prominent figures as John D. Rockefeller, Jr., Louis Brandeis, Samuel Gompers, and J.P. Morgan. The research, findings, and report of the Commission, although centering on economic and attendant social issues, provides the first informed and comprehensive factual look at U.S. foundations and insight into the public perception of them. The international aspect of benefices of foundations does not appear to have been treated, and no significant action regarding foundations was taken by following Congresses.

During the interim period between the two world wars there was one major study of foundations conducted in the 1930s, by an individual, Eduard C. Lindeman. He estimated that there were only about three hundred foundations in existence at that time and he lamented that he would not have undertaken the study had he known how difficult it would be to get information from or about them. He examined one hundred foundations on whom he could get reliable information during the decade from 1921 to 1930 and published his 135-page result, *Wealth and Culture,* in 1936.[3] Approximately half of the volume is devoted to his generally critical comment on the impact of U.S. foundations on American culture and half to statistical tables and graphs. There is no comment on their international activities or programs other than his calculation that in 1921, 1.3 percent and in 1931, 1.6 percent of total expenditures were devoted to international relations.

World War II to Present

Harrison and Andrews

In the period 1944-1946 Shelby M. Harrison and F. Emerson Andrews analyzed 505 foundations of some size and significance. Depending upon the varying information available about these foundations and stipulating that there might be some overlapping, they narrowed this number to 335 foundations reporting fields of interest for 1944. Out of ten classification fields, they reported that twenty-six of that number conducted programs in international relations. Also, they calculated, out of total grant expenditure for the 335, the field of international relations then amounted to 7.8 percent[4]

Following the pre-World War I investigation conducted by the Walsh Commission, it was not until 1950 that U.S. foundations again received any substantial examination by the Congress with the creation of the Buchanan Committee, named for its Chairman, Frank Buchanan.

Buchanan Committee

The impetus for the creation of this Committee grew out of the significant increase in lobbying activities at the federal level during and after World War II. A notable change in that growth was the augmentation of organizational lobbying as contrasted with lobbying by individuals, the primary organizations being corporations, foundations, labor unions, farm organizations, and governmental entities. Therefore although still concerned with individuals, the committee primarily focused its concern on these organizations and whether or not they were seriously violating statutes regulating lobbying.

The resolution creating the Buchanan Committee stated:

> The committee is authorized and directed to conduct a study and investigation of (1) all lobbying activities intended to influence, encourage, promote, or retard legislation; and (2) all activities or agencies of the Federal Government intended to influence, encourage, promote, or retard legislation.[5]

Although the committee ruminated at length about defining what constituted lobbying, in a section *On defining lobbying,* it concluded that:

> In the final analysis, there are only two practical gauges of lobbying activity-intent and some substantial effort to influence legislation. The means employed are secondary, and any attempt to define lobbying by listing specific methods of influence is inevitably and almost immediately out of date.
>
> These criteria do not define lobbying, but they do set forth the essential conditions without which lobbying does not exist. We feel that that these are the only criteria inclusive enough to span the entire present system of pressure politics. They are the only criteria which would have enabled this committee to lay the full facts before Congress and the people.[6]

In carrying out its investigative mandate, the committee zeroed in on the activities of a few individuals and several specific organizations in the various categories mentioned above. One group investigated for lobbying activities included such individuals and organizations as members of the du Pont family and J. Howard Pew; B.F. Goodrich Company, United States Steel Corporation, and the Alfred P. Sloan Foundation, Falk Foundation and Kresge Foundation. A second group similarly included Oscar M. Ewing and Raymond F. Foley; the U.S. Federal Security Administration and Housing and Home Finance Agency; the American Federation of Labor (AFL) and Congress of Industrial Organizations (CIO) and the American Farm Bureau Federation and National Council of Farmer Cooperatives.[7]

While recommending several amendments of an expository nature to the existing lobbying statutes, the committee concluded that the investigative authority of Congress, through standing and special committees, such as the Buchanan Committee, constituted a safeguard against lobbying abuses. The press and inquiring reporters were also cited as a further check on the expenditure of funds in questionable lobbying activities. It emphasized, however:

> We need more information on lobbying and lobbyists. This, at the moment, is the most feasible approach. Every group has the right to present its case, but at the same time Congress and the public have a right to know who they are, what they are doing, how much they are spending, and where the money is coming from—in a word, full disclosure of the relevant facts.[8]

The minority members of the committee concurred with these views but, citing a lack of objectivity by the majority members, maintained that in gathering evidence and reporting:

(1)   the majority of the committee was determined to prove that lobbying by Government agencies is in the public interest and not subject to criticism.
(2)   The majority of the committee was determined to prove that lobbying by organizations openly opposed to Fair Deal legislation was selfish and reprehensible while lobbying in support of Fair Deal objectives was perfectly all right.[9]

Although foundations were not specifically mentioned in (2) above, by inference, those foundations previously investigated and cited in committee reports did provide support for such "reprehensible" purposes. Also by inference, although only a relatively few were mentioned, it seems that the earlier views expressed in the Walsh Commission proceedings and reports that most foundations were conservative or even reactionary still held sway with the congressional majority and its staff. Since the Buchanan committee was entirely concerned with domestic lobbying there was, similarly, little or no interest expressed or concern with the foreign activities of any foundations including the relatively few investigated and mentioned.

Cox Committee

In contrast to the thinking largely inspiring the Walsh and Buchanan congressional investigations and their conclusions, the 1952 Cox committee origination was very much different. First, instead of liberals viewing foundations as forces for reaction and conservatism, by the 1950s many conservatives were charging that they had been captured by liberals and were engaged in communist/subversive activities. Second, there was more interest in the foreign activities of foundations against the backdrop of the perceived threat to the United States by Russia and the communist system associated with it. As this writer stated at the time:

the United States, confronted with the problems of traitors and subversives within its own borders to an extent never existing before, sought the reasons. What would cause the well-bred and educated, those who stood to benefit most from our way of life, to embrace communism? Was our educational system at fault? Was it at fault in its interpretation, or conduct of the social sciences, and of economics and economic history particularly?

In a search for the answer to these and related questions, inevitably interested persons would attempt to assay the role played by the foundations. In view of their importance to the educational world, the diversity and range of their operations, their freedom of action, their venture-capital concept, it is understandable that a spotlight would be turned on them.[10]

In addition to these broad forces, it appears that there were three more or less defined and distinct groups, successfully calling for the creation of the resultant Cox committee investigation. Although they had a common purpose, the motivation of each group was different. The first group may be labeled the "Brickerites"; associated with then Republican Senator John Bricker of Ohio. He and this group was opposed to U.S. ratification of various proposed international treaties because they believed, without proper safeguards, such action would undercut or negate certain provisions in the U.S. Constitution. With some of our larger foundations supporting organizations which called for such ratification, the group wanted to put them all on the carpet as allegedly engaging in subversive activities and thus helping to carry this viewpoint. The second group was motivated by domestic political considerations. They wanted Republican Senator Robert A. Taft of Ohio to be the Republican Party's nominee for president in the 1952 election. The possible nomination of General Dwight D. Eisenhower, then president of Columbia University, appeared to pose the greatest threat to their favorite. They concluded that the best way to make him unavailable as a candidate was to launch a campaign that associated him with influential supporters, such as John Foster Dulles and Paul Hoffman, who were officials of foundations. If they could reveal that communists had infiltrated or received aid from these foundations then it would tar them all with a communist guilt by association and reduce Eisenhower's chances for the nomination. The same guilt by association ploy could also be played if President Eisenhower's Columbia University could be revealed as a hotbed of leftists and communists supported by foundation largesse. Finally, a third and smaller group of journalists and academics, centered in Chicago, were personally distrustful of and disliked the 1940s and 1950s head of the University of Chicago, Robert M. Hutchins. They published articles and books[11] attacking him as a semi-subversive liberal associated with and supported by large foundations of the same ilk. When Hutchins left the University in 1951 to become an Associate Director of the newly enriched Ford Foundation, this group supported a general investigation of all foundations as a way to attack Hutchins because of his new association with that foundation. Individuals in these three groups expressed their condemnation of foundations orally and in writing to a receptive long time conservative Democratic Congressman E. Eugene Cox of Georgia which eventually led to the creation of the Cox Committee.[12]

Initially expected to be a witch-hunt similar to other congressional committees of the 1950s, the committee did not turn out that way largely due to the independent and competent staff employed. For example, the

Director of Research was not forced to employ political hacks. As a result, he was able to hire a then relatively unknown Roger H. Mudd as one of several able research assistants. The committee and its staff probed deeply into the communist/subversive charges through its circulation to large and small foundations of a questionnaire[13] which, while devoted to eliciting replies from them on the charges, also called for and elicited a great deal of other information about foundations. Its staff also conducted extensive interviews with individuals allegedly communist/subversive in their views and work or in a position to comment on such individuals. As to these charges, its final report stated: "The committee believes that on balance the record of the foundations is good." It added that

> It seems paradoxical that in a previous congressional investigation in 1915 the fear most frequently expressed was that the foundations would prove the instruments of vested wealth, privilege, and reaction, while today the fear most frequently expressed is that they have become the enemy of the capitalistic system. In our opinion neither of these fears is justified.[14]

The committee and its staff, however, engaged in a much broader study and analysis of foundations, including the wisdom and efficacy of their international activities. Two lengthy sections, E and F, of the nine-section questionnaire submitted to fifty-four larger foundations for replies were concerned with such activities; particularly those of a political or educational nature. Also, numerous witnesses appearing at committee hearings were queried on various aspects of the subject. These included trustees and staff of many of the larger foundations plus key officials from the then Bureau of Internal Revenue, now the Internal Revenue Service, the U.S. governmental supervisory agency for foundations. By far the greatest foreign activity reported was that provided by the three largest: Ford, Rockefeller, and Carnegie. Only one quarter of the fifty-four stated that they had ever engaged in any foreign giving or activity. During the period 1947-1952 these foundations averaged about ten percent for expenditures abroad in proportion to total amounts expended in the United States. Highest was the Rockefeller Foundation which disbursed about twenty-five percent of its giving abroad. Out of the fifty-four foundations, only six had set up offices and employed staff in foreign countries. At that time foreigners employed per foundations there averaged about five or six persons. Among the six, the smallest employer was the John Simon Guggenheim Memorial Foundation with several informal part-time representatives in various countries in the Western Hemisphere being paid small amounts of money to cover their expenses. The largest employer, soon to be overshadowed by the Ford Foundation, was the Rockefeller Foundation with forty-six full-time staffers in its offices located in countries all over the globe. None of the fifty-four foundations believed that there should be a prescription as to what percentage of their grant funds should be expended abroad. Typical of this thinking was that expressed by Paul G. Hoffman, then president of the Ford Foundation, when asked about the wisdom of granting of tax exemption for foundation expenditures abroad. He stated:

> If your goal is peace, contributing toward peace—remember, I said a little bit in a few places—if your goal is that, what you want to do is find the places where those dollars will prove to be most effective in their use.
>   Now, from the standpoint of this goal, it makes no difference whether the money is spent in Arkansas, if I may say so, or in India, We want a world at peace, and I think that every dollar we have spent abroad can be related intimately and closely to the interests of the American people.[15]

As a result, in its final report the committee concluded:

> Considering the picture as a whole, those foundations operating on an international scale are very few in number, but because they are well known and their expenditures comparatively great, the attention focused on their foreign activities is disproportionate. Those foundations which are concerned with internationalism along political lines appear to center their activities around projects which support the Government policy of participation in United Nations activities. All foundations deny participation in politics or political propaganda. The committee believes that that these international activities and foreign expenditures of the foundations are motivated chiefly by consideration of the welfare of the American people and as such are entirely praiseworthy.[16]

Reece Committee

The Reece Committee investigation of 1953 can aptly be described as a fall-out from the Cox Committee investigation. Congressman B. Carroll Reece, a long time supporter and friend of Senator Robert A. Taft, endorsed and wanted him to be the 1952 presidential nominee for the Republican Party. When Congressman Reece, who had been a minority Republican member of the Cox Committee, and the groups instrumental in bringing on the Cox Committee investigation, realized they could not accomplish their goals, he and they lost interest in it. He and all of the other members of the Cox Committee assented unanimously to its final report but Congressman Reece significantly added at its conclusion that "the select committee has had insufficient time for the magnitude of its task" and "the inquiry might be continued with profit."[17] After the Cox

Committee efforts ended on January 1, 1953, Congressman Reece, this time spurred on and encouraged in large measure by the Chicago group mentioned above, eventually engineered the passage on July 27 of that year of a House resolution authorizing a new committee to investigate foundations. It was rumored at the time that Congressman Reece had anticipated being named Secretary of the Treasury in the event of Senator Taft's nomination by the Republicans and his election as President. If so, his chagrin when this did not take place was probably also a factor in his move for the creation of a new investigating committee hard on the heels of the preceding one of which he had been a member. In any case, by that time he maintained that:

> Some of these institutions [foundations] support efforts to overthrow our government and to undermine our American way of life. These activities urgently require investigation. Here lies the story of how Communism and socialism are financed in the United States, where they get their money. It is the story of who pays the bill. There is evidence to show there is a diabolical conspiracy back of all this. Its aim is the furtherance of socialism in the United States. Communism is only a brand name for socialism and the Communist state represents itself to be the only true form of socialism.[18]

The Reece investigation, directed to make a report by January 3, 1955, centered on proving this previously announced thesis rather than ascertaining facts. It published a series of lengthy staff reports purporting to buttress this thesis and the principal witnesses at its hearings were the same staff members. Allegedly because of the continuing and acrimonious wrangling between majority and minority members of the committee, it was abruptly announced on July 2, 1954 that there would be no further hearings. Foundation officials and others who had been waiting to appear were not heard but were later afforded the opportunity to file written statements which a few of the larger ones did.[19] Thus the final report of the Reece Committee appearing on December 16, 1954 consisted of a 416-page majority report highly critical of foundations and an eleven-page minority report even more highly critical, specifically and generally, of the majority members and staff of the committee and of its report. It vehemently objected to the denial of a fair hearing to foundation representatives and concluded:

> The proceedings and the majority report evidence the tragedy of the men and women of the committee's staff who having lived and prospered under freedom, yet do not believe in due process and American fair play; who fear the thinkers and those who dare to advance the new and the unaccepted; who believe that universal education for our people can be risked only if the teachers and their pupils accept their doctrine and are shielded from the mental contamination of other thoughts and beliefs. They would deny the right of individuals to seek truth without limit or restriction.[20]

Although not a participant in the minority report, Congressman Angier Goodwin, who had been a member of both the Cox and Reece committees, added a vitiating addendum to the majority report: "Nothing," he stated, "has transpired in the proceedings of the present [Reece] Committee to cause me to alter or modify the views expressed in the Cox Committee report. I take this opportunity to again re-affirm."[21]

The foreign activities of the foundations, mainly the larger ones, and their grantees and projects in the area came in for criticism on ideological grounds throughout the majority report[22] but were not specifically touched on in the minority report. Somewhat surprisingly, however, the majority report, in its "Concluding Observations" also stated regarding

Foreign Use of Foundation Funds:

> In this area this Committee has not been able to do sufficient study to come to a final evaluation. However, we offer this suggestion tentatively and subject to further investigation of the extent and significance of foreign grants and grants for foreign use- that such grants be limited to ten per cent of the annual income of the foundation or, if it is disbursing principal, ten per cent, in the aggregate, of its principal fund. An exception should be made in the case of religious organizations, such as foreign missions, and perhaps in some other instances of peculiar and historic nature.[23]

In contrast to the overwhelming media commendation for the efforts of the Cox Committee, the Reece Committee's performance was either ignored or generally condemned. Typical of such views was that expressed by an article appearing in the *New York Times* and titled "Another Stupid Inquiry." It stated, in part, "Under the conditions laid down by Chairman Reece the suspension of public hearings by the special House of Representatives committee to investigate foundations is inexcusable.... The history of this committee has been a disgrace to Congress. There was no need for it to begin with."[24] A book length[25] rebuttal to such views was eventually made in 1958 by the General Counsel for the Reece Committee, Rene A. Wormser. Prefaced with an introduction by Congressman Reece, in his Introduction Wormser disparages any altruistic motives in those establishing foundations. This writer's analysis of the book found:

> The approximately 300 pages in the main body of Wormser's book are wholly devoted to an alleged "interlock" of foundations and intermediary organizations, controlled by an "elite" group of trustees and administrators, who are "subverting" the U.S. government and society from a capitalistic, free society to a controlled, socialistic-communistic one. The final pages of this book are used primarily to justify the means and methods followed in the work of the Reece Committee, with extensive quotations from the committee's *Hearings* and *Report*.[26]

Following the Cox and Reece investigations, many philanthropic foundation observers and some foundation executives believed that the two had pretty much cancelled each other out, thus signaling a favorable future for philanthropy and foundations. Still, a number of key foundation executives came to the conclusion that this was an erroneous view. To the contrary, they believed that there was a real need for long range efforts to be mounted that would provide greater insight by the public into the need for and the continued maintenance and even augmentation of our philanthropic and particularly foundation structure and activities. An initial leader in launching this effort in the 1950s was H. Rowan Gaither, then president of the Ford Foundation.

Cambridge and Princeton Study Groups

In 1954, at Gaither's initiative, a study group consisting of academic and legal scholars knowledgeable about foundations was organized. Meetings of the group centered in Cambridge, Massachusetts during the 1950s and early 1960s. The deliberations of the Cambridge group were the catalyst for a series of U.S. meetings of academicians and foundation representatives which eventually resulted in outcomes of great significance in foundation history. It marked the beginning of support by an increasing number of the larger foundations for more permanent studies of philanthropy in general and foundations in particular through the establishment and/or support of other organizations for this purpose. Tangentially, this gave rise to an increase in information available to the public about U.S. as well as foreign foundations. One initial result of the Cambridge meetings was the impetus for subventions supplied by the Ford Foundation which aided in eventually bringing to completion several seminal studies covering the history of English philanthropy and foundations from 1480 to 1960.[27] Donald Young, then president of the Russell Sage Foundation, shared Gaither's views. He was the organizer and a principal participant in a 1956 conference in Princeton, New Jersey which resulted in enlisting the interest of intellectual historian Merle Curti and others of wide ranging political, scientific, and other fields of history in turning to philanthropy, including foundations, as a sphere of interest.[28] More than a score of books and articles eventually resulted from this impetus including several by Curti himself, including his previously cited *American Philanthropy Abroad, A History*. Probably the principal immediate result of such activities, however, was the creation in New York in 1956 of the Foundation Library Center (its name changed to Foundation Center in 1968). The prime mover in this endeavor was President John W. Gardner of the Carnegie Corporation of New York, abetted by the aforementioned Donald Young.[29] Under Gardner's recommendation, the Corporation supplied the first funds for its operation, supplemented in later years by a host of foundations, large and small. The setting up of the Foundation Center was followed in succeeding decades by the founding or metamorphosis of a host of U.S. academic, journalistic, and commercial organizations interested in and often engaged in publication about special or general aspects of philanthropy and foundations.[30] In the 1950s and 1960s, however, other forces affecting philanthropic foundations were also at work.

Patman Committees

John William Wright Patman was born in 1893 to a poor farming couple in a then poverty-stricken area of East Texas. His hard work resulted in his attaining a law degree and his eventual election to Congress in 1928 from a district located there. He served consecutive terms in the House from that district until his death in 1976. Undoubtedly influenced by this background, it is understandable why ... "Patman fought big banks, foundations, and the Federal Reserve and enjoyed a reputation as the House's last 'populist'."[31] Because of his longevity and hard work, he became one of a small number in the House of Representatives termed 'Barons' because of the power they attained and exercised.

Patman's legislative attacks on big banks in general and on the Federal Reserve System in particular were grounded in his belief that they exercised undue financial control on interest rates charges, particularly those charged farmers and small businessmen. Thus oversight of these bodies from the 1950s onward became "an issue that he would support for the remainder of his career."[32] Coupled with this animosity,

> Patman had, throughout his congressional career, built up a reservoir of distrust for the practices of the nation's largest businesses. He believed they employed unethical and illegal procedures in their competition with smaller concerns. It was from this perspective that his attack on foundations originated. Patman complained that foundations did not pay taxes on revenue, usually generated from investments, whereas their small business competitors enjoyed no such luxury.[33]

In furtherance of his goals to rein in these entities, he succeeded in the establishment of the House Select Committee on Small Business in 1941 with him as chairman. His long service there and on the key House Banking and Currency Committee eventually resulted in his being named its chairman in 1963, a post which he held until his death in 1976. While he achieved mixed success in the other target areas, Patman's significant role and impact on the regulation of philanthropic foundations is clearer cut.

There are a number of anomalies which differentiate the Patman inquiry of foundations from the previous investigations. It was a long and continuously running one (1961-1972) and it concentrated on the economic effect or significance of foundations rather than the nature, content, and conduct of foundation programs. As a corollary, it zeroed in on numerous instances of foundation malfeasance and asserted that the Internal Revenue Service had proved incapable of policing and correcting such actions. In short, it was economically rather than ideologically oriented. Because of continuous differences with other committee members over the running of the investigation, it turned into what was essentially a one man show, Patman, with the aid of a few key assistants. Another anomaly, there were only two sets of short hearings dealing with foundations conducted under Patman's aegis. The first, in 1964, consisted of the questioning, mainly by him, of four government officials, the Secretary of the Treasury, the Acting Chairman of the Securities and Exchange Commission, and the Acting and Former Commissioners of the Internal Revenue Service (IRS), concerning possible violation of various statutes by foundations.[34] Bearing down on his consistent criticism of the latter agency, he raised questions of the Acting Commissioner of the IRS about the IRS's reluctance to provide information about the J.M. Kaplan Fund and its relationship to eight other foundations. Perhaps inadvertently, it was revealed that the Fund had been used as a conduit by the Central Intelligence Agency (CIA) for channeling money for its work.[35] The second hearing, in 1967, was devoted almost exclusively to the activities of an organization, Americans Building Constitutionally (ABC).[36] The latter purported to advise, for a fee, in the creation of foundations with an emphasis on the avoidance of taxes. Those persons associated with it were ultimately indicted for fraud.

In a 1961 speech opening his investigation of foundations, Patman opined regarding the tremendous growth of new foundations being established and their economic impact, particularly as they affected small businesses. He stated, however:

> Let us digress to say that we have nothing but praise for the work that has been done and is being done by foundations in many fields such as education, health, social welfare, scientific research, humanities, religion, international affairs, and government. So our thought today is not to criticize, but to urge Congress to take a fresh look. What has brought about this feverish growth?[37]

In addition to the aforesaid two hearings and frequent speeches on foundations before the House and in testimony at its committees, Patman's investigation resulted in seven *Chairman's Reports*[38] and an eighth *Staff Report*.[39] Patman made many recommendations for change anent foundations, accompanied by an enormous and wide array of statistics and examples to buttress such recommendations. Accompanying them was convincing evidence that a significant number of foundations had engaged in malfeasances of various types. Attributing much of this to a poor and lax supervision of foundations by the Treasury Department's Internal Revenue Service, he called for a moratorium on tax exemption granted foundations and added:

> Consideration should be given to a regulatory agency for the supervision of tax-exempt foundations.
>
> In the area of foundations, the Treasury Department has been so lax in enforcement of the law and regulations that it amounts to irresponsibility and a virtual abdication from the task of administration. This might have been overlooked 40 years ago, but times have changed. The increase in the number and size of foundations has drastically altered the situation. Under present-day conditions, the public consequences are much wider and more serious.[40]

Other major recommendations regarding foundations made by Patman included: a limitation of twenty-five years on their life instead of allowing them to exist in perpetuity; they should be prohibited from engaging in business; foundation ownership of the stock of a corporation should be limited to three percent; in figuring the accumulation of income, contributions to and all capital gains should be considered as income and not capital gains; and better reporting by the foundations to the IRS and the public should be required. Patman made no recommendations concerning possible restrictions on foreign grants by foundations. His critical attitude towards such grants, however, is clearly revealed in many disparaging comments. He complained, for example:

> As of December 31, 1967, the Rockefeller Foundation had 211 employees in the United States and 112 in foreign countries, excluding nationals hired locally. The Rockefeller Foundation sent 75 percent more money out of the country in 1966 than it spent here. It spent $17.8 million for the benefit of foreign institutions or persons, while institutions and persons in this country received only $10.9 million.... The foundation spent $1,693,762 in India, but not a penny in Arkansas. It spent half a million dollars in Uganda, but not a cent in Idaho. It spent more than $1 million in Uganda, but not a cent in Idaho. It spent more than $1 million in Nigeria, but could bring itself to spend only $1,000 in Kentucky.... It spent nearly $2 million in Colombia, but it spent nothing at all in South Carolina, or Wyoming, or Maine, or Delaware.[41]

While the Congress and the administration searched feverishly for funds to finance essential urban rebuilding programs, the Richard King Mellon Foundation sent $50,000 to Ireland for the "preservation of historical buildings."[42]

The shortage of physicians in America is critical, so the Commonwealth Fund of New York sends $208,141 to Canada for medical education.[43]

Also, for example, one philanthropist in alluding to Patman's criticism of the foreign activities of U.S. foundations and one instance of his own in particular, quoted Patman as describing "the Bollingen Foundation as having been concerned with grants for 'the development of trivia into nonsense."[44]

Informed opinion regarding the Patman investigation was mixed; some favorable other unfavorable. The foundation world was also divided as to its merits. For example, its most strident critic, a former head of the Foundation Center, concluded:

At this stage the [Patman] investigation has utterly failed to present a rounded picture of the place of the philanthropic foundation in American society or even in the domestic economy. It has set a most unfortunate example of how a Congressional investigation should never again be conducted.[45]

On the other hand, a former long time Rockefeller Foundation executive maintained:

There is no doubt that the illumination furnished along with the heat of Patman's spotlight has resulted in more stringent reviews of foundation conduct and important movement toward tighter regulation of the areas of permissible functioning. This is undeniably good.... It has revealed that a very few foundations have behaved badly; and that the laws and regulations should doubtless be somewhat altered to prevent such misbehavior.[46]

Treasury Department Study

Undoubtedly stirred by the ongoing Patman investigation and the diverging opinion as to its merit, in the early 1960s the Treasury Department launched an extensive study of private foundations and the tax laws pertaining to them. In 1964 the Committee on Ways and Means of the House of Representatives and the Committee on Finance of the Senate requested the Treasury Department to prepare a report on the activities, particularly those of a tax and financial nature, of private foundations and forward its conclusions and recommendations to the committees. The Department's 1965 *Report*[47] made no mention of foreign grants or activities of foundations. It recommended against putting a time limit on the lives of foundations and rejected the need for setting up a separate agency other than the IRS to oversee foundation activities. Rather, it alluded to and discussed at length a number of abuses by a minority of foundations under current tax law and then proposed six recommendations to correct them. The *Report*'s overall conciliatory and encouraging nature towards private foundations can be seen from the following quote from that document:

> The recommendations seek not only to end diversions, distractions, and abuses, but to stimulate and foster the active pursuit of charitable ends which the tax laws seek to encourage. Any restraints which the proposals may impose on the flow of funds to private foundations will be far outweighed by the benefits which will accrue to charity from the removal of abuses and from the elimination of the shadow which the existence of abuse now casts upon the private foundation area.[48]

The Congress took four years to digest the Treasury *Report* and during that time no action was forthcoming from it to make any changes called for. Meanwhile, as has been related, this inaction took place against the backdrop of the continuing Patman investigation of foundations. By 1968-1969, however, perspicacious foundation officials had become concerned about the future facing foundations. Alan Pifer, then head of the Carnegie Corporation of New York, for example, in 1968 warned:

> The danger which foundations have faced in recent years, and perhaps never more so than today, is that public loss of confidence in them, occasioned by limited, but continuing and well publicized disclosure of abuses will become great enough to precipitate Congress into a hasty and clumsy piece of legislation.... It is evident, therefore, that the foundations which are carrying out genuine philanthropic purposes, which are well managed, and are making a strong effort to serve the public interest, must take energetic steps themselves to put the foundation house in better order. They have no grounds for thinking that because they have escaped restriction in the past they will necessarily continue to do so in the future. A field which has grown from less than 200 members 40 years ago to 20,000 today will, of course, come under even closer scrutiny by public authorities. And the concern of these officials, once aroused, may not stop at regulation which simply prevents wrongdoing or the grosser forms of mismanagement, however inappropriate more extensive government regulation may be.[49]

Peterson Commission

John D. Rockefeller III was undoubtedly the prime mover in the creation of both the Peterson Commission and its follow up Filer Commission.[50] He was the eldest son and had the namesake of the family and it was accompanied by his own deep interest in philanthropy in general and the Rockefeller foundations in particular. As his oral and written observations show, he was deeply convinced of the need for the maintenance and growth of philanthropy, what he categorized as the third sector, i.e. charitable giving for social purposes at all levels of American society. For example, he wrote:

> At the broadest level, my concern is over the strength and vigor of this sector of our society as compared with the other two, business and government, which have grown so enormously in size and power in recent decades. And, specifically, my concern is over the private nonprofit sector to play fully and effectively in part in resolving our complex social problems.[51]

With the historic and continuing role of the philanthropic foundation as the primary method for Rockefeller munificence, it is readily apparent why, particularly following the death of his father in 1960, he became ever more deeply involved with the affairs of the Rockefeller foundations. When the Rockefeller and other foundations came under increasing questioning and attack in the 1950s and 1960s, he was among the leaders in defending philanthropy and foundations.[52] As the foregoing biographers perceptibly observed:

> One of the more remarkable aspects of JDR's [John D. Rockefeller III] career was his self appointed role as the caretaker of philanthropy. Many wealthy people engage in philanthropic activity, and some even make it a full-time occupation as JDR [John D. Rockefeller] and his father did. But JDR was unique in his time in the extent to which he exerted leadership to protect, reform, and enhance philanthropy generally in the United States.[53]

It is against the foregoing background that, in the period 1968-1969, John D. Rockefeller III invited Peter G. Peterson, then head of the Bell and Howell Corporation, to chair a commission to study American philanthropy in general and private foundations in particular. Privately funded, albeit with some difficulty,[54] the commission consisted of thirteen distinguished and informed members of diverse backgrounds, aided by a six-member staff composed of lawyers. Its research and deliberations eventually resulted in the 1970 publication of a report consisting of three parts, plus Appendices: Part One. Philanthropy; Part Two. Foundations; and Part Three. Recommendations.[55] Part One consisted of thirty pages with the remainder of the report taken up with the other portions.

The problem that the commission unequivocally and repeatedly complained about was the lack of information about foundations.

> It began its work with confidence that its primary task would be to formulate judgments on the principal policy questions raised by the role of foundations in our society, not to collect facts.... The shock of disillusion was not long in coming. Some of the data

on hand were quite extensive, but available statistics were not responsive to certain questions central to the commission's inquiry ... when the commission cast about for relevant data, there was very little hard evidence on hand which either refuted or supported the allegations [of foundation misconduct] made.... Information gaps of every kind abounded.[56]

The commission felt that adequate supervision by the individual states was only being carried out in a few of them. It surmised that the Treasury Department and the Internal Revenue Service did not provide sufficient funds or staff to provide such information or to adequately supervise the national or international activities of foundations. In the latter case, it stated, "IRS auditing of foundations grants abroad is virtually nonexistent, largely, we believe, because of inadequate budgets."[57] The commission concluded at that time international activities were conducted by about nine percent of all U.S. foundations. During the years 1967-1968 total expenditures for such purposes amounted to approximately $221 million. Seventeen of the then twenty-five largest foundations accounted for about eighty-two percent of the latter figure. The largest share of foundation money spent for foreign activities was devoted to programs in Asia, Africa, and Latin America.[58]

The commission recommended, therefore,

For the time being, the commission accepts continued reliance on the Internal Revenue Service as the primary regulatory agency at the federal level. The commission believes, however, that the IRS's performance in this area must be improved. Not the least of the reasons why is a general lack of public confidence in the foundation as an institution. In point of fact, evidence gathered by the commission shows that the vast majority of foundations do not engage in any of the activities which form the core of the current concern. But to eliminate those abuses which do exist, and as a take-off point for the restoration of public confidence in foundations, greatly intensified auditing by the Internal Revenue Service is desirable.[59]

Consequently, one of the commission's major recommendations stipulated that in the future an Advisory Board on Philanthropic Policy be created and it spelled out the purpose, function, and makeup of such a body. Simultaneously with the work of the Peterson Commission, however, hearings on tax reform took place in 1969 in both the U.S. Senate and the House of Representatives.

Tax Reform Act of 1969

Major portions of the 1969 hearings in both the Committee on Ways and Means of the House of Representatives[60] and the Committee on Finance[61] of the Senate were devoted to the subject of tax exempt organizations, including foundations. The first witness to be called and heard by the House Committee was Congressman Wright Patman. And, early on, he appears on the roster testifying before the Senate Committee. His testimony was followed by that of hundreds of other witnesses including the executives of practically all of the major foundations and ancillary organizations. From the outset it became clearly apparent that a severely critical attitude towards foundations had developed. Underlying much of the voluminous material gathered at the hearings was the question of the fairness of the various tax exemption privileges, particularly by the establishment of foundations, afforded those of wealth which were not really available to those of lesser means. Also, it was asserted that many foundations were controlled and operated for the benefit of the donor, members of his family, or heirs. Arguments were advanced that some limits should be placed on charitable deductions. An overwhelming number of witnesses agreed that there was grossly inadequate auditing and supervision of foundations at the state level and by the IRS at the federal level. Against this background there was a cascade of testimony alleging fraudulent activities of foundations accompanied, in many cases, with documentary proof. Some witnesses questioned the wisdom of allocating foundation funds abroad when there was a need for such expenditures by them in the United States. Also, queries were made as to the efficacy of putting time limits on the life of foundations. Questioning by House and Senate members of various foundation officials and ancillary organizations served to buttress or exacerbate such testimony. For example, there was repeated questioning of the president of the Ford Foundation as to the propriety of his approving the awarding of grants by the foundation to former staffers of Senator Robert Kennedy. Similar queries were made regarding the funding provided by the foundation for voter registration programs and drives in various sections of the country. Perhaps the greatest stir occurred among those present at the hearings when John D. Rockefeller III made an eloquent plea for the necessity of maintaining a favorable climate for philanthropy as a needed and good public policy. In commenting on his own giving he testified that his philanthropic giving had qualified for the unlimited charitable deduction on income taxes every year since 1961, i.e., he had paid no income taxes from that year to the present.

Chairman Peterson of the Peterson Commission had presented much of the deliberations and work of his commission at the House and Senate hearings. Such evidence undoubtedly helped to avert more drastic measures advanced at these hearings. The denouement in this intensive scrutiny of foundations, however, was the passage of the Tax Reform Act (TRA) of 1969. Although some more drastic measures affecting foundations, such as a limit of twenty-five or forty years on their existence, were not passed, the legislation did include new regulatory and supervisory laws for foundations. The major new laws included a tax of four percent of investment income on foundations to pay for the cost of auditing their operations; certain restrictions on grants made to individuals; a requirement that expenditures must at least be the same as income within a year with invasion of capital if such income did not reach a percentage set annually by the IRS; additional restrictions on financial dealings between a donor and the created foundation; and amplified and more stringent reporting requirements. Also passed was the revised classification, for IRS purposes, of kinds of foundations. If assets came from a single donor (individual, family or company) they are classified as private foundations. If their assets came from multiple sources, such as community trusts or other charities, they are classified as public foundations. The new legislation exempted the latter from taxes and restrictions applicable only to the private foundations.

Ditchley Conference

The passage of the Tax Reform Act of 1969 appeared to many observers to confirm the fears expressed earlier by Alan Pifer. It is against this background that he lead in the calling together in 1972 of a conference in Ditchley, England attended by him and others from the United States and England to consider the current problems confronting U.S. philanthropy and foundations against the backdrop of English experience. Although the conferees discussed other problems relevant to philanthropy and foundations, its comments about the events affecting foundations in the 1960s and 1970s were probably the most trenchant and perceptive. For example,

> The discussion did not make clear why American foundations had not "set their own house in order" before having new requirements imposed upon them or why, since tax and audit requirements existed before 1969, these had not been enforced. American members in turn regretted there was no body in the United States equivalent to the British Charities Commissioners which could advise and assist tax-exempt organizations as well as regulate them. The conference members were told that the Peterson Commission recommended the formation of an Advisory Board on Philanthropic Policy to oversee the whole field of philanthropy, but members were not hopeful that decisions about the charitable status for tax exemption could be wrested from the Internal Revenue Service. Even so, they agreed that some kind of special advisory agency, perhaps along the lines of the British Charity Commission, would be desirable[62]

Some observers at home and abroad viewed the TRA of 1969 not only as drastic and punitive but as threatening the very future existence of foundations. Particularly alarming to them was the fact that, for the first time, foundations had been singled out as the charitable organization subject to an excise tax for their auditing. Called an excise tax, what it amounted to was an actual tax on their operation. It was against this background and in the turbulent climate associated with the interpretation and implementation of the overall legislation that various proposals by philanthropists and philanthropoids were advanced to make a better case for philanthropy and foundations. In addition to the aforementioned Ditchley Conference, a number of conference committees with varying titles and composed of different individuals were formed in the early 1970s for this purpose. They advanced varying ideas as to the title and exact makeup and function of bodies that might be set up to advance this cause. This ferment concerning foundations, their founding, operation, and supervision resulted in the creation of the 1973 Filer Commission.

Filer Commission

The leading figure in the 1973 creation of the Commission on Private Philanthropy and Public Needs was John D. Rockefeller III.[63] The Commission came to be named the Filer Commission because of its chairman, John H. Filer, then also chairman of the Aetna Life and Casualty Corporation. In financing its operations,

> JDR [John D. Rockefeller III], Aetna, and the Ford Foundation each contributed $25,000 to get the project started. Before it was over, $2 million was raised from some seven hundred contributors, mainly due to the efforts of Philip Klutznick, a commission member and philanthropic leader from Chicago, and the American Association of Fund Raising Counsel.[64]

In addition to the 31 members agreeing to serve on the commission, consisting of men and women from a variety of backgrounds, over 150 staff and consulting experts were eventually enlisted in its efforts. From its beginnings and throughout its work, the Filer Commission maintained close connection with key officials in the Congress and the U.S. Treasury Department. It utilized the expertise of some officials on leave from the department and the voluminous results of the commission's labor were published in 1977 under departmental imprint.[65]

The *Report* and *Research Papers* cover most areas of philanthropy, particularly its economics aspects and the role of the federal government in relation to it. In the portions dealing with foundations there is limited discussion of the founding and domestic and foreign activities of foundations. A great deal is said about the tax and supervisory laws affecting them, particularly those made in the Tax Reform Act (TRA) of 1969. The principal recommendations of the Filer Commission regarding foundations included a diminution in the four percent governmental tax levied on them for auditing by the TRA to one more accurately reflecting the actual costs of such auditing, reducing a required payout rate of foundation granting from six percent to five percent, personnel diversification for both trustees and staff, and easing the restrictions on lobbying government by tax exempt groups. A concluding recommendation stated "in terminating its own work, the Commission put forward as one of its major recommendations: *That a permanent national commission on the nonprofit sector be established by Congress.*"[66] It then spelled out the purposes, formation, members, funding, and term of existence of the proposed commission. This recommendation was vitiated, however, by a previous recommendation in the report: "That the Internal Revenue Service continue to be the principal agency responsible for the oversight of tax-exempt organizations."[67]

The 240-page *Report* included, however, twenty-five pages of dissenting comments by various members of the commission. In addition, a smaller fringe group composed of individuals who openly criticized the scope and direction of the commission's efforts established itself as a self-styled "Donee Group." This group eventually co-opted with the commission but the group finally stated that to a large extent it had failed in its attempt to have the commission accept most of the views or positions it advanced. It did succeed, however, in having them included as a semi-separate brief document within the *Research Papers.*[68] Their major concerns regarding foundations can be summarized as follows:

(1) expanded and more broadly disseminated information about programs and activities of foundations; (2) broader geographical, public, and non-profit sector and especially gender and minority representation on foundation governing boards and staff; and (3) a variety of changes in governmental regulations affecting foundations, particularly the removal of the IRS as a supervisory agency and the simultaneous creation of a new independent governmental commission for that purpose with direct congressional oversight provided for it.[69]

As has been noted, the *Report* of the commission only endorsed the creation of a "semi-governmental advisory commission" on foundations while retaining the IRS as their major supervisory body. The "Donee Group" views on the matter were strongly endorsed by two members of the commission. Graciela Olivarez stated:

I maintain that the regulatory function of the IRS should be transferred to another agency, specifically the proposed commission on the nonprofit sector. Recent questionable activities of the IRS alone make that agency suspect. Apart from that, however, placing charitable activities under the scrutiny of IRS seems to be a tradition rooted in the wisdom that any sector accorded special tax status automatically be regulated by the central tax authority. Philanthropy, I maintain, is a far broader concept and practice than 501(c)(3) [IRS audit form], and should fall within the regulatory purview of a special entity created for and sensitive to that purpose.[70]

In a lengthier, stronger, and more specific dissenting statement, Frances Farenthold maintained that:

The Commission's report has no greater blind spot than its refusal to acknowledge the recent revelations of past and continuing perversions of government agencies for political purposes. The unprecedented abuses of power still being exposed in the wake of the Watergate phenomenon make it clear that the Internal Revenue Service should not be the agency regulating exempt organizations.

Citing specific examples of such abuses under the administrations of Presidents Truman, Eisenhower, Kennedy, Johnson, and Nixon, she remonstrated, "Even without their continuing history of politicization of the regulation of exempt organizations, most observers agree with Alan Pifer. He said that present regulation is "quite ineffective, it is characterized by a negative rather than a positive attitude toward charity and it is located in the wrong place within the government." Farenthold then gave specific examples as to why the IRS was not set up or could be set up to perform regulatory functions anent tax exempt organizations. In urging the transfer of power from the IRS to a new independent regulatory commission, she concluded: "The new commission would also have greater credibility and more potential for performing the research and advocacy function envisaged by the Commission report for the proposed permanent national commission on philanthropy."[71]

The Filer Commission *Report* and the statement of the "Donee Group" had both endorsed the creation of some kind of commission on philanthropy for the future. In 1975-1976 there was a welter of individual and group meetings by their members and others interested in bringing such a commission into being. Eventually a 24-member group was officially set up as the U.S. Treasury Department's Advisory Committee on Private Philanthropy and Public Needs with Douglas Dillon as its chairman. By the time the committee held its first meeting on January 6, 1977, however, a new administration under President-elect Jimmy Carter had been formed. With the belief that the prospective new Secretary of the Treasury approved of the continuance of the activities of the committee, it next met on April 7, 1977. At that meeting, however, Treasury Department officials, already embarked by the new administration on a drive to reduce the number of such advisory committees, suggested that the committee should reconstitute itself as an informal, i.e., unofficial body. There were strong protests by committee members at the time regarding this announcement.[72] This was later in the year followed by correspondence and several meetings by various committee members and others in an increasingly divided attempt to resurrect it. The death knell for such a movement at that time, however, has been aptly summarized:

> Nevertheless, although the battle lines had been drawn, it was still almost a year before the somewhat parallel, but clearly more visionary, concept of a permanent commission on philanthropy was dealt its final blow. This happened when John D. Rockefeller III was killed in a car accident on July 10, 1978. With his death the idea of a national commission lost its most powerful supporter and no longer seemed to be viable.[73]

Foundation Center Studies

The latest major studies on foreign activities by our foundations have been two in the 1990s managed by Vice President Loren Renz of the Foundation Center. Conducted by the Center in cooperation with the Council on Foundations, they have been the only ones devoted exclusively to international funding by U.S. foundations. The results of the studies were published as *International Grantmaking: A Report on Foundation Trends* (1997) and *International Grantmaking II: An Update on U.S. Foundation Trends.* (2000). Together they cover the entire decade of the 1990s and provide an astounding array of data and statistics and view the international grantmaking of U.S. foundations from every conceivable angle. As President Sara L. Engelhardt of the Center stated, in a summarizing Preface to the first work:

> The result is the first comprehensive analysis of international funding by U.S. foundations. This is a complex topic, encompassing international funding in both its geographic and substantive contexts. Based on an analysis of grants over half a decade (1990-1994) and on survey data, we have identified trends, depicted the current state of international grantmaking, and even predicted future directions. Foundations have contributed insight into policy and procedural issues in international grantmaking, and a comparative picture is drawn by the three authored articles.[74]

Both studies defined international grantmaking by U.S. foundations to include domestic grants for broadly defined international purposes. As to the database used in both studies, the second report noted: "The number of international funders identified in the Foundation Center's grants database (the source of the data for the trends analysis in this report and in the first benchmark study) climbed to 576 in 1998 from 479 in 1994."[75]

A major conclusion drawn was that:

> Bolstered by a booming stock market and a spectacular rise in the value of foundation assets, international giving by U.S. foundations grew rapidly in the late 1990s. In 1998, it reached an estimated $1.6 billion, a 66 percent rise over 1994 levels. (By comparison, from 1990 to 1994, international funding grew 26 percent). Relative to total foundation giving, the share going to international programs slipped from 11.5 percent in 1994 to 10.9 percent in 1998. Nevertheless, in absolute terms, the more than $600 million increase in giving over that period represents an unprecedented infusion of resources. Not only did the amount of giving surge, but these funds came from many more grantmakers.[76]

Notes

1. A notable exception to this relatively light opposition, primarily directed against the General Education Board that was incorporated in 1903, was Bishop Warren A. Candler's pamphlet Dangerous Donations and Degrading Doles, or A Vast Scheme for Capturing and Controlling the Colleges and Universities of the Country. Privately printed, Atlanta, Georgia, 1909.

2. See *Industrial Relations.* Final Report and Testimony Submitted to Congress by the Commission on Industrial Relations, U.S. Senate, 64th Congress, lst Session Senate Document 415. Government Printing Office, Washington, D. C., 1916. 11 vols. The material concerning foundations appears primarily in: vol. 8, pp. 7427–7748 under the heading "Centralization of industrial control and operation of philanthropic foundations" and in vol. 8, pp. 7761-8013 and in vol. 9, pp. 8015–8948 under the heading "Proceedings related to Colorado strike, large foundations, and industrial control." In the Final Report, similar material regarding philanthropy and foundations is primarily to be found in (vol. 1, sections I, II, III, and IV, pp. 17-269).

3. Eduard C. Lindeman, *Wealth and Culture: A Study of One Hundred Foundations and Community Trusts and Their Operations during the Decade 1921-1930.* Harcourt, Brace and Co., New York, 1936.

4. Shelby M. Harrison and F. Emerson Andrews, *American Foundations for Social Welfare.* Russell Sage Foundation, New York, 1946, p. 79.

5. U. S. House of Representatives, 81st Congress, 2d Session, House Report 3138, *General Interim Report of the Select Committee on Lobbying Activities.* Government Printing Office, Washington, D.C., 1950, p. 1.

6. Ibid., p. 6.

7. Ibid., pp. 1-67. See also, U.S. House of Representatives , 81st congress, 2d Session, House Report 3239, *A Report of the Select Committee on Lobbying Activities.* Government Printing Office, Washington, D. C., 1950, Part 1, pp.1-58 and Minority Views, Part 2, pp. 1-11.

8. *General Interim Report,* p. 61.

9. *A Report of the Select Committee on Lobbying Activities,* Part 2, p. 3.

10. Joseph C. Kiger, *Operating Principles of the Larger Foundations,* Russell Sage Foundation, New York, 1954, p. 91.

11. See, for example, Frank Hughes, *Prejudice and the Press,* The Devon-Adair Company, New York, 1950. See particularly Chapter 10, The Bias of Great Wealth, pp. 285-324.

12. See Joseph C. Kiger, *Philanthropic Foundations in the Twentieth Century*, Greenwood Press, Westport, Connecticut, 2000, pp. 24-28.

13. Hereafter cited as *Answers to Questionnaire*. The larger and lengthier questionnaire was submitted to 54 larger foundations by the Select Committee.

14. U.S. House of Representatives, 82nd Congress, 2nd Session, *Final Report of the Select Committee to Investigate Foundations and Other Organizations*. House Report No. 2514. Government Printing Office, Washington, D.C., 1953, pp. 8, 10.

15. U.S. House of Representatives, 82nd Congress, 2nd Session, *Hearings before the Select Committee to Investigate Tax-Exempt Foundations and Comparable Organizations*. Government Printing Office, Washington, D.C., 1953, p. 232.

16. *Final Report of the Select Committee to Investigate Foundations and Other Organizations*, p. 12.

17. Ibid., p.14.

18. B. Carroll Reece, *Congressional Record*, Vol. 29, No. 141, July 27, 1953, p. 10188.

19. For example see, *Statements of the Carnegie Corporation of New York*, New York, 1954, pp. 1-46 and *Statement of the Rockefeller Foundation and General Education Board*, New York, 1954, pp. 1-72 and Appendices.

20. U.S. House of Representatives, 83d Congress, 2d Session, *Report of the Special Committee to Investigate Foundations and Comparable Organizations*. Government Printing Office, Washington, D.C., 1954, pp. 431-432.

21. *Report of the Special Committee to Investigate Foundations and Comparable Organizations*. p. 226. The following note on the foregoing page refers to this addendum; "(Mr. Goodwin's added remarks were not received in time to be include in this printing of the report, but will be included when the report is reprinted.)" It should be added that the report has never been reprinted.

22. See particularly, "Internationalism and the Effect of Foundation Power on Public Policy," *Report of the Special Committee to Investigate Foundations and Comparable Organizations*, pp. 169-194.

23. *Report of the Special Committee to Investigate Foundations and Comparable Organizations*, p. 220.

24. "Another Stupid Inquiry," *New York Times,* July 5, 1954, p. 10.

25. Rene A. Wormser, *Foundations: Their Power and Influence*. Devon-Adair, New York, 1958.

26. Joseph C. Kiger, *Historiographic Review of Foundation Literature: Motivations and Perceptions*. Foundation Center, New York, 1987. p. 17.

27. W.K. Jordan, *Philanthropy in England, 1480-1660: A Study of the Changing Pattern of English Social Aspirations,* Russell Sage Foundation, New York, 1959 and David Owen, *English Philanthropy, 1660-1960,* Belknap Press of Harvard University Press, Cambridge, Massachusetts, 1964.

28. See *Report of the Princeton Conference on the History of Philanthropy in the United States*. Russell Sage Foundation, New York, 1956.

29. For a longer but still brief account of the formation and history of the Foundation Center see Joseph C. Kiger, *Philanthropic Foundations in the Twentieth Century*, pp. 67-69.

30. See *Ibid.,* pp. 69-81 for a detailed identification and discussion of the major actors in these categories.

31. Jordan A. Schwartz, "John William Wright Patman, " *Dictionary of American Biography,* Simon & Schuster Macmillan, New York, 1995, Supplement 10, p. 619.

32. Nancy Beck Young, *Wright Patman: Populism, Liberalism, and the American Dream*. Southern Methodist University Press, Dallas, Texas, 2000, p. 159.

33. Ibid., p. 208.
34. U.S. House of Representatives, Select Committee on Small Business, 88th Congress, 2nd Session, *Hearings before Subcommittee No. 1 Foundations.* Government Printing Office, Washington, D.C., 1964.
35. Ibid., p. 182, 191.
36. U.S. House of Representatives, Select Committee on Small Business, 90th Congress, 2nd Session, *Hearings before Subcommittee No. 1 Foundations.* Government Printing Office, Washington, D.C.,1967.
37. Wright Patman, *Congressional Record* 107, no.73 (May 2, 1961), p. 6560.
38. U.S. House of Representatives, Select Committee on Small Business, 87th through 91st Congress, *Chairman's Reports. Tax Exempt Foundations and Charitable Trusts: Their Impact on Our Economy.* Government Printing Office, Washington, D.C., 1962 through 1969, Installments 1 through 7.
39. U.S. House of Representatives, Committee on Banking and Currency, Subcommittee on Domestic Finance, 92nd Congress, 2nd Session, *Staff Report. . Tax Exempt Foundations and Charitable Trusts: Their Impact on Our Economy.* Government Printing Office, Washington, D.C., 1972, Installment 8.
40. *Chairman's Report,* 1962, Installment 1, p. 134.
41. U.S. House of Representatives, Committee on Ways and Means, 91st Congress, 1st Session, *Hearings, Tax Reform.* Government Printing Office, Washington, D.C., 1969, Part 1, p. 14.
42. Ibid., p. 16.
43. Ibid., p. 17.
44. Paul Mellon with John Baskett, *Reflections in a Silver Spoon; A Memoir.* William Morrow and Company, New York, 1992, pp. 331-332.
45. F. Emerson Andrews, *Patman and Foundations: Review and Assessment.* Occasional Papers, Number Three, The Foundation Center, New York, 1968, p. 55.
46. Warren Weaver, *U.S. Philanthropic Foundations: Their History, Structure, Management, and Record.* Harper and Row, New York, 1967, pp. 183, 185.
47. U.S. Department of the Treasury. *Treasury Department Report on Private Foundations.* Government Printing Office, Washington, D.C., 1965.
48. Ibid., p. 10.
49. *Annual Report for 1968.* Carnegie Corporation of New York, New York, 1968, pp. 8-9.
50. Eleanor L. Brilliant, *Private Charity and Public Inquiry: A History of the Filer and Peterson Commissions.* Indiana University Press, Bloomington, Indiana, 2000. See particularly, Chapters 5 and 6.
51. John D. Rockefeller III, *The Second American Revolution.* Harper & Row, New York, 1973, p. 114. See also, pp.81-82, 97-98, and 113-130.
52. John Ensor Harr and Peter J. Johnson, *The Rockefeller Century.* Charles Scribner's Sons, New York, 1988. See particularly, Chapter 29.
53. Ibid., p. 289.
54. Eleanor L. Brilliant, *Private Charity and Public Inquiry: A History of the Filer and Peterson Commissions.* p. 91.
55. *Foundations, Private Giving and public Policy: Report and Recommendations of the Commission on Foundations and Public policy.* University of Chicago Press, Chicago, 1970. See also, *A Summary of Findings and Recommendations.* University of Chicago Press, Chicago, 1970.
56. Ibid., pp. 3-5.
57. Ibid., p. 62.

58. *Foundations, Private Giving, and Public Policy: A Summary of Finding and Recommendation.* University of Chicago Press, Chicago, Illinois, pp. 81-82.

59. Ibid., p. 170.

60. U.S. House of Representatives, Committee on Ways and Means, 91st Congress, 1st Session, *Hearings. Tax Reform.* Government Printing Office, Washington, D.C., 1969. Parts 1-15. See particularly Parts 1, 2, and 3.

61. See U.S. Senate, Committee on Finance, 91st Congress, 1st Session, *Hearings. Tax Reform Act of 1969.* Government Printing Office, Washington, D. C., 1969. Parts 1-7. See particularly Parts 3 and 6.

62. John J. Corson, and Harry V. Hodson, eds., *Philanthropy in the 70's: An Anglo-American Discussion.* Council on Foundations, New York, 1973, p. 12.

63. See Eleanor L. Brilliant, *Private Charity and Public Inquiry: A History of the Filer and Peterson Commissions.* pp. 99-114, for a detailed discussion of the players involved in these tangled negotiations.

64. John Ensor Harr and Peter J. Johnson, *The Rockefeller Conscience.* Charles Scribner's Sons, New York, 1991, p. 377. For a detailed account of this fund raising effort, see John J. Schwartz, *Modern American Philanthropy: A Personal Account.* John Wiley & Sons, New York, 1994, pp. 101-106.

65. U.S. Department of the Treasury, *Giving in America: Report of the Commission on Private Philanthropy and Public Needs.* Government Printing Office, Washington, D.C., 1975 and *Research Papers Sponsored by the Commission on Private Philanthropy and Public Needs,* vols. 1-5. Government Printing Office, Washington, D.C., 1977.

66. *Giving in America: Report of the Commission on Private Philanthropy and Public Needs,* p. 191.

67. Ibid., p. 167.

68. "Donee Group Report and Recommendations" *Research Papers,* vol.1. part 1, pp. 49-85.

69. Joseph.C. Kiger, *Philanthropic Foundations in the Twentieth Century,* p. 37.

70. *Giving in America: Report of the Commission on Private Philanthropy and Public Needs,* p. 214.

71. Ibid., pp. 214-216.

72. Urban C. Lehner, "Treasury Stuns New Philanthropy Panel with Word That It Doesn't Have a Future," *Wall Street Journal* (April 11, 1977), p. A8.

73. Eleanor L. Brilliant, *Private Charity and Public Inquiry: A History of the Filer and Peterson Commissions.* p. 143.

74. Loren Renz, Josefina Atienza, et.al., *International Grantmaking: A Report on U.S. Foundation Trends.* Foundation Center, New York, 1997, p. vii.

75. Loren Renz, Josefina Atienza, et.al, , *International Grantmaking II: An Update on U.S. Foundation Trends.* Foundation Center, New York, 2000, p. 1.

76. Ibid., p. 1.

4

Rockefellers, Jones, Pew, Starr, Tinker, Packard, and Hewlett

Rockefellers

The five sons of John D. Rockefeller, Jr. were John D. III (1906-1978), like his father devoting much of his life to philanthropy; Nelson (1908-1979) governor of New York from 1958 to 1973 and then U.S. vice president from 1974-1977; Laurence (1910-2004) conservationist; Winthrop (1912-1973) governor of Arkansas from 1967 to 1970; and David (1915-) associated with the Chase Manhattan Bank from 1946 on and latterly its chairman. The five brothers established the Rockefeller Brothers Fund in 1940 and were shortly joined by their sister Abby Rockefeller Mauze (1903-1976).

Rockefeller Brothers Fund

The Rockefeller brothers all served as the fund's initial trustees. Their founding motive was to carry on in the family philanthropic tradition and simultaneously engage in joint giving. Initially funded by annual grants from them, the fund remained a relatively small one until the 1950s, restricting its grants to New York City. The projects and programs funded by it in that period tended to coalesce around the interests of each founding member. In 1951-1952 the fund received a $58 million endowment gift from John D. Rockefeller, Jr. augmented with additional sizeable bequests from him and his wife in the 1960s. Also, a 1999 merger with the Charles E. Culpepper Foundation considerably augmented the Fund's assets which now stand at approximately $700 million.

With the accretion of assets in the 1950s and 1960s, in ensuing decades the Fund expanded the composition of its board of trustees to include non-Rockefellers as trustees. Simultaneously it shifted its emphasis from the local and increasingly concentrated on the national level and, even more so, on the international scene. By the 1980s the

> RBF activities at the international level, during these years, included grants for South American and Asian agricultural development, education in the Near and Middle East, improved Asian-American relations, and the economic development of West African nations.[1]

In 1993 the Fund announced:

> Since June 1984 the principal part of the Fund's grant making program has been organized about the theme of One World, with two major components: sustainable resource use and world security.... The major portion of grant funds are applied to the One World program. Projects are located for the most part in East Asia, East Central Europe, the former Soviet Union or the United States.[2]

In other words, the individualistic philanthropic motives of the founders, largely of a local character, were supplanted by an increasingly concentrated international one. Changes of such magnitude were accompanied and implemented by a significant increase in professional staff, headed by Dana S. Creel (1968-1975), William M. Dietel (1975-1987), Colin G. Campbell (1988-2000), and since then by Stephen B. Heintz. Successive generations of the Rockefeller family, however, have served on the board of trustees and have consistently maintained a working interest in the Fund's grant making programs. One of them, Steven C. Rockefeller, is currently chairman of the board.

Jones

W. Alton Jones was born on April 19, 1891 on a small farm in southeastern Missouri near Joplin. He was the youngest of seven children and began working at various non-farm jobs at an early age and attended local public schools. He eventually earned enough money to enroll in Vanderbilt University but was forced to leave after his freshman year to support the Jones family as a meter reader for a gas company near home. It was during this period, in 1914, that he married his childhood sweetheart Nettie Marie Martin and the couple subsequently had two daughters, Patricia Jane and Elizabeth Marie. He became a secretary for a larger gas company in Joplin after having completed a bookkeeping course while working. In 1920 he moved to New York City for work with the prominent petroleum and utilities Cities Service Company. Following a rise through several executive positions and playing a major role in steering the company successfully through the depression of 1929, Jones was named president in 1940 and chairman of the board of trustees in 1953. In the process he became a power in the natural gas and petroleum industries and a very wealthy man. Also he became a close friend of numerous influential business and military leaders including General and then President Dwight D. Eisenhower. The latter was in attendance at his funeral following his death in 1962 in an airplane crash while en route from New York to California for a projected fishing trip with the former president. He left the major part of his fortune, consisting in large measure of shares in the Cities Service Company, to the W. Alton Jones Foundation.

W. Alton Jones Foundation

In 1944, relatively early in his business career, Jones had set up the foundation bearing his name in New York. The charter describing its statement of purpose opened with "to promote the general well-being and general good of mankind throughout the world." From a relatively small initial corpus the foundation assets grew to about $4 million by 1953. Until his death in 1962, W. Alton Jones was president with his wife and two daughters serving as directors of the foundation. With additional funds from his estate, plus donations from Mrs. Jones, the assets of the foundations stood at about $24 million in 1969. In 1980 the foundation moved its offices to Charlottesville, Virginia where Mrs. Jones lived until her death in 1991.

Despite the broad purpose avowed at its founding, from its inception and up until 1982, the Jones Foundation overwhelmingly made grants to educational and scientific organizations, museums, and art and cultural institutions almost wholly in the United States. About that time, however, two things happened which caused a shift in policy. First, there was a buy-out of Cities Service Company by Occidental Petroleum Corporation that resulted in a tremendous boost in the value of the company shares held by the Jones Foundation. Second, the foundation, with assets now at about $100 million, shifted its grant making program and became a major national funding agency for projects in the conservation and environmental area together with anti-nuclear research and other efforts designed to prevent nuclear war; with many of these grants made to entities and organizations located outside the United States. By the 1990s and the death of Mrs. W. Alton Jones the foundation grants, amounting to about $9 to $10 million annually, were almost totally concentrated in these areas.

It was against this background that the Jones Foundation, governed by six members of the Jones family including daughter Patricia Jane, now Mrs. Patricia Jones Edgerton, as president, and Dr. John Peterson Myers as director, supported and funded a study and resultant publication by Theo Colborn, Dianne Dumanoski, and John Peterson Myers of *Our Stolen Future: Are We Threatening Our Fertility, Intelligence, and*

Survival?—A Scientific Detective Story, (Dutton, New York, 1996). Alleging the deleterious effects of the use of various chemicals on the environment and humans, this book initially received widespread and favorable publicity. The study/publication soon proved, however, to be very embarrassing to the authors and the foundation because the scientist, upon whose research the work rested, was forced to completely retract his earlier findings.[3]

There is speculation that the foregoing matter played a considerable role in the subsequent closing down of the W. Alton Jones Foundation. This action was followed by the subsequent splitting up of its endowment of some $350 to $400 million among three new foundations established in 2002: the Oak Hill Fund, headed by William A. Edgerton; the Blue Moon Foundation, headed by Mrs. Patricia Jones Edgerton and her daughter Mrs. Diane Edgerton Miller; and the Edgerton Foundation, headed by Bradford W. Edgerton. Each of these individuals had been officers or directors of the now defunct W. Alton Jones Foundation. In 2002 officials of the Oak Hill Foundation announced that the foundation will center its grants on education and for the support of affordable housing units and concentrate its grants in the southeastern United States.[4]

Pew

John and Elizabeth (Vaughan) Pew settled in then frontier Mercer County Pennsylvania in 1796. A son, John, acquired a farm there, married Nancy Glenn, and on July 25, 1848, the founder of the Pew fortune, Joseph Newton Pew, was born to the couple. By 1866, while working on his father's farm, Joseph had acquired a creditable elementary and secondary education which was followed by his teaching school for two years and then opening a real estate office in nearby Titusville, Pennsylvania. Early on he recognized the potential economic value of the petroleum oil initially produced there in 1859. He began to acquire oil producing properties in Pennsylvania and elsewhere and in the 1870s Pew started organizing a series of companies for the production of oil and its byproducts such as natural gas and gasoline. These endeavors culminated in the setting up in 1901 of the Sun Oil Company; probably the best known and most lucrative of his ventures. He was a devout and staunch Presbyterian with an aversion to alcoholic beverages. Joseph Newton and his sister Sarah were staunch abolitionists and Sarah spent time in the South after the Civil War in efforts to educate the newly freed blacks.[5] Later he served for many years as a trustee of the Bryn Mawr Presbyterian Church together with a similar tenure at the Presbyterian affiliated Grove City College. Of the College he stated that "he was more interested in the College than in the business enterprises which were taking so much of his strength and time."[6] In any case, by the time of his death in 1912 Pew had acquired a sizeable fortune which he bequeathed to his wife, Mary Catherine (Anderson) and five children: the eldest, Arthur Edmond, of whom little is known, J. Howard (1882-1971), Joseph Newton, Jr. (1886-1963), Mary Ethel (1884-1979), and Mabel Anderson Myrin (1889-1972) Pew.[7]

Pew Charitable Trusts

Joseph Newton Pew's philanthropic giving was characterized by its personal and anonymous character. Building on the parental fortune and led by his sons J. Howard and Joseph Newton Pew, Jr., it was greatly augmented by a vast expansion of the family business spanning two world wars and even profiting during the interim depression years.[8] In addition to the acquisition of more oil properties here and abroad, this included the setting up of refineries and the creation of pipe lines and tankers for the movement of oil, gasoline, and natural gas. Subsidiary ventures included shipbuilding and publications. Thus, by 1948 the Pew family fortune was one of the largest in the country. In addition to their business interests J. Howard Pew and, to a greater extent, Joseph Newton Pew, Jr. were behind-the-scenes financial supporters of the Republican Party, particularly its conservative wing. They detested most of the policies of President Roosevelt's New Deal of the 1930s and 1940s, particularly what they viewed as the ever increasing intrusion of the federal government into business matters. They contributed millions of dollars to candidates and causes in a generally failing effort to defeat or thwart these New Deal measures. Joseph W. Martin, Jr., Speaker of the House and a longtime powerful Republican Congressman in those decades eulogized:

> Throughout these bleak years I could, fortunately, still count on financial support from some of the men and women who have remained loyal in good times and bad. Joseph N. Pew, Jr. of Pennsylvania, head of the Sun Oil Company, is an outstanding example. In his dedication to the preservation of the Republican Party he has given millions. Yet in all the years I have known him and have been close to him in campaigns and other party activities he has never asked me for a single favor. When almost no one else was giving any money his contributions kept coming in; without them the party might have utterly dried up for lack of funds.[9]

It is against the religious and political background above that the earlier Pew family philanthropic endeavors took place. Prior to 1948 their benefactions were directed to schools, hospitals and similar organizations almost wholly in the Philadelphia area; Presbyterian churches; and to national conservative public policy institutions. Reflecting their political and religious beliefs, such aid was rendered personally and anonymously. Beginning in 1948, however, the four Pew brothers and sisters set up seven foundations, six of which were smaller ones designed to carry out their specific individual concerns. The seventh chartered in that year was the Pew Memorial Foundation. With initial assets of about $50 million it was by far the largest of the seven. In 1956-1957 a reorganization took place in which the foundation's name was changed to the Pew Memorial Trust and its assets and eventually those of the other six were transferred to a newly created Glenmede Trust Company. Chartered under the state banking statutes of Pennsylvania, it acts as the trustee and administrator for the seven foundations. Requests for grants to any of the foundations were and are directed by an officer of the Glenmede Trust Company to an appropriate foundation for action. This reorganization, however, did not affect the control and administration of the trusts which rested almost entirely in the hands of the four Pews with a miniscule assisting staff. Up until the end of the 1970s, by which time the four had passed away, the pattern of giving and its administration essentially continued as described above.

Their deaths ushered in a new generation of inheriting Pews who maintain a continuing and pervasive interest in the programs of their foundations. Six members of the Pew family now sit on a ten-member board of trustees of the combined seven foundations, presently designated the Pew Charitable Trusts, with the Glenmede Trust continuing to act as trustee. By this time, too, the corpus of the foundations saw a steady increase, so that today the Pew Memorial Trusts assets rank among the top ten with a corpus of about $5 billion.

The change in the makeup of the board of trustees was accompanied by a dramatic change in the administration and geographic thrust of the combined foundations. There was a significant augmentation in the size of the staff and an enlargement in the decision making power afforded a new president, Robert Smith, appointed in 1977. The first annual public report of the foundation was made in 1979 and since then there has been a continuing increase in publications concerning the conduct of the program and activities of the foundation.[10] Smith was succeeded in 1986 by Dr. Thomas W. Langfitt. Health care and education in the United States were the largest areas of concern of the Pew foundations during their tenures. Rebecca W. Rimel, the present incumbent and also with a medical background, joined the Pew foundations in 1983, and was named executive director in 1988. Although Dr. Langfitt remained on the foundation's board of trustees, following his retirement as president in 1993, Ms. Rimel was named president in 1994.

Rimel's first annual report, when she had been named executive director of the foundation, contained the following statements foretelling change in the trusts programs:

> During 1988 we undertook a major, comprehensive evaluation of our programs and organizational structure, which has resulted in a new template that will better position the Trusts to serve the needs of our many constituencies in the years ahead.... The grantmaking of the Trusts has changed significantly in its programmatic focus, geographic distribution, and response to societal needs.... If foundations are to require interdisciplinary responses from the grantee community that transcend institutional, departmental, and geographic boundaries, then we too must be willing to approach problems and review proposals in a similar way.[11]

The foundation's annual reports during the 1990s reflect this shift. The most dramatic change in its program was the globalization of its efforts. References therein are increasingly made to the global nature of the problems confronting society and ergo the foundation. Statistically, while a majority of grants in sizeable amounts were still made by the foundation in the Philadelphia area and at the national level in the 1990s, increasing interest in the international area took place. Thus, by 1997, such grants were amounting to about $35 million annually out of total annual grants in excess of $250 million. In 2005, international grants totaled about $10 million while national and regional ones amounted to about $127 million. Most striking in this connection was the foundation decision in the 1990s, following the relatively sudden collapse of the Communist regimes in Central and Eastern Europe, to concentrate and use much of its resources there.

Starr

Cornelius Vander Starr was born in Fort Bragg, California on October 15, 1892. He was the son of a locomotive engineer and his father died when he was two years old. Entering the University of California, Berkeley in 1910 he waited on dining hall tables to pay his way. There followed various other jobs while he studied law at night with a San Francisco attorney and Starr passed the California bar examination in 1913. In 1915 he organized and ran his first insurance company; sold it for a $10,000 profit in 1917, and with the onset of U.S. involvement in World War I enlisted in the U.S. Army. Following the end of the war and being mustered out from the Army, Starr wound up in Shanghai, China in

1919. Starr established an insurance company there in 1921 and, branching out from Shanghai, by the 1930s he had created and was operating an insurance empire covering China and Southeast Asia. In addition, he invested in real estate in Shanghai, founded a newspaper there, and was managing several automobile agencies in the region. His opposition to growing Japanese expansion in Asia led to his return to the United States in 1940 and the beginning of his expansion of his insurance business into Latin-America which soon matched his Asiatic interests. With the end of World War II, Starr reopened and expanded his business activities in the Far East and eventually worldwide. For example, following the war his companies were insurer to U.S. military forces in occupied Japan. By the time of his death in 1968, he was operating 100 insurance companies in some 130 countries under the title American International Insurance Group. In the process, he had become a wealthy man and, with no immediate survivors, he left the major portion of his fortune of millions of dollars to the Starr Foundation that he had established in 1955. Under Starr's guidance, its activities were focused on education, including scholarships for U.S. citizens and Asians, particularly for children of employees of his companies.

Starr Foundation

Upon Starr's death in 1968 and bequest to the foundation, its assets consisted of approximately $2 million and its grants amounted to about $100,000 annually. For the next few years, its activities followed the path charted by Starr. The 1970s, however, witnessed a continuing awesome growth in its assets from $143 million in 1979 to its present day approximately $2.5 billion. In addition to this growth, the 1980s marked the beginning of a period of change in the pattern of giving of the foundation in terms of amount and kind. While continuing its scholarship programs, (it has continued it down to the present) the foundation began making and has continued to make substantial grants to institutions: hospitals and medical research facilities, universities, and organizations devoted to the arts, such as the Metropolitan Opera Association of New York. Many of these grants were made for international purposes with a focus on China and Asia, such as those to the Asia Society.

The principal architect in the spectacular post-Starr expansion of the business and the accompanying growth in assets and change in giving at the Starr Foundation was Maurice R. "Hank" Greenberg. He served on the board of directors of American International Group, Inc. (AIG), and the successor firm to those launched by Starr, for three decades, much of it as its chairman. Greenberg also occupied and played a similar role at the Starr Foundation. Such asset growth in the foundation was due to his engineering the donation of stock to the foundation by the directors of AIG. At the same time, he and these same directors occupied similar and controlling interests in the Starr Foundation. This relationship came to an end in 2005, however, when Greenberg was forced to resign as AIG chairman amid charges of dubious transaction and improper accounting practices leveled at it by federal and state investigatory bodies. The Starr Foundation held only two percent of the total AIG stock but the investigations did raise questions about some of its grants. In particular, the propriety of the foundation making a multimillion dollar grant to the American Museum of Natural History, where Greenberg was a director, shortly after the museum's president was named to the foundation's board of directors.[12] Subsequently, Greenberg resigned from the museum's board of directors as well as that of the Asia Society where he had also served for many years.[13] It remains to be seen what these events bode for the future of the Starr Foundation.

Tinker

Edward Larocque Tinker's paternal ancestors were New England ship owners and sea captains of Puritan descent. His grandfather moved to New York City in the early 1800s, invested in New York real estate in the pre-Civil War period and established and practiced in a law firm. He prospered greatly, building an impressive home on Park Avenue where Edward Larocque Tinker was born in 1881. His maternal ancestors were French Huguenots who had emigrated to Savannah, Georgia at the time of the French Revolution.

Born to wealth, Tinker graduated from prep school in New York City and attended and graduated from Columbia University in 1902. Attaining a law degree three years later from New York University, he was admitted to the bar. There followed a one year stint with the Legal Aid Society and three as an assistant district attorney in New York City. Tinker had developed a deep interest in Mexico, however, following boyhood trips there with his parents, and he then moved to the Mexican border town of El Paso, Texas to set up safety standards for railroads. For the next few years he also got caught up in and was a keenly interested observer of the Mexican Revolution against Diaz that included a colorful sojourn with the forces of Pancho Villa and the direct observation of a battle. Tinker thought that, although the revolution resulted in the deaths of thousands and devastated the country, it helped the common man. Later, in his 1970 memoirs, he presciently warned;

> What made the revolt inevitable was the greed and callousness of a small ruling minority. This should be a lesson to those Iberian-American countries where the same conditions exist today for, if these tiny dominant groups do not develop in time a generosity, a sense of fairness and a desire to help the underprivileged, they, too, will suffer the same holocaust as Mexico, and all their possessions will be swept away.[14]

In 1916, he left Mexico for the United States where he met and was married to Frances McKee of New Orleans. They bought a house on St. Charles Street and lived there during the winter months. This marked the beginning of the scholarly and academic part of his career and until Frances' death in 1958 she was an active participant in the stream of publications by him that followed. With his residence there, Tinker became a devotee of New Orleans and Louisiana history and literature and in 1924 he published a biography of Lafcadio Hearn.[15] Another best known work of his was inspired by his belief that "The horsemen of the Americas—the *huasos* of Chile, the *gauchos* of the Rio de Plata, the *llaneros* of Venezuela, the *vaqueros* of Mexico, or the cowboys of the United States, call them what you will—are brothers under the skin."[16] His conclusion that these differing nations produced men so similar was probably a major motivating factor in his later establishment of the Tinker Foundation as a bridge for better understanding between North America and Latin America.

While Tinker continued the practice of law and the management of his real estate interests in New York City—and he was competent in these occupations—his major interest became his aforementioned literary and artistic endeavors. As a consequence Tinker acquired advanced academic degrees in law and the humanities at universities in the United States and abroad. In this process, while traveling widely and writing and publishing extensively, he early on developed an interest in all things Hispanic both in the old and new world.

Tinker Foundation

The Tinker Foundation was established in 1959 by him as a memorial to his wife, Frances McKee Tinker, and his paternal ancestors. His purpose in its founding was the utilization of its resources in the promotion of better understanding among the peoples of the United States and Latin America, Spain, and Portugal. He was active in the affairs of the foundation until his death in 1968 leaving no immediate survivors.

Tinker bequeathed the foundation some $20 million. By the 1980s its assets grew to about $35 million and have since grown to about $100 million today. The foundation almost immediately launched a grants program which has been continued at home and abroad to promote the purpose of its creation.

Packard

David Packard was born on September 7, 1912 in Pueblo, Colorado. A 1995 autobiographical volume, devoted almost entirely to his business career, states: "My father was a lawyer and my mother a high school teacher. They met at Colorado College in Colorado Springs, and after they were married they moved to Pueblo which was my father's home. My younger sister, Ann Louise, was born in 1915."[17] There follows a description of his youth in a small city which he characterizes as a "Western frontier" town. The family was a moderately well to do one; Packard notes that a future U.S. Senator studied law in his father's law office. He attended and distinguished himself in academics and sports at the local high school and, following graduation, was admitted to Stanford University. Already decided on a concentration in the electrical engineering field, he and by then close friend and fellow student William R. Hewlett fell under the influence of Professor Fred Terman who acted as a mentor to both men. Following graduation and a stint working with the General Electric Company in Schenectady, New York, Packard returned to Stanford in 1938 to engage in graduate work, defrayed by a fellowship arranged for him by Professor Terman. In that same year, he married Lucile Salter, a fellow student with him while at Stanford. Also, he was reunited with Hewlett who, following study and receipt of a master's degree from the Massachusetts Institute of Technology, had returned to California to engage in research work; similarly engineered by Professor Terman. The married couple rented a small house in proximity to the Stanford campus; subletting a small building in the back to bachelor Hewlett. It was in the one car garage of this home that, in their spare time, the two partners launched what was to become the Hewlett-Packard Company. Parenthetically, in 1989 the garage was designated a California Historical Landmark and the birthplace of Silicon Valley. Materially aided by Packard's wife and in 1939 by newlywed Hewlett's wife, Flora Lamson, initial products of the partners were electronic measuring instruments. Showing profits from its beginnings, U.S. participation in World War II augmented them and 1947 saw the incorporation of the Hewlett-Packard Company. A name that was decided on by the flip of a coin as to which name would come first. The inauguration of the computer and the corporation's response was the catalyst that propelled the tremendous growth of the company. As Packard states, "In 1994 HP's sales in computer products, service, and supports were almost $20 billion, or about 78% of the company's total business. In 1964, our sales totaled $125 million and were entirely in instruments. Not a penny was from computer sales."[18] He added, "Hewlett-Packard now produces and sells thousands of products in more than 650 plants located in over 120 countries around the world."[19] This tremendous company growth saw a corresponding growth in Packard's personal fortune and he and co-founder Hewlett became two of the wealthiest men in the United States.

In a final chapter in his autobiography,[20] Packard maintains that American businesses and businessmen have a responsibility to society beyond making a profit. He cites the fact that he grew up in the depression of the 1930s and the impulse to help and share with those who suffered during that period as the background for his strong feelings in this matter. In carrying through in his own case, Packard, in addition to his business affairs, served in numerous capacities on many regional and national non-governmental organizations such as Stanford University and the Hoover Institution, together with government where he served in Washington as U.S. Deputy Secretary of Defense from 1969 to 1971. In his autobiography, he extols philanthropic giving by his and other business corporations. The only mention of the foundation he created, however, is the following: "Unrelated to the corporate philanthropy of the Hewlett-Packard Company are the philanthropic foundation [David and Lucile Packard Foundation] established by my late wife and me in 1964 and the William and Flora Hewlett Foundation, incorporated in 1966."[21]

David and Lucile Packard Foundation

David and Lucile Packard were the original president and vice-president of the foundation they established with several of their children forming a majority on its board of trustees. The foundation grew from small original assets to about $1 million by 1970 and with annual grants amounting to several hundred thousand dollars. At that tine its grants consisted of funds for education and social welfare, together with a few grants for conservation and population issues. Such giving was centered on the San Francisco and Monterey areas in California. By the 1980s the foundation's assets had grown to about $35 million with annual grants of about $1.6 million and the focus of its grants and activities remained about the same. With the death of David and Lucile Packard in the 1990s the foundation's assets soared:

through bequests from the late David Packard (deceased in 1996) and also due to strong appreciation in the foundation's holdings of Hewlett-Packard stock. In 1998, Packard became the nation's third largest foundation, with assets valued at more than $9.5 billion. Growth in resources spurred the foundation to greatly expand funding for its population and conservation programs. Packard's international giving jumped from a modest $3.6 million in 1994 to more than $37 million in 1998, a tenfold increase.... This share is likely to expand in the future. In 1998, Packard announced a five-year commitment to donate at least $375 million for reproductive health and population planning efforts, mainly in eight developing countries[22]

With the death of their parents, firm control and conduct of the activities of the foundation passed to and remains with the four children of the Packards. The 2004 by-laws of the foundation, as to the composition and power of its board of trustees, provide the following

Membership: The Packard Foundation is a Family Foundation, created and funded by David and Lucile Packard. The Packard Foundation is structured to have one class of "Members." The members have rights and powers specified in the Bylaws, but have no ownership of the Foundation's assets. Only members of the Packard family, which is defined as the children of David and Lucile Packard, their spouses and children, are eligible to be Members of the Foundation.

The four children of David and Lucile Packard are the current Members: David Woodley Packard, Nancy A. Burnett, Susan Packard Orr, and Julie Packard. Members may serve for their lifetime, or they may resign or transfer membership to another member of the Packard family or their membership may be terminated.

Powers: Members have the powers set forth below: The powers of the Members are exercised by a majority of the Members then holding office:

(1)   Approve any amendment, revision or deletion of the Bylaws.

(2)   Determine the authorized number of Members.

(3)   Elect additional Members whenever a vacancy occurs.

(4)   Remove any General Trustee without cause or explanation or cancel the election of any person as General Trustee.

(5)   Elect the family Trustees. The Members select five representatives from among themselves, their immediate families, or other people who represent the family's interests to serve as Family Trustees.

Thus, although the Packard Foundation presently has some 100 staff and employees, headed by an executive director, its significant expansion internationally has essentially been determined by its four Members listed above.

Hewlett

The son of a doctor on the University of Michigan medical faculty, William Remington Hewlett (1913-2001), was born in Ann Arbor, Michigan. His father relocated to the Stanford University faculty when he was three years old and his formative years were spent in the San Francisco, California area. Although his father died when Hewlett was twelve, his family lived on under comfortable circumstances. It was there that he was enrolled and graduated, without much in the way of academic distinction, from the Lowell High School. His enrollment at Stanford University followed and resulted in a bachelor of arts degree conferred in 1934. This was followed by study at and the receipt of a master's degree in engineering in 1936 from the Massachusetts Institute of Technology. Returning to pursue further graduate study at Stanford saw Hewlett teaming up with close friend and fellow student, David Packard, to eventually form the Hewlett-Packard Company in 1947. The company was first located in the garage at Packard's home and the initial capital was $538. The same year marked Hewlett's marriage to Flora Lamson and the subsequent birth of five children to the couple. Following four years of service in the U.S. Army during World War II, Hewlett resumed his work with Packard. He continued as a chief executive with the emergent Hewlett-Packard Company for the remainder of his life and in the process amassed one of America's large fortunes. With the company's early and growing interest internationally there was a corresponding one in Hewlett's. His:

> interests extended around the world: to population issues and the status of women, their education, and economic opportunities in Africa, Southeast Asia, and Latin America; to conflict resolution, particularly in eastern and southern Europe, the former republics of the Soviet Union, and the Middle East; to U.S.—Latin American relationships[23]

According to the eulogizer of Hewlett quoted above, "Never stifle a generous impulse" was one of his favorite and best-known phrases and, as was his custom, he practiced what he taught."[24]

William and Flora Hewlett Foundation

In 1966 William Hewlett set up the W.R. Hewlett Foundation with him, his wife, and son, James S. Hewlett, its trustees. During the period 1972-1975, this son resigned from the board and the Hewlett's two other sons plus two non-family members were added. By 1977 the foundation's former assets of some $500,000 with expenditure of about $140,000 had grown to about $40 million and with expenditures amounting to some

$3 million annually. In that same year Hewlett's wife died. In her honor the name of the foundation was changed to its present William and Flora Hewlett Foundation. Up until this time the foundation had engaged primarily in local giving in California but now a massive reorganization took place which underpinned a considerable increase in foreign activities. As Hewlett announced at the time:

> It is our intention that the Foundation be a national foundation, unlimited by geography in its scope. At the same time, we plan to have a program of local grant-making to which a modest proportion of disbursable funds will be allocated. In all probability, this local granting activity will be concentrated largely in the San Francisco Bay Area.[25]

While Hewlett remained as chairman of the board of trustees of the foundation, a telling indicator and a key factor in the changes that began in 1977 was the naming of Roger W. Heyns as president. His first annual report in that year was a subtle announcement that change was in the works. By 1982, he stated:

> In spite of increasing reference to the interdependence of the United States with the economic, political, and social movements of other nations, our national understanding of this interaction is imperfectly and inadequately reflected in our national debates. Increased understanding of the international dimensions of our lives is clearly needed. We have neglected those instruments whose task it is to increase our knowledge of other countries. Agencies which have undertaken to increase public understanding of international affairs clearly warrant our greater support.[26]

In 1985 Heyns explained that his annual report was "to report on the Foundation's grantmaking since 1977." He noted its sizeable grants program in the California and particularly San Francisco areas, one which has continued to the present day. Regarding the international area, he commented on the Hewlett Foundation's escalating programs. For example, he stated:

> Another set of grants with international significance is the support of national security/arms control studies. A number of special projects have also been in support of organizations primarily involved in international affairs. The total Foundation funds granted for international activities in all areas is approximately $40 million, slightly more than a quarter of the total [$150 million] since 1977.[27]

Heyns' 1986 statement was devoted entirely to international affairs. He opined: "Global interdependence has steadily increased since World War II. Never before, however, have our national security and our economic welfare depended so much upon our external relations." After describing the foundation's international activities, he concluded:

> In the ten years from 1977 through 1986, grants with international implications totaled $49 million; most of these funds were allocated in the four areas described above. We

have formed exciting and gratifying partnerships with institutions and organizations in these areas, and we expect this pattern of serious involvement in international grantmaking to continue.[28]

Heyns' retirement and the election of David P. Gardner as president of the Hewlett Foundation in 1993 marked the continuation of its strong interest in the international area. Major changes since then were his 1996 announcement of the expansion of its longstanding U.S.-Mexico program into a U.S.-Latin American relations program.[29] Also, it was announced in 2003 that:

the Hewlett Foundation launched a three-year exploratory initiative in Global Affairs to explore issues of global significance. It may not fit within any single Program's funding strategies, but will have an appreciable impact on the problems tackled by the Foundation.[30]

William Hewlett, chairman of the board of trustees of his foundation, certainly approved of this involvement in international affairs. In a 1999 eulogium to Gardner he stated:

During David's time in office, the Foundation's assets have increased from approximately $800 million in 1993 to over $2 billion as of this report. Staff has increased from eighteen to thirty-six, and grants have increased from $35 million in 1993 to $84 million in 1998. David has attracted professionals of the highest caliber to the program staff while managing this rapid growth in an orderly manner.[31]

Following the death of William Hewlett in 2001, his son, Walter Hewlett, was named chairman of the foundation's board with other members of the family presently serving there. The son's accession together with the naming of the present president, Paul Brest, saw the foundation maintaining its previous course.

Notes

1. Amy P. Longsworth, "Rockefeller Brothers Fund," Harold M. Keele and Joseph C. Kiger (eds.) *Foundations*. Greenwood Press, Westport, Connecticut, 1984, pp. 361-364.
2. Rockefeller Brothers Fund, *Annual Report,* 1993, p. 15.
3. For a detailed, albeit highly critical, article on the matter see, Ronald Bailey, "Leading the Charge *The W. Alton Jones Foundation's environmental scare tactics,*" *Philanthropy Magazine*, July/August, 1998, no page number.
4. Lisa Provence, " Green offshoots: W. Alton Jones Foundation sprouts Oak Hill Fund," *The Hook,* vol. 37, October 17, 2002,
5. *In Memoriam; Joseph Newton Pew and Issac Conrad Ketler.* pp. 5-6, no date and place of publication. One of the few, if only, copies of this eulogy is located in the Oberlin College Library, Oberlin, Ohio.
6. *Ibid.,* p. 12.
7. Considering the eventual size of the Pew fortune, there is a remarkable lack of factual and objective information published about the founder and first generation

of the family. There are biographical sketches about them in the *DAB* and similar publications, articles in popular magazines such as *Time*, obituaries, and disparaging and largely undocumented comments about them in general foundation works such as Waldemar Nielsen's *The Big Foundations,* 1972 *and The Golden Donors,* 1985. An exception is the previously cited *In Memoriam: Joseph Newton Pew and Issac Conrad Kesler.*

8.   The eldest Pew son and the two sisters did not figure prominently in the carrying out of this business expansion although they did share in the proceeds emanating from it.

9.   Joe Martin (Joseph W. Martin, Jr.), *My First Fifty Years in Politics; as told to Robert J. Donovan.* McGraw-Hill Book Company, Inc., New York, 1960, p. 123.

10.   See the following recent examples published by the foundation: *Sustaining the Legacy, A History of the Pew Charitable Trusts,* 2001; *The Pew Fund Story* (2002), and *Planning and Evaluation at the Pew Charitable Trusts,* 2001.

11.   *The Pew Charitable Trusts, Annual Report, 1988.* Philadelphia, Pennsylvania, 1988, pp. 14-15.

12.   Diane Brady and Marcia Vickers, "AIG: What Went Wrong," *Business Week,* April 11, 2005, pp. 32-36.

13.   Elizabeth Bernstein and Monica Langley, "Greenberg resigns From Two Non-profits," *Wall Street Journal.* April 11, 2005, p. B1.

14.   Edward Larocque Tinker, *New Yorker Unlimited: The Memoirs of Edward Larocque Tinker.* University of Texas Press, Austin, Texas, 1970. p. 146.

15.   Edward Larocque Tinker, *Lafacadio Hearn's American Days.* Dodd Mead and Company, New York, 1924.

16.   Edward Larocque Tinker, *The Horsemen of the Americas and the Literature They Inspired.* University of Texas Press, Austin, Texas, 2nd ed., 1967, p. 118.

17.   David Packard, *The HP Way: How Bill Hewlett and I Built Our Company.* Edited by David Kirby and Karen Lewis. Harper Collins Publishers, New York, 1995, pp. 3-4.

18.   Ibid., p. 103.

19.   Ibid., p. 72.

20.   Ibid., pp. 165-189.

21.   Ibid., p. 189.

22.   Loren Renz, Josefina Samson-Atienza, and Steven Lawrence, *International Grantmaking II : An Update on U.S. Foundation Trends.* Foundation Center, New York, 2000, p. 36.

23.   David Pierpont Gardner, " William Reddington Hewlett," *Proceedings of the American Philosophical Society,* Volume 127, Number 2, June, 2003, p. 165.

24.   Ibid., p. 165.

25.   William and Flora Hewlett Foundation, *10 Year Cumulative Report, 1966-1976,* 1976, p. 5.

26.   William and Flora Hewlett Foundation, *Annual Report,* 1982, p. 6.

27.   William and Flora Hewlett Foundation, *Annual Report*, 1985, p. 11.

28.   William and Flora Hewlett Foundation, *Annual Report,* 1986, p. 5.

29.   William and Flora Hewlett Foundation, *Annual Report*, 1996, p. 4.

30.   William and Flora Hewlett Foundation, *Global Affairs,* 10/5/2004, p. 1.

31.   William and Flora Hewlett Foundation, *Annual Report,* 1998, p. xi.

5

MacArthur, Soros, Templeton, Kerkorian, Turner, and Gates

Although early on not nearly as well known as his father, several of his seven siblings, or his cousin General Douglas MacArthur, John D. MacArthur (1897-1978) became a notable, colorful and, in many ways, enigmatic figure in the history of American business and philanthropy. He was the youngest of four sons and three daughters of William Teller MacArthur and Georgiana Welstead. Born in Pittston, Pennsylvania, his father eventually rose from being a coal miner to a nationally renowned evangelistic minister. Reverend MacArthur, until the time of his death was held in awe by all of his children and undoubtedly was a major force in molding their characters and left a deep imprint on them.[1]

As a youth, John D. MacArthur's attendance at school was conspicuous by its relative absence: he never attended beyond the eighth grade. Following the death of his mother in 1915, he moved to Chicago where his three older brothers were then located and began work for one of them, Alfred, as a very successful salesman in the latter's life insurance company. MacArthur put in a brief stint as a reporter for a Chicago newspaper following failed attempts to become an active participant in World War I. His two other brothers, Charles and Telfer, had already launched their successful journalistic careers and, undoubtedly, influenced John in the venture. The early 1920s saw him returning to the insurance business, carrying on successfully through the Great Depression. His hallmark was the purchase of small moribund insurance companies and rejuvenating them. In 1935 he purchased the Banker's Life and Casualty Company for $2,500 and it became the primary vehicle for his creation of an insurance giant through his introduction of various innovations such as the selling of life insurance by mail and the introduction of low-cost policies to middle-class Americans. MacArthur had become a wealthy man by the early 1950s with such methods. In that same decade, he and his second wife, Catherine T. Hyland (1909-1981), took up permanent residence in Florida where he expanded his holdings to include a wide variety of investments there: banks, hotels, and Florida land in excess of 100,000 acres. Thus, by the time of his death in 1978, MacArthur was one of the nation's handful of billionaires.

During the course of acquiring his wealth, MacArthur married his first wife, Louise Ingalls in 1919. The couple had two children, a son J. Roderick and a daughter Virginia nee Cordova, prior to their divorce in 1937. Apparently the father's relationship with his children, particularly his son, was as bad as that with his first wife. From the 1950s on John and Roderick engaged in widely publicized personal and business battles. Eventually "Rod" struck out on successful business ventures of his own and he had become a millionaire in his own right by the time of his father's death. Some of the animus developed here may have been due to the fact that, after a very brief spending stint when he began to make big money, by the 1950s Roderick can best be described as a paragon of frugality. There were innumerable stories, from John D. MacArthur, friends, and others, illustrative of this description of the man. He owned and drove an old Cadillac and always traveled economy class when traveling by air. He and his wife Catherine lived in a modest apartment overlooking the parking lot in a small hotel that he owned in Palm Beach Shores, Florida. Minus a retinue of staffers of his own, he was not averse to pitching in to help if the hotel staff was shorthanded. More often than not he made and carried out his business deals and other transactions from a table in the hotel's coffee shop. Thus this billionaire was often times mistaken for a bellhop or other clerk at the hostelry.

Retirement Research Foundation

Relatively little is known of John D. MacArthur's private giving prior to 1950. During that year he established the first and lesser-known of his two foundation philanthropic endeavors, the Chicago-based Retirement Research Foundation. The present day assets of the foundation are about $185 million. With the stated purpose of improving the quality of life of old people in the United States, the impetus for its creation probably stemmed in large part from the fact that a considerable portion of those insured by his companies fell in this category.

John D. and Catherine T. MacArthur Foundation

The John D. and Catherine T. MacArthur Foundation was incorporated in 1970 by MacArthur, accompanied in the same year by his establishment of a trust which specified that upon his death all of the then approximately $700 million in assets of his bellwether Bankers Life and Trust Company would fall to the foundation. His will specified that his wife would receive about $40 million and his two children about $20 million each.[2] In creating the foundation he simply asked that the foundation be operated for "charitable, religious, scientific, literary, and educational purposes," and that it award money to "exceptionally talented individuals." In addition to this very general wording as to purpose, MacArthur very clearly reiterated his hands-off policy as to its future, following his death.

In a personal letter written in March 1977, Mr. MacArthur said: "I have established a foundation, and one thing I had in mind was to give the trustees autonomy. I know of a number of foundations where the donors tried to run them from their graves. I have guaranteed to the trustees that when I am gone they can run the show." He made a more graphic challenge in telling one director, "I figured out how to make the money. You fellows will have to figure out how to spend it."[3]

The original seven-member board of directors of the foundation consisted of MacArthur, his wife and son, and four close business associates and friends of the donor. MacArthur died on January 6, 1978 followed by his wife on December 15, 1981. As an inkling of what was to follow, the surviving wife could not agree with the two children on an appropriate wake, also called for in MacArthur's will, so two separate wakes were held, one sponsored in Chicago by the wife and the other in Florida by the children.[4] By 1981 John E. Corbally, a former president of the University of Illinois, had been installed as the chief executive officer of the foundation, a gradual expansion of the staff took place, and the foundation began to make a few grants. In the next few years there was an acrimonious debate within the board as to the future program and operation of the foundation. Roderick MacArthur wanted by far the major portion of the foundation's giving to be concentrated on a program awarding grants to talented individuals. The deaths of Mrs. MacArthur in 1981 and Roderick MacArthur in 1984 (his sister was not active in foundation affairs) saw an end to the controversy. Also, an enlarged and more diverse eleven member board of trustees was elected in 1984. Simultaneously, a Fellowship Program which expended about $13 million out of about $73 million in total grants was authorized in that year. Since that time, the fellowship program, while making princely grants to its recipients, now constitutes only about five percent of the foundation's total grants.

At the same time the foundation was embarking on the fellowship program, it became very active in foreign activities. In 1984, for example, an International Security Program was announced which, in addition to sizeable grants to U.S. institutions, included some to those located abroad. The election of Adele Simmons as president of the foundation in 1989 began an increase in such foreign undertakings by the foundation. Her entire 1993 presidential report, for example, was devoted to globalization and the importance of non-governmental groups in the workings of this process. By 1994 more than forty percent of foundation grants were made outside the United States. During her regime, the foundation concentrated its foreign activities in the former Soviet Union, Nigeria, Mexico, Brazil, and India. A major and continuing interest of the foundation, begun in 1992, was the former Soviet Union where the foundation opened an office in Moscow and has expended about $4 million annually. By the end of the decade, the staff of the foundation, domestic and foreign, had expanded to include in excess of two hundred people. At that time, Ms. Simmons was succeeded as president by Jonathan F. Fanton, a former staff member of the Rockefeller Brothers Fund.

Soros

George Soros, the son of Jewish parents, Tivadar Soros and Erzebet Szucs, was born on August 12, 1930 in Budapest, Hungary. The family was a middle upper class one and the elder Soros, an attorney, by various stratagems managed to save his son from the effects of the 1944 German occupation and the resultant death of many other Hungarians. Hungary fell under a repressive Russian occupation following the defeat of the Nazi regime. George Soros left Hungary in 1947 for a freer London. While working his way through the London School of Economics, he came under the influence of Professor Karl Popper, who expounded on the overwhelming benefits of societies which encouraged and fostered freedom in all aspects as opposed to those in which a controlling group repressed them. Soros worked for a few years in England as a salesman and as an assistant in a bank after graduating in 1952. He then departed for New York in 1956. During the next ten years he worked as a broker in various financial firms, concentrating on arbitrage trading and foreign securities. Becoming a naturalized U.S. citizen in 1961, in that year he married Annaliese Witschak. Divorcing the latter in 1981, he married Susan Weber in 1983 whom he also divorced. Soros had three children from his first marriage and two from the second. In 1969 he set up his own Quantum Fund and, although he has had some substantial financial reverses, losing millions in 1987, 1994, and 2000, he acquired an ever-increasing fortune. In 1992, for example, he personally amassed some two billion dollars in successful speculations on the chaos in the currency markets accompanying devaluation of the British pound in that year.[5] Soros attributes such financial success to his development and application of a semi philosophical term, reflexivity, to his financial affairs. In his autobiography he states: *"The Alchemy of Finance,"* the first of a considerable number of financial, philosophical, geopolitical books and articles authored by him, "was an important breakthrough for me because I managed to state the idea of reflexivity, which is crucial to my analysis of market behavior." Soros added that "I can summarize the main idea [reflexivity] in a few words—two words, in fact: imperfect understanding"[6]

Open Society Funds

In the process of acquiring his fortune, Soros "openly disparaged philanthropy," and as he continued to examine and expand his life and activities in the late 1970s it did not seem to offer him a particularly fruitful option. " I had a very negative view of philanthropy," he recalled.[7] At that time he did provide aid to organizations, such as dance companies or parks that interested him and his wife but gave nothing to Jewish causes or aid to the poor or destitute. Nevertheless, he eventually developed his own formula for the giving of some of his vast wealth: support for open societies.

The derivation for this formula appears to have come from two major sources. First, the repressive regimes that Soros had encountered in his youth in Hungary. As he comments in his autobiography, "An open society is one in which a person like me can live and prosper. As a Jew in Hungary I was hunted by the Nazis, then later I had a foretaste of communist rule in that country, so I know whereof I speak."[8] Second, he was motivated by the philosophical, economic, and political influence of the thoughts and teachings of Professor Popper during his university days. Thus the latter not only provided much of the basis for his money making ability but also the formulation and application of this wealth for the establishment and maintenance of open societies. Acknowledging this debt, Soros' authorized biographer observes:

When George Soros first ventured deeply and innovatively into international philanthropy in 1981-1982, he called his first foundation the Open Society Fund, and he named the scholarships he was handing out to East Europeans in honor of Karl Popper, who was still alive. Later, as his charitable undertakings spread around the world, Soros consistently praised and honored Popper at every opportunity.[9]

Because he disliked philanthropy/charity, in structuring his philanthropy Soros did not generally follow the foundation concepts utilized by Carnegie, Rockefeller, and other philanthropists. As he expounded at length:

I was very leery of foundations. I had some strong prejudices against them. I still do. I think that charity tends to turn the recipients into objects of charity, and that is not what it is intended to accomplish. I call this the paradox of charity. I also think that philanthropy is basically a corrupting influence; it corrupts not only the recipient, but also the giver, because people flatter him and never tell him the truth. It's the role of the applicant to find a way to get money out of the foundation, and it's the role of the foundation to prevent people from taking advantage of it. To protect itself from people who want to take advantage, a foundation needs to be either very bureaucratic and have very strict rules, like the Ford Foundation or the state, or it should keep a low profile, working quietly in the background. I chose the latter alternative, you know: "Don't call us; we'll call you.[10]

In other words, the foundations/funds he established were essentially provided assets based on his determination of their initial and continuing needs. If their efforts did not meet his success criteria in their operation he could and did terminate his funding of them. It was this method of funding that gave rise to the questioning as to whether or not they were indeed foundations. In any case, his initial Open Society Fund was set up in 1979 and its target was the repressive apartheid regime then operating in South Africa. He admits that his effort there was a failure. Consequently, his funding there ceased. As he said later: "When I got into this business of philanthropy it was definitely a process of trial and error. From '79 to '84 was a period of painful experimentation. I didn't know what the hell I was doing, and I made some wrong steps. I felt very embarrassed at times. I would break into a cold sweat. I was playing a certain role and it didn't quite fit me."[11]

The philanthropic breakthrough for Soros came in 1983 with his creation of a Soros Foundation in his native Hungary and its subsequent activities there. It was followed by the creation of similar entities all over Central and Eastern Europe. To coordinate what has since become an internationally scattered network of organizations, in 1993 Soros founded the Open Society Institute in New York City. This was followed by the creation of other Open Society Institutes in Brussels, Budapest, Paris, and

Washington, D.C. Sums expended for their respective operations in 1999 were: $85,010,000; $582,000; $21,000,000; $144,000; and $748,000.

At present, Soros oversees the funding and activities of some fifty philanthropic organizations in countries all over the world. Such activity, prior to 1996 and since, was not carried on without controversies, abroad and at home. Abroad, they included accusations by leaders in some countries that Soros' foundations and resultant activities were camouflages for nefarious plots against them by the U.S. government. More recently, at home, many conservatives allege that Soros' Open Society Institute in the United States has engaged in a thinly veiled campaign to discredit the conservative ideology. This, despite vehement disclaimers from Soros and the Open Society Institute of New York that political activities by him were financed completely from his own private financial resources. Such activities included an all out unsuccessful attempt to defeat President George W. Bush for re-election in 2004, costing an estimated $26 million, in which he made many speeches and paid for anti-Bush ads in newspapers all over the country. Since then in an interview: "Soros said he's no longer actively investing and is primarily interested only in earning enough to support $300 million in annual spending on philanthropic and political projects."[12]

Templeton

John Marks Templeton's grandfather, Dr. John Wiley Templeton, had been a surgeon in the Confederate Army during the Civil War and married Susan Jones of Canton, Mississippi. The grandfather had later practiced medicine for forty years in Tennessee and ultimately retired and died in the small town of Winchester. John Marks Templeton's father, Harvey Templeton, had built a house there for his bride, Vella Handly, shortly after they were married and became an affluent, although not rich, lawyer and businessman. Their son, named for his paternal grandfather and for his mother's prominent ancestors, the Marks family, was born on November 29, 1912. As a youth, John had a great variety of interests and graduated at the top of the town's high school class. This was capped by his admission to Yale University in 1930 where, by a combination of scholarships, self-employment plus very limited family financial aid, he graduated with honors and was awarded a Rhodes Scholarship at the University of Oxford. There followed his immersion for two years in the English higher educational approach, which was concluded by a worldwide trip, on the cheap, through thirty-five countries in Europe, the Middle East, and Asia.

Oxford was followed by a return to the United States and in 1937 John was married to the socially prominent Judith Dudley Folk of Nashville, Tennessee. A move by the couple to New York, interspersed with a short business sojourn in Texas, resulted in the launching of John's legendary career as an investment counselor. The result was that many investors profited greatly from his advice and his acquisition of a considerable fortune for himself, with dwellings in various locales and eventually an elegant one in Lyford Cay in the Bahamas where he has permanently resided since 1968. His becoming a British citizen in that year, his long acquaintance with Britain, and his business and philanthropic renown, resulted in his being knighted in 1987. Sir John Templeton had three children prior to his first wife's tragic accidental death in 1951. A second marriage followed in 1958 to Irene Reynolds Butler, a divorcee, with two young children. Prior to her death in 1993, both parents and children had melded into a happy and close-knit family. These events were accompanied by an ever increasing interest by John Marks Templeton in philanthropy, much of it of an international nature.

John Templeton Foundation

John Marks Templeton along with his business endeavors had engaged in philanthropy years before he incorporated the John Templeton Foundation in 1988 in Tennessee. His philanthropic efforts ran side by side and were accompanied by deep and abiding religious convictions.[13] He served for forty-two years on the board of trustees of the Princeton Theological Seminary, twelve years as chairman. Such convictions ran far beyond denominations, sects, and creeds, however, and it is from this background that, in 1972, he created his best known charitable endeavor: the Templeton Prize for Progress in Religion. Permanently funded through the John Templeton Foundation, the prize would be for "progress in religions of all types, so no child of God would feel excluded." To confirm this idea, Templeton convened a panel of nine prestigious judges, with at least one judge from each of the five major religions. In addition, at least half the judges would not be religious professionals. "In this way," he said, "they would be more likely to be receptive to new ideas." He also set up an extensive system of nominators representing all denominations of the Christian Church and several other religions.[14]

The first recipient of the prize in 1973 was Mother Teresa and successive annual recipients have followed on a world wide basis. The prize amount has been calculated each year so as to exceed Nobel Prizes and, now in excess of $1 million, it was and has remained the world's largest annual monetary award. With present day assets of about $850 million, the foundation is committed to the provision of aid for the furtherance of religion and spirituality, particularly cooperation between science and religion. In furtherance of these aims the foundation makes grants of about $35 million annually, a considerable percentage of this amount expended in England, Indonesia, and other countries abroad. Included in these foreign projects were the funds provided for the 2003 organization of the International Society for Science and Religion. The Templeton Foundation has a sixteen-member board of trustees consisting of Sir John as chair and includes a half dozen members of the Templeton family. The staff includes some ten full-time and six-part time members and the foundation is administered from a headquarters presently located in Philadelphia, Pennsylvania. Also located there is the Templeton Foundation Press. Established in 1996, the Press has published some sixty-two titles, some by Templeton, centering on the scientific/religion interests of the Templeton Foundation.

Kerkorian

A 1970s biographer summed up Kirk Kerkorian's career with the following. "Kerkorian, the unassuming, easygoing man, is complex and deceptive. Behind the mild façade lies a true entrepreneur—a master of the cold-blooded skills of risk-taking. He has put his life, his fortune, and all his earthly possessions on the line repeatedly."[15]A more recent physical description of the man avers:

> His dark motionless eyes are set below thick salt-and-pepper eyebrows. The tanned deeply lined poker face reveals nothing. He may be amused, bored, or about to knock his interviewer through the second-story window of his Beverly Hills, Calif., office. He still looks capable of demonstrating why he was called "Rifle Right Kerkorian" in the boxing ring. [16]

Kerkor "Kirk" Kerkorian was born in Fresno, California on June 6, 1917. His grandfather, Kaspar, and his father Ahron, were both Armenians. The grandfather emigrated to the United States in 1888 and brought his seventeen-year old son Ahron there in 1905. The latter soon sent back to Armenia for his future wife Sushon, who adopted the American name Lily. Buying and selling fruit, the close knit Kerkorian family prospered. Preceded by two brothers, Art and Nishon, and one sister Rose, by the time Kirk was born, Ahron had acquired farm land to grow fruit that was valued in the 1920s at about $100,000. In the process, however, the father became financially over extended and the depression beginning in 1929 left the Kerkorians in straitened circumstances. In the effort to provide for his family, Ahron moved to an estimated twenty various California locations but eventually settled in the 1930s in Los Angeles where Kirk spent his teenage years.

From his boyhood on, Kirk made money to help his family. He sold newspapers; he turned to boxing in matches for the small prizes provided. In 1934 he put in a six month stint in the depression-spawned U.S. Civilian Conservation Corps. Following that, it was back to boxing again where he became a Pacific coast champion amateur welterweight. Then, in 1939, came the event that was to change his life: flying. Kerkorian was working for a man who installed wall furnaces, Patrick O'Flaherty, who was an avid part time flyer and who got Kerkorian to fly with him. Thirty-two years later, O'Flaherty remembered: "He was sold on it right then. He had never been up in a plane before. But I'm telling you, after that first flight he went right at it. The very next day he was back out at the field to take his first flying lesson. I never saw a person more eager to learn."[17] By the time the U.S entered World War II in 1941 Kerkorian had acquired the flying time and skills to become a flight instructor for the U.S. Armed Forces. The onset of war was also a catalyst in his 1942 marriage to Hilda "Peggy" Smith. The couple had no children and that fact, frequent separations, plus Peggy's difficulties in adjusting to being part of a close knit Armenian family, saw the marriage end in divorce in 1951. It was during this period that Kerkorian made the move that provided him with the experience and the money to launch his spectacular business career.

With the onset of war and his success as an aviator but with little formal education, Kerkorian could still write his own ticket by becoming an officer in the Army Air Corps and continuing on as a flight instructor. Instead he moved to Canada, accepted a Royal Air Force Air Transport Command commission, and began ferrying planes to England at $1,000 per trip. It was extremely hazardous duty and many of the planes and pilots went down. Kerkorian, however, flew thirty-three successful missions and saved most of the money he earned. The end of the war ushered in his acquisition of an increasing number and types of planes, initially for instruction and later for transportation of goods and passengers by his own airline. By 1969, when he sold out his aviation interests, he had amassed a fortune in excess of $100 million.

Meanwhile in the late 1940s, Kerkorian had begun visiting Las Vegas, Nevada where he stayed and gambled in the then embryonic entertainment/gambling establishments. He soon stopped this activity and began considering the money making opportunities of what was to be known as the "Strip." It was there that he met Jean Maree Hardy, a Las Vegas resort dancer from England, whom he married in 1954. The couple had two daughters, Tracy born in 1959 and Linda adopted in 1965. This marriage, too, ended in divorce in 1983, to be followed in 1999 by a marriage to tennis professional Lisa Bonder which lasted thirty days.

In the midst of these marriages, Kerkorian began and has continued to acquire land in Las Vegas together with the erection and control of a series of mega hotels/casinos there, including the MGM Grand and the International. He suffered serious financial reverses at times in the process. For example, to stay financially afloat at one point, he had to sell stock previously worth $180 million for $16.5 million and in 1980 he had to successfully face the economic consequences of a devastating fire in the MGM Grand which caused 85 deaths and hundreds of injuries. At the same time, Kerkorian also became interested in the U.S. film industry and in 1969 acquired control of the ailing Metro-Goldwyn-Mayer Studios that, in addition to other valuable assets, included an archive of past movies, to become priceless with the advent of their being leased to be shown on television. In summary, his profits from the airlines, the movies, and Las Vegas were the basis and provided the means for subsequent investments in the automobile industry and other business enterprises. Parenthetically, in the spring of 2005, Kerkorian bought shares, at a cost of a little less than $1 billion, which raised his holdings to about nine percent in a financially ailing General Motors Corporation. In its recent list of super rich individuals, Forbes estimated his present-day fortune at $8.9 billion.

Lincy Foundation

It comes as no surprise that relatively little is known about his earlier philanthropy given the life, temperament, and character of Kerkorian. He rarely granted interviews, seldom made speeches, generally avoiding meetings and eschewing the results of gifts from him bearing his name. A large portion of his recent largesse has also apparently been distributed anonymously. Characteristically, in setting up the Lincy Foundation in 1989, he is not listed as an officer but merely as a member of the board of directors. The officers and other members of the board are primarily Armenians and other friends or close associates of Kerkorian and the staff appears to be miniscule in view of its assets and its activities. Indicative of typical Armenian close familial ties was his naming of the foundation for his two daughters, Linda and Tracy. The holding company through which he conducts most of his business dealings, the Tracinda Corporation, is also named for them. As to size, the foundation has listed annual assets in the millions of dollars. Kerkorian announced in 1995, however, that he planned to give stock worth $550 million to the foundation but it apparently continues to rely on annual increments from him to carry on.

It has become known that Kerkorian has made significant gifts to worthy causes in the Las Vegas area and much of it through the Lincy Foundation. For example, the Nevada Cancer Institute in Las Vegas has received at least $5 million through the foundation. Most of the programs and projects carried out by the Lincy Foundation have been overwhelmingly concentrated on Armenian causes, both in the U.S. and abroad. Domestically, the foundation has made grants in the millions of dollars to the Armenian Fund, Armenian Assembly, and the Armenian Church. Similar or larger sums have been awarded for projects in Armenia. A prime example was the millions of dollars donated for relief in Armenia and also Turkey as the result of the disastrous earthquake in the region in 1988. Other grants have included ones to the Armenian Technology Group and funds for the restoration of the Armenian Drama Theater.

Turner

In the Introduction to his 1993 biography of Robert Edward "Ted" Turner III, Porter Bibb correctly states "Ted Turner is a journalist's dream"[18] In addition to Bibb's book-length biography of Turner, four other works of a biographical nature have appeared[19] plus innumerable articles about him and his career. Although Turner accepted advances from several publishers, later returned, to write an autobiography, one has yet to appear.

As to his ancestry, Ted Turner was of English, Scotch, and French ancestors on his father's side and German, Irish, and Dutch on his mother's. His paternal great-great grandfather, Simon Theophilus Turner, was part of the western population movement in the eighteenth century from North Carolina across the Appalachian Mountains and into Memphis, Tennessee. There he met and married Mary Ann Eddings. The couple had two sons, Robert Edward Turner and Frank Wellons Turner, and in the 1850s the family moved south to Mississippi. Despite the ravages of the Civil War, enough land was acquired and held for the family to profitably engage in farming. Robert Edward, "R.E." Turner, Ted Turner's grandfather, eventually settled in Sumner, Mississippi where he farmed and operated a general store. In 1908, he married a local girl, Maggie Dill Gaston, and it was here, in 1911, that Ted's father, Robert Edward "Ed" Turner, Jr., was born. In 1929 Ed was sent off to the University of Mississippi, "Ole Miss" in Oxford. After a brief study stint there, the onset of the Great Depression forced Ed to depart and he eventually wound up as a tremendously successful automobile salesman in Cincinnati, Ohio. In that city Ed married Florence Rooney, an Irish Roman Catholic. Although professing no religion of his own, Ed adamantly insisted and Florence forsook hers and she eventually turned to as an Episcopalian. The couple had two children: Ted, born November 19, 1938, and his sister Mary Jane born in 1941.[20]

The onset of World War II witnessed the beginning of the puzzling relationship between father and son. Ed enlisted in the U.S. Navy after our entry into the war; departing from Cincinnati with his wife and daughter for a series of assignments at naval installations on the Gulf Coast. Ted was left with his grandmother in Cincinnati and at the age of six was enrolled in a boarding school. Returning to Cincinnati after the war, Ed Turner in a few years successfully established himself in the billboard advertising business. In 1947, in that connection, he moved the wife and daughter to a home in Savannah, Georgia. Ted, at age nine, was then enrolled in the Georgia Military Academy on the outskirts of Atlanta. Then, in 1950, he was sent to the McCallie School in Chattanooga, Tennessee, a preparatory school which at that time also had a military department. Ted was initially recalcitrant and troublesome at McCallie but, as he maintained later: "But then I turned it around. I'd been the worst cadet and I was determined to be the best."[21] By 1993 at age 54, he said: "I love this school a lot. It did a lot of good for me.... A lot of times you don't appreciate things as much when you are there as when you have the opportunity to look back on them from a number of years." He added: "I thought the education I got here was terrific. I learned to think for the first time."[22] It was during this period that the love-animus relationship between him and his father became obvious to all who came in contact with them. Apparently much of this relationship developed out of the father's unrelenting drive, including physical punishment, to advance his son, and the son's natural reciprocal feeling of not being loved by the father. Probably exacerbating this father/son relationship was the death of Ted's only sister that both loved deeply. The fact that he spent most of the summer vacations from school with his grandparents was not conducive to rapport with his father. Driven in part by these familial events, in part by his inability to star in other sports, and in part by his desire to excel, his love for sailing that began on a lake adjacent to McCallie, ultimately resulted in his 1977 winning of the America's Cup, yachting's preeminent prize.

Admission to, attendance at, and eventual expulsion from Brown University was followed in 1960 by Ted's marriage to Chicagoan Judy Nye, a fellow sailing enthusiast. The newlyweds moved to Macon, Georgia where Ted took up employment at his father's billboard advertising firm. The couple had two children, Laura Lee and Robert Edward IV, prior to divorce in 1962. Two years later, Ted married Jane Smith of Birmingham, Alabama. Three children, Rhett, Beauregard "Beau," and Jeannie "Jennie" resulted from their twenty-five years of marriage, which ended in divorce in 1989; followed by a 1991 marriage to the actress Jane Fonda, which also ended in divorce in 1999.

Despite their acrimonious father/son relationship, all agree that Ted Turner had proved to be a success with his work in his father's billboard advertising business. At that time, however, the father had become increasingly concerned about the company's future and was engaged in a convoluted business arrangement with others which was a significant factor in his suicide in 1963. His son was thus confronted with but prevailed in negotiations that saw him emerge as the head of a profitable and strengthened operation. In the 1970s Ted Turner bought stations in Atlanta and Charlotte, North Carolina in the budding television industry and several years later he moved into cable television, pioneering with the utilization of the new U.S. satellite system. In the 1980s he launched a revolutionary live-news network and acquired a costly programming library of old films to air over his network. For example, he paid Kirk Kerkorian $1.5 billion for the latter's MGM films and other assets. Along the way, he purchased two sports franchises: the Atlanta Braves in baseball and the Atlanta Hawks in basketball. He also became one of the largest individual U.S. landowners, eventually buying some two million acres of land in nine American states plus acreage in Argentina. Then in 1996, his media holdings were merged into a giant Time Warner conglomerate. Thus, by the turn of the century, Ted Turner had amassed a fortune of some two to three billion dollars. Yet, in the words of his latest biographer:

The year 2000 turned out to be among the most miserable of Ted Turner's life. His marriage to Jane Fonda had ended, after eight years, and this was announced in January. In addition, two of his grandchildren were diagnosed with a serious illness; he smashed his foot in a skiing accident; his beloved black Labrador, Chief, contracted coonhound disease and was temporarily paralyzed; his back hurt and he thought that he needed surgery. Most adults have the support of a spouse and family, friends, and a job; Turner didn't have a spouse, didn't have-with the possible exception of his close investment advisor, Taylor Glover-any intimate friends, and no longer ran his own company. "I felt like Job," said Turner, adding, not for the first time, that he felt "suicidal." In the new world of AOL Time Warner, it was not premature to write Ted Turner's business obituary.[23]

Turner Foundation

Against this roller coaster life coupled with his ebullient personality and with vast sums of money still at his disposal, it comes as no surprise that Ted Turner has engaged in numerous philanthropic endeavors. Earlier these centered on the local and the regional and were generally palliative in nature. By the 1980s, however, he had formed the Better World Society to produce TV programs aimed at accomplishing the societal title. He also underwrote and sponsored the Goodwill Games, sporting events abroad designed to mitigate Cold War tensions. Also, particularly as he acquired more land, his philanthropies increasingly centered on environmental concerns. The creation of the Turner Family Foundation, now Turner Foundation, in 1990, marked the beginning of much of his philanthropy through the foundation structure. The Turner Foundation's stated purpose is "the preservation and conservation of the environment throughout the world." Incorporated and headquartered in Atlanta, Georgia, with present day assets of about $200 million and a small staff, the foundation makes relatively small grants to fulfill its purpose. Ted Turner has always been chairman of its board of directors. Jane Fonda served for a time as a board member, but his five children now comprise its membership. In addition to the work of the Turner Foundation, Ted Turner has provided major funding for smaller organizations with similar purposes: the Captain Planet Foundation organized in 1991 and the Nuclear Threat Initiative created in 2001.

United Nations Foundation

In 1998, Ted Turner created the United Nations Foundation and pledged funds to it in the amount of $1 billion spread over a ten year period. In a speech delivered at the United Nations in 2002, he stated that he believed that the organization and its work were vital to prevent wars. Although later financial reverses have caused him to extend the ten-year gift period to fifteen years, he has donated millions annually to the foundation. Turner has served since its inception as chairman of its board of trustees. The other ten board members include a gender and racially diverse group from all over the world. The staff, headed by President Timothy E. Wirth, a former U.S. Senator, is similarly diversified. To date, the foundation has concentrated on grants for health, environment, peace, and population projects. Much of the latter are carried out through various United Nations agencies.

Gates

William Henry "Bill" Gates III was born on October 28, 1955 in Seattle, Washington. He was the only son and the second child of William H. Gates II and Mary Maxwell Gates. The family was a well to do one; his father was a prominent Seattle attorney and his mother was the daughter of a wealthy banker and active in social and civic affairs. As a youth Bill was enrolled and attended the local and academically rigorous private Lakeside School. While there he was exposed to the embryonic computer and began programming them at age thirteen. Up until the time he graduated from the school in 1973, he and several friends engaged in various ventures involving computers that proved to be very lucrative for someone of his years, several of them providing him with thousands of dollars. In 1973 he was admitted to Harvard University with an admittedly vague intention of becoming an attorney. Still, as a freshman at Harvard, Gates and several friends again became engrossed with the intellectual and financial lures of computers. At the end of his sophomore year he dropped out of Harvard, which led in 1975 to the founding of the Microsoft Corporation and his embarking on a meteoric fulltime career in computers. Measuring his success in dollar terms, by March 1987, at the age of thirty-one, Gates became a billionaire. Since that time, although he has given due credit to the executives associated with him in what has been called the Microsoft empire, it is universally agreed that it was his drive and unceasing devotion to the technological as well as the business side of the development and marketing of computer hard and soft ware that soon made him one of the richest men in the United States and the world. Ruminating about the Gates family and the women associated with him, a 1992 biography about Gates and the persons allied with him in the creation and operation of Microsoft observed: "he [Gates] comes from a close-knit family with traditional values…." and added "For the last few years, Gates has had an on-again, off-again romance with a product manager in Microsoft's marketing division. Neither will comment about the relationship."[24] Apparently this reference was to Melinda French who was married to Bill Gates in 1994. A daughter, Jennifer Katherine Gates was born to the couple in the same year and subsequently they had two other children.

Gates has authored two bestselling books, given many speeches, and written numerous articles that are primarily devoted to his business career, his pioneering and spectacular success in taking the lead in the development of the computer and the information age, and his all out endorsement and encouragement of them as hearkening a better future for mankind worldwide. For example, in the Foreword to his 1996 *The Road Ahead,* he commented:

> in this book I draw on the history of the computing industry and my own history for what they can teach us. Yes, I even talk about my house. But anyone expecting an autobiography or an account of what it's like to be as lucky as I have been will be disappointed. When I've retired, I might get around to writing that book. This one looks primarily to the future.[25]

In the first chapter, however, he provides a brief account of his youth and early interest and ventures in computers but the remainder describes his role and that of others in the development of the personal computer and the information age, and concludes with his views as to the resulting future. His 1999 book *Business @ the Speed of Thought; Using a Digital Nervous System* is largely a book for company executives and managers to make full use of the tools of the information age to ensure their success in business. He admits that:

> With my insistence on eliminating paperwork, I must sound "antipaper." I am against paper forms, but even I still print out long electronic documents I want to read and annotate. Most people, when they're trying to organize a long document, like to spread out the pages on a table so that they can see them all at once—hard to do with a PC!" He follows with the semi-caveat, however: "Until we get a breakthrough in flat-screen technology—and furious research is going on at Xerox, the MIT Media Lab, Kent State, Microsoft, and other academic and corporate research sites in the United States and Japan—books and magazines still can't be beat for readability and portability.[26]

Reflecting his "antipaper" views the foundations he established have adopted the policy of not printing their annual reports. They are made available for printing, however, on computer websites.

Both of his books emphasize the tremendous impact on and encouragement for globalization that the computer has already wrought. He praises this dramatic change and maintains that its continuation can and will be beneficial into the future. In this connection, too, Gates emphasizes and extols the importance and need for the introduction, fostering, and utilization of the computer and allied technology at all educational levels. He offers no comment, however, on the Huxley/Orwell implications that have been raised as the computer use is applied in educational and biological/medical areas. There is no mention of philanthropy or foundations in either book although the profits from both books have been donated to non profit organizations and used for educational technological development. The 1996 book specifically states that the proceeds from the sale of the book will be given to a National Foundation for the Improvement of Education to fund education through the use of technology. Such decisions plus his observation that "the greatest benefit of this communications revolution will be using interactive technology for learning, both inside and outside the classroom,"[27] do provide clear evidence of one of the major motives for and aspects of his earlier and later philanthropic efforts

Bill and Melinda Gates Foundation

Gates' interest in and philanthropic activities were undoubtedly encouraged by the fact that both his parents were deeply committed to giving time and wealth for others. While he was a youth at home, they were very active in a number of educational and social welfare agencies. Mary Gates was the first woman president of the Seattle United Way and she served for a number of years on its national board. Coincidentally, Gates noted that the first electronic form used at Microsoft was for the United Way campaign at the company. Reference having been made above to the close-knit aspect of the Gates family, it comes as no surprise that Bill Gates' father appears to have been a prime architect in the setting up in 1994 of the first of the Bill Gates foundations, the William H. Gates Foundation. In a long 2004 speech to a foundation group, the younger Gates ruminated about the questionable practice of making money and giving it away (philanthropy) at the same time, but concluded: "And so my dad started working on me and eventually convinced me, OK, I'll do some philanthropy at a young age. And particularly the kind of impact we could have by renewing the excellence of education and by solving some of these big health problems, those seemed like things that really couldn't wait."[28]

Named for his father, the William H. Gates Foundation was established in 1994 with a program that focused on global health problems. In 1997, Bill Gates and his wife established the Gates Library Foundation. Its name was shortly changed to the Gates Learning Foundation to reflect its commitment to aiding the introduction and use of computers in U.S. and foreign libraries and to also help low-income and minority students to attend colleges and universities. In 1999 these two foundations were merged into the Bill and Melinda Gates Foundation. With assets then of approximately $17 billion it was and continues to be, by far, with assets presently of about $32 billion, the largest independent foundation in the United States and the world.

From its inception to the present, the Gates Foundation's stated purpose and program has been the bringing of innovation to health and learning. In addition to asset size, it has been notable on a number of other counts. It has always operated from modest offices, albeit expanding somewhat in the last few years. At the beginning the offices were located in the senior Gates' basement and in rooms over a pizza parlor. Similarly, the number of members of its board of trustees and its professional staff has always been miniscule when compared to other large U.S. foundations with relatively fewer assets. In 1999, for example, Bill Gates and his father, together with Melinda, and Ms. Patty Stonesifer, who has been there from the beginning to the present, plus six program officers were running the show. In that year, the foundation awarded grants amounting to approximately $2 billion (93.1% of total expenditures); paid federal taxes of about $147 million (6.8% of total expenditures); and $2.6 million for administrative and program expenses (0.1% of total expenditures). Of the grants made, over $1.2 billion was designated for expenditures to improve health in the world, most of this sum made in or for aid in developing countries, notably for the AIDS epidemic in Africa. The remaining grant distribution was concentrated in educational projects, a major one consisting of making computers available to persons all over the United States. In addition, moneys were devoted to aid for low income and minority students and smaller sums were appropriated for special projects undertaken in the Pacific Northwest. In 2003, Ms. Stonesifer, in a two-page summary, reported that the foundation had continued "to improve health in some of the poorest countries of the world" and that the foundation had helped "reach the goal we set seven years ago. If you can reach a public library in the United States, you can reach the Internet."[29]

Notes

1. Interview by this author with deceased attorney William Kirby, longtime friend and confidant of John D. MacArthur.
2. W.M.P. Dunne, " John D. MacArthur, *Dictionary of American Biography,* Supplement 10, Charles Scribner's Sons, New York, p. 478.
3. The John D. and Catherine T. MacArthur Foundation, *Report on Activities, 1980-1981,* p. 2.
4. See the following article for details, Bob Tamarkin, "Rival Wakes," *Fortune,* June 11, 1979, 114.
5. Robert Slater, *Soros; The Life, Times, & Trading Secrets of the World's Greatest Investor.* Irwin Professional Publishing, Burr Ridge, Illinois, New York, New York 1996, pp. 163-189. These pages provide a detailed monthly and then daily account of Soros' transactions that resulted in this financial coup.
6. George Soros, *Soros on Soros; Staying Ahead of the Curve.* John Wiley and Sons, Inc., New York, 1995, pp. 65, 66.
7. Michael T. Kaufman, *Soros: The Life and Times of a Messianic Billionaire.* Alfred A. Knopf, New York, 2002, p. 167.
8. George Soros, *Soros on Soros,* p. 113.
9. Michael T. Kaufman, *Soros,* p. 73.
10. George Soros, *Soros on Soros,* p. 113.
11. Michael T. Kaufman, *Soros,* p. 178.
12. Internet, Bloomberg.com., "Soros Says Kerry's Failings Undermined Campaign Against Bush," p. 3, dated and viewed, January 30, 2005.
13. For a thorough discussion of the great influence of the religious beliefs of his mother on the development of his beliefs see, William Proctor, *The Templeton Touch,* Doubleday & Company, Inc., Garden City, New York, pp. 101-105. This 228-page volume is divided about equally between an account of Templeton's business career and methods and his interest and activities in the juncture of science and religion. It also includes a biographical sketch of him together with ones dealing with the first ten recipients of the Templeton Prize.
14. Ibid., p. 125.
15. Dial Torgerson, *Kerkorian: An American Success Story.* The Dial Press, New York, 1974, pp. 6-7.
16. A.D. Hopkins and K.J. Evans, *The First 100: Portraits of the Men and Women Who Shaped Las Vegas,* "Kirk Kerkorian." Huntington Press, Las Vegas, Nevada, 1999, p. 241.
17. Dial Torgerson, *Krekorian: An American Success Story.* p. 35.
18. Porter Bibb, *It Ain't as Easy as It Looks; Ted Turner's Amazing Story.* Crown Publishers Inc., New York, 1993, p. ix. A paperback reprint of the foregoing biography was published by Johnson Books, Boulder, Colorado, 1997.
19. Christian Williams, *Lead, Follow, or Get Out of the Way: The Story of Ted Turner.* Times Books, New York, 1981. Robert Goldberg and Gerald Jay Goldberg, *Citizen Turner: the Wild Rise of an American Tycoon.* Harcourt, Brace and Co., New York, 1995. Janet Lowe, *Ted Turner Speaks: Insight from the World's Greatest Maverick.* John Wiley& sons Inc., New York, 1999. Ken Auletta, *Media Man: Ted Turner's Improbable Empire.* W.W. Norton & Co., New York, 2004.
20. More details on Ted Turner's ancestry can be found in Porter Bibb, *It Ain't as Easy as It Looks; Ted Turner's Amazing Story,* pp. 5-10.
21. Janet Lowe, *Ted Turner Speaks: Insight from the World's Greatest Maverick,* p. 30.

22. Ibid., p. 33.
23. Ken Auletta, *Media Man: Ted Turner's Improbable Empire.* pp. 17-18.
24. James Wallace and Jim Erickson. *Hard Drive; Bill Gates and the Making of the Microsoft Empire.* John Wiley and Sons, New York, 1992, p. 416.
25. Bill Gates, with Nathan Myhrvold and Peter Rinearson, *The Road Ahead.* Revised Edition. Penguin Books, New York, 1996, p. xv.
26. Bill Gates, with Collins Hemingway, *Business at the Speed of Thought, Using a Digital Nervous System.* Warner Books, New York, 1999, pp. 53-54.
27. Bill Gates, *The Road Ahead,* p. 317.
28. Microsoft com., Internet, "Remarks by Bill Gates, Chairman and Chief Software Architect, Microsoft Corporation Community Foundation of Silicon Valley Santara Clara, California, p. 6, dated October 1, 2004 and viewed January 6, 2005.
29. Bill and Melinda Gates Foundation, *Annual Report, 2003,* p. 2.

6

Central and Eastern Europe

Over fifty years ago Lyman C. White, in his seminal work on the subject of international non-governmental organizations, complained in his Introduction:

> Perhaps no aspect of international relations has received less attention, even from students of international organizations, than the part which non-governmental organizations have played in world affairs … the study of their function has been almost completely ignored in textbooks, in university courses, and in the training of those who represent governments in international organizations.[1]

In his books published some fifty years later, historian Akira Iriye drew much the same conclusion. For example, in giving three reasons for the research and publication of a major work, he stated:

> First, there is the obvious fact that international organizations have steadily grown in number and in the scope and variety of their activities since the late nineteenth century, to such an extent that the contemporary world would be incomprehensible without taking them into consideration. Second, most writings on modern world affairs, especially by historians, have nevertheless ignored this fact. This scholarly void must somehow be filled. And finally, a focus on international organizations, rather than nations and states, as units of analysis provides a fresh perspective on the evolution of international relations and enables us to reconceptualize modern world history.[2]

Iriye might have added that the international programs of philanthropic foundations have received even less attention than the other organizations engaged in international activities that he describes. In complete agreement with such views and as a caveat to his own efforts, this author forthwith attempts to provide a chronological account of the movement of several U.S. foundations into Central and Eastern Europe from previous operation of essentially a domestic nature. It covers the period from the 1980s to the 1990s and then assesses their impact and effect on the region.

In the twentieth century, in contrast to Western Europe, there were relatively fewer foundations established internally in Central and Eastern Europe. Overwhelmingly, the Roman Catholic and Greek Orthodox Churches were the philanthropic entities operating there at the beginning of the century. This disparity can be traced to several historical factors including later industrialization in the region and concomitant delayed development of an affluent upper/middle and urban class. Tied in with this difference was the fact that the close linkage of church and state, with the aforementioned church dominion in philanthropy, was abruptly eliminated in Russia with the Communist upheavals and takeover there in the early twentieth century. A central feature of the Communist ideology was, of course, that "religion is the opiate of the people." It followed logically that the largely successful drive to suppress churches in Russia by the triumphant USSR communist state following World War I took place. A somewhat similar effort, although a less effective one, followed in Central Europe following World War II with the establishment of the Comintern which projected USSR influence and control into the region. During the decades when these events took place, foundation establishment and operation within the region or sponsored from without was discouraged and/or essentially outlawed. The Communist ideological grounds for this opposition were that private philanthropic organizations of any type were not needed in a country where all of the needs of the people were met by the state. Thus, the region was essentially left without the benefit of philanthropic giving by religious or other non-governmental organizations such as foundations. In other words, a relatively omnipotent state was to render them unnecessary. There were a few exceptions. This writer had a 1984 discussion concerning academies and foundations in Zagreb, Yugoslavia with Vice President Andre Mohorovicic of the Yugoslav Academy of Arts and Sciences. Mohorovicic maintained that Yugoslavia occupied an intermediate position between the capitalist West and Communist East. As examples, he offered the less centralized state financial support underpinning his own academy as compared to that in Russia and other Communist bloc countries. He also vaunted that the Academy had been provided funds, by a prominent violinist in the United States, for it to nominate and defray the expenses of a violist for study at Harvard University. Although this last claim could not be confirmed subsequently, it does appear significant that it could have been advanced at all by a prominent academician at that time in a country still committed, on balance, to a Communist ideology or approach.

Viewed from the external standpoint, prior to the twentieth century U.S. foundation activity in Central and Eastern Europe was relatively slight. The foundations created by Andrew Carnegie and John D. Rockefeller, in the first decades of the twentieth century, really inaugurated significant overseas activities by our foundations. They were the major players in the international area in the pre-World War II period and the primary ones with the assets and staff that might have moved into Central and Eastern Europe. The mission statements of the two largest foundations Carnegie and Rockefeller established: "the advancement and diffusion of knowledge" in the case of the Carnegie Corporation of New York and, even more clearly, the Rockefeller Foundation "to promote the well being of mankind throughout the world" provide ample evidence of the potential worldwide thrust of these foundations. Then too, many of the other foundations that Carnegie and Rockefeller endowed were specifically created to operate internationally in specific global states and areas. Spurred by his affection for his native Scotland, Carnegie set up several foundations there with assets running in the millions of dollars. England and the Commonwealth nations, particularly South Africa, also benefited from his largesse. Chiefly through foundations, he scattered money on libraries and churches worldwide but little in Central and Eastern Europe. His goal of attaining international peace saw the establishment by him of foundations, such as the Carnegie Endowment for International Peace and the World Peace Foundation, both with a global sweep. His founding of a Carnegie Hero Fund was also conceived by Carnegie as contributing to international peace through its rewarding of non-military acts of heroism. His creation of such a fund in the United States eventually led to the setting up of similar ones in nine other countries abroad but not in Central and Eastern Europe.

Following the 1918 end of World War I, the Rockefeller Foundation disbursed over $22 million primarily in Western European countries devastated in that war, much of it to alleviate hunger and for health purposes. International programs in health and medical research in other areas abroad were also launched by the foundation. An outstanding example was the establishment of the China Medical Board. The board devoted most of its funds in the post-World War I decades to the 1921 founding and operation of the Peking Union Medical College. In turn, the college revolutionized the teaching and practice of medicine in China. Tied in with these programs were agricultural ones conducted abroad to aid in the production of more and better foods and fibers. Thus, the Rockefeller

Foundation embarked on its "Green Revolution" agricultural program to increase food production in Mexico and India. It also conducted various other programs in Asia, the Middle East, and Africa. By the 1960s this foundation, operating in fifteen foreign countries, had a foreign staff totaling more than 140 persons. Thus a large portion of these and other foundations engaged internationally devoted their aid to foreign countries for programs in agriculture, health, and medicine. They also provided aid of various types to a score of foreign universities located all over the world. Despite these worldwide activities, during these decades relatively little aid for such purposes was provided by them to countries in Central or Eastern Europe. Why?

In Carnegie's case this was due in part to the fact that he restricted much of his giving to his native Scotland and the Commonwealth nations, particularly South Africa. In the case of Rockefeller Sr. and Jr., it was due in part to their early strong Baptist and missionary ties, much of it to the Far East plus the burgeoning medical and agricultural programs centering there that eventually spread to Mexico and India. In large part, however, it appears that the major reason for their relatively late involvement, and in the twentieth century that of other U.S. foundations, in Central and Eastern Europe stemmed from the belief of their founders, trustees and staff that foreign activities could and should be undertaken in countries with reasonably stable governments and in countries where they would not meet with outright hostility and could expect some measure of governmental agreement and cooperation. To an overwhelmingly degree, such conditions were absent in the countries of Central and Eastern Europe during the World War I period and continuing into the post World War II decades. This is not to imply that U.S foundations were averse to promoting ideas and methods abroad that could have been viewed as revolutionary by some foreign elements. In the last analysis, however, the considered answer for the absence of U.S. foundations philanthropic activity in Central and Eastern Europe is the following one advanced by this writer in the 1960s:

> There has also been some questioning of foundation insistence upon local support and cooperation in the conduct of foreign programs. The foundation reply here is that this approach has been tried and tested successfully in national as well as international programs and that unless such local support is freely given the long-range prospects for the success of any program are negligible.[3]

Despite such foundation convictions, this did not prevent some post World War II U.S. government agencies, particularly the U.S. Central Intelligence Agency (CIA), from secretly cloaking some of their programs abroad in "dummy" foundations they created for that purpose or channeling monies through a few others for clandestine purposes. At the height of the Cold War in the 1960s and 1970s there appears to have been some activity of this type anent the USSR and its client countries in Central Europe. Overwhelming foundation sentiment against such practices, however, is reflected in the following observation by F. Emerson Andrews, who wrote extensively on philanthropy in general and foundations in particular and served for eleven years as the first head of the Foundation Center:

> I opposed the whole practice, and any cooperation with it by foundations or individuals. This was not on moralistic grounds—though for individuals this might be decisive—but on appraisal of total effects. Any strategic information which could be obtained by these means had to be weighed against the poison spread in foreign minds about all of our genuinely independent research, or our efforts to aid. Glib speeches supporting American views at foreign conferences would be heavily discounted when it was discovered that any of these delegates was government-paid.[4]

Regarding such developments and viewpoint, this author concluded:

> While it is apparently true that a few probably small foundations have been used as "cover" for operations of an intelligence nature (the recent Patman revelations of the C.I.A. / J.M. Kaplan Fund relationship is one example) … such operations appear to be miniscule relative to the overall activities of the larger foundations.[5]

Nevertheless, during the Cold War period many governmental officials in the USSR and many in Central Europe persisted in the belief that "foundations which operate programs in international affairs are merely disguised agencies of the United States government."[6] All of these factors, therefore, contributed to the lack of interest in and funding for programs in Central and Eastern Europe by major U.S. foundations throughout most of the earlier decades of the twentieth century.

In the 1960s and 1970s as the Cold War between the USSR and its communist satellite states heated up, however, there was increasing apprehension that it might lead to a nuclear holocaust that sane men on either side wanted to avoid. It was against this background and the inherent ideological distrust of the West on the Communist side that there gradually developed at the academic and higher educational level increasing contact between intellectuals from the Iron Curtain countries and the West who were acutely aware of this threat of nuclear war. Increasingly, particularly at meetings devoted to disciplines in the natural sciences and held in both regions, the distrust gradually weakened in the face of the nuclear war threat facing both sides. The result was a discernable thawing in the Cold War which was noticeable in both regions.

Although relatively little noticed at the time, a significant development in this rapprochement between East and West was the 1980s break in the monolithic Communist structure in the USSR that essentially had outlawed philanthropic organizations such as churches and foundations. Regarding the latter, some Kremlin leaders began to think favorably about establishing and operating them internally and/or their operating with funds provided from without. A major catalyst in this change regarding foundations was the conciliative efforts in the 1980s of two men: David A. Hamburg, president of the Carnegie Corporation of New York from 1983 to 1997; and Mikhail S. Gorbachev, Secretary-General of the Communist Party in the USSR from 1985 to 1991. In his first report as president titled "The Context for Carnegie Corporation's New Grant Program," Hamburg stated that its new program would be pursued under four new rubrics and the first one was the avoidance of nuclear war, i.e., a drive for peace. Detailing the specifics in this first rubric, he stated:

> The present moment in history is so decisive for the human future that the Corporation will work vigorously through its grants to increase the chances that good ideas for managing and preventing crises involving the risk of nuclear war will be subjected to constructive critical examination; it will try to engage the ablest and best-informed minds over a wide range of perspectives in generating new options; and it will work to build a broad public understanding of ways in which the risk of nuclear war can be diminished. The foundation will also explore possible contributions of the behavioral sciences to the conduct of negotiations, decision-making, and conflict resolution. Finally it will look at possibilities for fundamental, long-term change in the relationship between the United States and the Soviet Union.[7]

He concluded:

> Given the immense risks and costs of the nuclear arms race, is it at least conceivable that the basic relations between the two nations might change for the better in the decades ahead? If so, should somebody be thinking about ways to get from here to there and on what basis? At the moment, this is not a subject of widespread active inquiry. The Corporation will make a few grants to explore and delineate long-term possibilities for improving the basic U.S. Soviet relationship, taking into account their view of us as well as our view of them[8]

The Carnegie Corporation's annual reports for several years following are replete with grants made in furtherance of these goals. In 1985, for example, a grant was made to our National Academy of Sciences to further meetings between U.S. behavioral scientists and their counterparts in the Soviet Union addressing the prevention of nuclear war. From 1985 through 1989, grants for the same purpose, but employing differing means and personnel but again stressing joint U.S. Soviet participation, were made to the Rand Corporation, the International Research and

Exchanges Board, the Aspen Institute for Humanistic Studies together with those to such universities as Harvard, Columbia, and New York University. Meanwhile, in 1985 Mikhail Gorbachev became General Secretary of the Communist Party in the USSR. He worked to reform the Communist party and the government in general, encourage freedom of speech, and a resuscitation of the moribund state economic system through the introduction of a threefold program: *glasnost* ("openness"), *perestroika* ("restructuring "), and *uskorenie* ("acceleration"). From the foundation standpoint, this program represented a successful drive for the overturning of the previous restrictions against their creation and operation within the Soviet Union.

The culmination of these trailblazing efforts were meetings held in the USSR and a number of other countries in 1987-1988 attended by outstanding scientific, religious, and business leaders from within and without the USSR. The conferees in the latter year decided on the establishment in the Soviet Union of an International Foundation for the Survival and Development of Humanity[9] with its central office located in Moscow. All of this was carried on with the direct support and encouragement of Gorbachev, who said at a Moscow conference on the subject that such a foundation "would encourage research on the burning international issues and contribute toward drafting projects on the problems facing humanity…. We would welcome the active participation of the Soviet public—both material and intellectual—in the activities of such a fund."[10] The resultant foundation's board of directors consisted of thirty-one distinguished members from all over the world. With Hamburg serving as a principal advisor, its initial substantial funds of some several million dollars were provided by individuals and organizations from within and without the Soviet Union. Such endorsement and action was soon followed by the establishment of other foundations in the country. For example, an Ecological Foundation, under the auspices of the Soviet Academy of Sciences and the Philosophical Society was established in Moscow at about the same time.

The freedom, democratization, and economic reforms exemplified in the setting up of such foundations in the USSR were accompanied by other better known dramatic political, economic and social reforms within the USSR and many of them were copied in its satellite nations in Eastern and Central Europe. The cumulative effect of all of these reforms, however, quickly led directly to a series of revolutions in these Communist nations culminating in its most dramatic event: the destruction in 1989 of the wall dividing West and East Germany. The unleashing effect of these changes, moreover, led to largely unforeseen events inside the Soviet Union: the ending of the supremacy of the Communist Party; the 1991 destruction of the Union; and the formation of the new Commonwealth of Independent States. This was followed in the same year by Gorbachev's resignation as head of the former Soviet Union and his replacement, as the *de facto* leader of the Commonwealth, by Boris Yeltsin. Simultaneously, the International Foundation became one of the founding institutions of the Gorbachev Foundation in Russia with Gorbachev as its chief executive officer. In his writings, Gorbachev makes only passing reference to such foundations. Yet, it appears that it has been and continues to be a major interest of him and his wife.[11]

The 1990 and 1996 Carnegie Corporation reports, commenting on its program to avoid nuclear war and its role in these momentous changes, stated:

> Given the recent dramatic changes in East-West relations, the program will support efforts to consolidate and codify the gains that have been made and to identify new opportunities for institutionalizing U.S.-Soviet and multinational cooperation in the prevention of war and the resolution of conflicts.[12]

Upon Hamburg's retirement in 1997 as head of the Carnegie Corporation, he reminisced in an article entitled "A Perspective on Carnegie Corporation's Program, 1983-1997":

> Unforgettably, we had the privilege of linking Mikhail Gorbachev with Western experts during his crucially formative early years in office. In 1985 a remarkable new generation of leadership took control in the Soviet Union. Building on my contacts with leaders of the Soviet scientific community that led to an enduring relationship with Gorbachev, the Corporation launched a vigorous attempt to expand cooperative projects between its U.S. grantees and their Soviet counterparts. The Soviet scholars and analysts who were involved in these contacts included several who were key advisors to Gorbachev in the early years of his reform efforts.[13]

In 1999, Vartan Gregorian, Hamburg's successor as president of the Carnegie Corporation, announced a "New Directions for Carnegie Corporation of New York" which amounted to a cessation of this effort of the 1980s and 1990s and one centering more on domestic concerns such as libraries in the United States.[14]

In the 1980s-1990s a number of other larger U.S. foundations were making grants for much the same purposes as those of the Carnegie Corporation that undoubtedly contributed to the foregoing dramatic changes in Central and Eastern Europe. A 1988-1989 study of 171 foundations then active in the fields of peace, security, and international cooperation showed that they made grants totaling about $124 million, much of it centering on Central and Eastern Europe. Leaders were the John D. and Catherine T. MacArthur Foundation and the Ford Foundation with grants of about $20 million annually each with third ranked Carnegie Corporation of about $10 million.[15]

The largest foundation in devoted assets, range, and scope of its international activities in the period from the 1950s through the 1980s was, of course, the Ford Foundation. One of the very first grants by the foundation and, tactfully, the reasons for making it for the Central and Eastern European region was announced:

> Through the East European Fund the Foundation has tried to assist exiles from the Soviet Union to become established in this country, and to add to the store of knowledge concerning conditions within the Soviet Union and Eastern Europe. The Fund has also organized a publishing house, The Chekhov Publishing Company, which plans to print in Russian some of the classics of Russian and Western literature and other books by Russians that are not now available in the Russian language. In this way it is hoped that the Russian people may resume touch with the common spiritual and cultural heritage of the world.[16]

In the 1950s, however, it concentrated initially on the Middle East and Asia and then expanded its grantmaking to include South America and Africa. Supporting joint research and planning programs with the governments in these areas of the world that welcomed its activities, these programs resulted in increased food production and health, medical, and educational advances. A Ford Foundation staff member in the early 1980s summarized that:

> Gradually, the foundation's international interests expanded to virtually every region of the globe. At one point, the foundation maintained more than twenty field offices in the developing countries, each with resident staffs and an array of project specialists. Indeed, in many places the foundation was the major, if not exclusive, aid-giving agency. Among the foundation's special interests abroad were agriculture, education, strengthening government institutions, rural development, and language problems.[17]

She added that Ford Foundation aid had been extended to aid Hungarian refugees in the 1950s and scholarly exchange programs between the West and Eastern European countries was undertaken in 1957. In her chronological account of international activities since that period, however, there was no further mention or discussion of foundation involvement in Central and Eastern Europe.[18] In the 1987 annual report of the Ford Foundation, the Central and Eastern European areas came center stage and major grants were discussed for: security studies involving the Soviet Union, Europe, and the United States together with a grant for nuclear site inspection involving the Soviet Union and the United States. Another example, in the 1988 annual report it was announced that:

> A better understanding of the scientific and technical policies and practices in the countries of Eastern Europe is desirable in view of the recent expansion of U.S. cultural and commercial relations with that region. With the aid of a $200,000 grant, the National Academy of Sciences, in cooperation with its counterpart organizations in Eastern Europe, will convene nine bilateral workshops for the exchange of information on this subject [19]

By 1997 Susan V. Beresford, newly elected president of the Ford Foundation, announced that:

> the foundation then employed about 600 employees worldwide; that approximately 25% of the total was non-U.S. citizens; that overseas grants accounted for about 40% of its annual giving of approximately $430 million; and that giving was planned for international activities in approximately that percentage in the future. She added though that $15 million was to be made available to major American universities to strengthen their international studies and exchange of scholars programs.[20]

She pointedly noted that, in addition to maintaining sixteen field offices globally, the foundation had established its latest one in 1995 in Moscow, Russia.

In 1983 the new president, John Corbally, of the relatively new but impressively large John D. and Catherine T. MacArthur Foundation, announced that the foundation was joining the Carnegie Corporation of New York in contributing to the search for international security. In 1984 this was followed by his announcement of a commitment by the MacArthur Foundation of $25 million over a three year period for an International Security Program with particular emphasis on the Soviet and Central European areas. With name changes in following years to International Security and Peace Program (1985) and Program on Peace and International Cooperation (1986), its grants during the 1980s under this program paralleled those of the Carnegie Corporation. In 1993, the Foundation announced that during the period 1989-1993 it had authorized grants totaling about $95 million for these programs, much of it centered in Central and Eastern Europe.[21]

The Rockefeller Brothers Fund was also an early participant in the movement of U.S. foundations into Central and Eastern Europe. By 1982, its international grants formed a significant part of its overall program and, in that year, its president, William M. Dietel, announced "the addition of Arms Control/Security as a discrete category" in that program. He added that it was "an effort that will lead to more dramatic steps in the Fund's evolution in 1983 and following years."[22] Almost a decade later the Fund's then-president, Colin G. Campbell, observed that Poland, Hungary, and Czechoslovakia were "those countries where the bulk of the Fund's grants and technical assistance for the region had been directed since the mid-1980s."[23] The Fund's 1993 report stated:

> Since June 1984, the principal part of the Fund's grantmaking program has been organized about the theme of One World, with two major components: sustainable resource use and world security…. The major portion of grant funds are applied to the One World program. Projects are located, for the most part, in East Asia, East Central Europe, the former Soviet Union or the United States.[24]

Other of the larger foundations making grants devoted to the Central and Eastern European region in the 1980s and 1990s included the Andrew W. Mellon Foundation, the Pew Charitable Trusts, the Charles Stewart Mott Foundation, and the philanthropies of George Soros. As has been described earlier, up until the mid-1980s the largest geographic areas of concern and activity of the first three were centered primarily in the United States.

In 1983, against the background of the Cold War between the United States and the USSR/Eastern Europe satellite states, and disturbed by the United States' relative lack of knowledge of the latter, the Andrew W. Mellon Foundation announced it was appropriating over $4 million to strengthen a broad spectrum of academic and research programs on the Russian/Soviet and East European areas at U.S. universities and other organizations. Such support was continued in succeeding years in the 1980s in about the same amount annually. The dramatic changes that took place in the USSR/Eastern Europe in the closing years of that decade resulted in the foundation's employment of an additional staff member, Professor Richard E. Quandt, to oversee the foundation's activities there. In 1993, it was announced:

> Largely as a result of Professor Quandt's active engagement with certain systemic problems in Eastern Europe, and with key institutions and individuals there, the Foundation has now (through 1992) appropriated $20 million for programs and projects in the region; and we expect to appropriate an additional $12 million to $15 million by the end of 1994.[25]

There then followed a 17-page report by Professor Quandt on this program that was subsequently separately published. It provides a fine and succinct discussion of the rationale and scope of the Mellon Foundation efforts there. In many ways it is illustrative of the perspective of other U.S. foundations engaged in similar programs at that time. The late 1990s was the high point of Mellon Foundation activity in Eastern Europe and the remaining years in the 1990s were marked by the Foundation's gradual but continuing reduction in its commitments there.[26]

The 1988 appointment of Rebecca W. Rimel to the new post of executive director and her subsequent election in 1994 as president of the Pew Charitable Trusts marks a period of dramatic change in the areas of interest of the Trusts. As she announced in 1988:

> During 1988 we undertook a major, comprehensive evaluation of our programs and organizational structure, which has resulted in a new template that will better position the Trusts to serve the needs of our many constituencies in the years ahead.... The grantmaking of the Trusts has changed significantly in its programmatic focus, geographic distribution, and response to societal needs. These changes and growth require new approaches, strategies, and mechanisms.[27]

In 1994 the major transition in geographic area of interest that ensued during the period was described as follows:

> The program's new focus targeting countries engaged in dramatic economic, political and security changes reflected a double transition for the Public Policy program. The change shifted support *away* from U.S.-based research institutions, and *toward* practical training, technical assistance and policy-related research regarding transitions to market-oriented democracies.... Because of the historical magnitude of the changes taking place in Eastern Europe, we decided to focus our attention there.[28]

Although the Trust made grants in the millions of dollars in the region during this period that included significant ones, such as the aid for libraries provided in Czechoslovakia, by the end of the decade its program in Central and Eastern Europe had in large measure been discontinued. Significantly, in a short history of the Trusts published in 2001, the emphasis is upon earlier and later domestic and national funding and no mention is made of that for Central and Eastern Europe.[29]

Quite similar to the dramatic changes in foundation interest and advancement into the Central and Eastern European areas described above were those that occurred at the Charles Stewart Mott Foundation. They are dissimilar, however in point of time of origin and length of stay. Throughout the 1980s much of the foundation effort and programs was directed to the Flint, Michigan area where it had originated or to other states in the U.S. for replications of such programs there. For example, in 1981 and 1982 only a miniscule one-half of one percent of total money appropriated by the foundation was for international grants. In 1984 it announced laconically that it supported "programs across the United States and on a limited basis internationally." In 1988-1989 the upheavals in Central and Eastern Europe took place. In these same years two things happened at the Mott Foundation; in 1988 C.S. Harding Mott, the son of founder Charles Stewart Mott and chairman of the board of trustees, died. In 1989 the president of the foundation, William S. White, announced the election of two new non-family members to the board, both with strong global interests and one of them with "extensive knowledge of Eastern Europe and the Soviet Union." By 1994 announcement was made of a full fledged program for the region:

> The goal of grantmaking in this program area was *to help emerging civil societies in Central/Eastern Europe, Russia and the Republics in their transitions to open, democratic and pluralistic societies and strong market economies by strengthening the nonprofit sector and providing technical assistance and training to the public and private sectors....* Also, the Foundation established a field office in Prague, Czech Republic, in 1994. This program will evolve as the field office expands in 1995-1996.

By 1998, in addition to its own grantmaking in Central and Eastern Europe, President White lauded the benefit of cooperating or coordinating its grants in the area with those of other foundations. He stated:

> In that part of the world {Russia} we have many close partners including the Charities Aid Foundation in England, the Ford Foundation, the Eurasia Foundation, the John D. and Catherine T. MacArthur Foundation, the Open Society Institute, and various U.S. and European government programs. In our Central/Eastern Europe grantmaking, we have also partnered with the Rockefeller Brothers Fund, the German Marshall Fund, the European Cultural Foundation and the King Baudouin Foundation.

The 2002 Annual Report of the Mott Foundation was entitled "Staying the Course." It was noted therein that economic trends had:

> a significant impact on many Civil Society grantees. Nonprofits faced heightened competition for fewer resources as the assets of most foundations dropped. Furthermore, international grantees—most notably in Central/Eastern Europe-faced additional pressures, because some traditional funders refocused their giving in other regions or on different issues.[30]

Faced with these developments, the Mott Foundation reports show that it continued its program of aiding hundreds of nongovernmental and civil society organizations in the area with funds amounting to over $15 million annually.

Undoubtedly the largest and most spectacular of U.S. foundation funds expended in Central and Eastern Europe programs and projects were those provided by George Soros. Reasonable estimates are that his philanthropy accounts for one-third to one-half of all support provided by all U.S. foundations in Central and Eastern Europe. Much of these funds were expended through an Open Society Fund which he had set up in 1981-1982 for the general purpose of what he called the creation of "Open Societies." In a 1991 book dedicated "To the people of the Soviet Union and Eastern Europe whose aspirations I have supported,"[31] he succinctly provided the rationale for his efforts there and elsewhere.

> It is a widely held view that that the transformation from a totalitarian to a pluralistic [open] society must be accomplished by the people concerned and that any outside interference is not only inappropriate but probably counterproductive. This view is false. People who have been living in a totalitarian system all their lives may have the desire for an open society, but they lack the knowledge and experience necessary to bring it about. They need outside assistance to turn their aspirations into reality.[32]

As has been remarked earlier, his first successful project in providing such assistance was the establishment in 1983-1984 in his native Hungary of the Soros Foundation. It initially provided funds for the purchase and use of books and copiers and was a resounding success. With innovative variations, he was to follow a similar pattern in the Soviet Union and other countries in Central and Eastern Europe. This was followed in 1987 with the creation of a Soros Foundation in the USSR, at about the same time that the International Foundation for the Survival and Development of Humanity was being set up. By 1994, as will be shown below, if one totals the annual giving amounts for that year through the Open Society Fund with that appropriated for the Central European University, his giving totaled $48 million for the year. Later Soros lamented, however,

> By the end of 1996, I had established a network of nonprofit foundations in 25 countries, including the United States. When I started out, I gave little thought to the long-term implications of my engagement. Had I done so, I would probably have shied away from establishing such a network. I was then and I remain today extremely critical of philanthropic activities.[33]

Much of the U.S. foundation aid provided in Central and Eastern Europe was used to support and rehabilitate existing learned societies and academies[34] and similar institutions located there or to create new ones modeled after those in existence in the United States[35] and other countries of the world. Probably an equal amount of aid was provided to existing universities or, in an outstanding case by George Soros, a new one was created. He provided some $65 million from 1990-1995 for the creation of a brand new Central European University established in Budapest, Hungary. This was followed in succeeding years by his appropriation of more millions for its operation, culminating in his pledge of over $200 million to the University in July 2005. This support brought its total endowment to about $500 million and was, of course, a material factor in its universally recognized successful record on the European and world scene.

Varied U.S. foundation projects were continued for several decades all over Russia and other Central and Eastern European countries. Undoubtedly the major foundations discussed here, together with minor ones such as the Carnegie Endowment for International Peace which opened a Carnegie Moscow Center in 1993, were by far the main players in the region compared to that provided by European foundations and those from other countries such as Japan. They were carried on with a surprisingly small number of governmental objections or actions in the recipient countries. In 1996 a few members of the Russian Duma denounced all of the foundations then operating there, but particularly Soros', as engaged in diabolical projects to mold Russia in a variety of nefarious ways. The allegations were couched in much the same capitalistic exploitative terms as those advanced by Antonio Gramsci and others mentioned previously in the Preface herein. Other members of the Duma and the Russian Minister of Science defended the foreign aid, however, and nothing came of the matter.[36] Similar allegations and unsuccessful attempts to outlaw outside philanthropic aid were made by some officials in a few Central European countries. Still, a Soros foundation operating in Belarus, Russia was forced to shut down, largely on such grounds, by local officials.[37] Also, in the summer of 2005, Russian President Vladimir V. Putin criticized foreign nongovernmental organizations (NGOs) with offices located in Russia with allegations of engaging in political activity. Later in the year the Russian lower house of parliament voted restrictions on domestic and foreign charitable and other NGOs, including foundations. Such legislation required additional governmental legislation to be implemented, however, and has been strongly opposed both within and outside Russia on the grounds that the establishment and operation of NGOs there should be encouraged rather than restricted or outlawed.[38]

The projects in the 1980s of U.S. foundations concerned with Central and Eastern Europe were undoubtedly a factor in the political, economic, and social changes resulting in the eventual collapse of the Communist Party and control in the region. They were, of course, dwarfed by other factors ultimately causing that collapse. An even more important role of our foundations appears to be the one they played in the late 1980s and 1990s. Two studies in the 1990s conducted by the Foundation Center in cooperation with the Council on Foundations shows that there was a tremendous increase in the amount of money expended by some of the foregoing and other foundations in Central and Eastern Europe during that decade relative to other areas of the world. For example, during the period 1990-1994 the amount of money flowing to countries there reflected a percentage growth of 548%. While several other areas of the world, Latin America and sub-Saharan Africa, still received more foundation aid during the period, their four year percentage growth of 121% and 52% respectively was a great deal less than that going to Central and Eastern Europe.[39]

Undoubtedly one of the most significant accomplishments of the aid provided by U.S. foundations in the region was that which resulted in the creation of hundreds of NGOs. Organizations of this type, of course, have played a major role in the operation of a democratic/capitalistic society in the United States and Western Europe. Their duplication throughout Central and Eastern Europe in the last decades of the twentieth century appears to be providing solid underpinning for the accelerating creation of a similar group of such organizations there. A very recent article on this process, although dealing primarily with European foundations activities, stressed the importance of foundation funding in fostering the creation of NGOs in the region:

> Foreign foundations have been the major source of funding for innovative civil society activities. Their agendas were to assist the shift to democracy and market economies, rather than become a replacement of the socialist state. But due to the drastic decline in state budgets, many found themselves taking on quasi-state responsibilities in areas such as arts, culture and education. [40]

Conceding that "early efforts were not entirely successful…." the article concludes that: "The role of foundations continues to be an important part of the debate on the role of the state and its relationship with its people."The importance of these NGOs in maintaining peaceful, stable, and prosperous countries in Central and Eastern Europe has been emphasized in a recent work by David A. Hamburg. As he succinctly explains:

> As a dynamic element of democratic societies, NGOs provide a wide range of analysis, services, and advocacy for action on many matters of public concern. Recent technosocial changes have enlarged their opportunities. The rapid spread of information technology, market-driven economic interdependence, and cultural pluralism within and among states have allowed NGOs to become key conveyors of information, ideas, financial resources, and technical assistance…. A matter of particular importance for the international community is the cultivation of peace-and-democracy NGOs in fragile democracies, especially by linking them with counterparts in established democracies.[41]

The foregoing major role played by United States and other foundations in the setting up of NGOs in Central and Eastern Europe appears

to have led to another significant accomplishment. It was a major catalyst in the internationalization of several European foundations and the
emergence of several new international organizations.[42] The present day
Charities Aid Foundation (CAF) began in the 1920s as an organization
designed to aid other charities and foundations in the United Kingdom.[43]
From its base there, it began to expand its operations internationally in
the 1980s with the opening of an office in the United States. This has
been followed by the opening of similar ones in Russia, Bulgaria, India,
South Africa, and Australia. Internationally such CAF aid has included the
facilitating of cross-border giving by individuals, foundations, and corporations through the development and implementation of legal and other
mechanisms to make such giving feasible and possible.[44] The European
Foundation Centre (ECF) is another example of such internationalization.
It was originally set up in 1954 in Geneva, Switzerland as the European
Cultural Foundation. By the 1970s it had moved to Amsterdam, Neth-
erlands and was operating a network of funds and institutes in sixteen
European countries to promote European cooperation in a wide variety
of cultural and social fields. One of these funds had offices located in
Brussels, Belgium and it was there in 1989 that seven European foundations[45] organized the European Foundation Centre to promote the work of
foundations and similar bodies in Europe and worldwide. Its founding chief
executive, John Richardson, succeeded by Gerard Salole in September 2005,
made the development of philanthropy in Central and Eastern Europe and the
fostering of civil society organizations there a top priority during his tenure.
Under his leadership, the EFC expanded its publications program, broadened
its membership to some 500 core and other members, and is linked with
thousands of networking organizations in countries worldwide.

The creation of the present day international nongovernmental World
Alliance for Citizen Participation (CIVICUS) also appears to have been
due in large part to the eventful developments in Central and Eastern
Europe in the 1980s and 1990s. CIVICUS was preceded by several other
organizations with a somewhat similar purpose and agenda: a World
Congress on Philanthropy which became defunct in 1990 and an International Standing Committee on Philanthropy (INTERPHIL). Founded in
1969 in Geneva, Switzerland by the executives of a number of European
foundations, the headquarters of INTERPHIL was located there until a
move was made to London, England in 1972 where it remained until
moving back to Geneva in 1994. The following statements explained its
purpose, structure, and goals:

"INTERPHIL" is a combination of the two words "international" and "philanthropy" and is a synthesis of all that these words imply. It is established to promote the principles and practices of philanthropy and is a voluntary, nongovernmental, nonprofit association working for the good of the community.[46]

INTERPHIL promotes the development of civil society, and specifically the idea and practice of modern philanthropy, i.e., private giving for community purposes. It thus complements the actions of other international bodies which focus on voluntary work. Its concern extends to NGOs, foundations and charities, fund-raising, corporate giving, legislation, fiscal policy, information exchange, capacity building, institutional development, advocacy and international cooperation. It has individual as well as corporate members.[47]

By the 1990s, there was increasing dissatisfaction among nongovernmental and philanthropic leaders, both in the United States and abroad, with its continuing meager financial support and small staff, thus drastically limiting the scope and effectiveness of INTERPHIL. A 1990 article capsules this view:

Interphil's critics, including several financial supporters and long-time members, say the organization has lacked the compelling vision and strong direction needed to propel it to the philanthropic front lines. They wonder whether an organization that has struggled for years in relative obscurity and with scarce resources can emerge as a leader to help channel the energies now driving private voluntary efforts in Eastern Europe, the Soviet Union, Latin America, and elsewhere….

Interphil's mission—to promote the principles and practices of philanthropy worldwide—is a lofty one, but its more down to earth achievements have reflected its scant resources. The organization, which has several hundred individual and institutional members representing more that fifty countries, has sponsored several major international conferences on philanthropy, most recently in New York City last October. It has also convened smaller regional or specialty meetings on various topics, such as a gathering in Budapest last summer to discuss philanthropy in Eastern Europe.[48]

Failed attempts to rejuvenate the organization led to the founding of CIVICUS in 1993 in Barcelona, Spain. Leaders in its establishment included a number of U.S. foundation executives, such as William S. White, president of the Charles Stewart Mott Foundation, then playing a prominent role in foundation aid being provided to the national civil society entities in Central and Eastern Europe. A major goal of CIVICUS was the aiding and fostering of the growth of activist civic organizations in countries and regions which had discouraged their founding and growth in the past. The headquarters of CIVICUS was initially located in the U.S. in Washington, D.C. with financial support in excess of $2 million. Its first executive head was Miklos Marschall, a Hungarian.

He was succeeded in 1999 by Kumi Naido, a native of the Republic of South Africa, and the headquarters was then moved to Johannesburg in that country. Since its founding CIVICUS has compiled an impressive worldwide membership base, conducted bi-annual world congresses in various countries, and conducted a significant publishing program in carrying through on its goals.

In view of the significant increase in international concerns reflected in the foregoing changes, it comes as no surprise that the academic world took notice of the increasing internationalization of foundations and other civic and nonprofit organizations. A result was the founding of an International Research Society for Voluntary Associations, Nonprofit Organizations, and Philanthropy in 1992 in Indianapolis, Indiana. The unwieldy name was soon changed to a simpler and present International Society for Third Sector Research (ISTR). With a multi-national board of directors an inaugural conference was held in Pecs, Hungary in 1994 where a mission statement was drafted outlining its purpose of providing for and aiding research and teaching for those involved in philanthropy, especially at the international level. Its membership in excess of 600 has always included a significant number from outside the U.S. and its headquarters office is located in Baltimore, Maryland. ISTR has convened biennial conferences all over the world and has inaugurated a successful publication program.

The most recent addition to the list of international organizations in the philanthropic area is the International Meeting of Associations Serving Grantmakers. Its title aptly states its purpose and it was initially launched at a 1998 meeting in Oaxaca, Mexico of some eighty representatives from twenty-six countries as a means for bringing grantmakers and those actively associated with them together to view their increasingly global work.

In summary, the 1980s and 1990s activities of the larger U.S. foundations in Central and Eastern Europe played a significant role in the changes in the region's political, economic, and social structures. They then followed through with aid for the establishment of civic organizations to foster these changes and, finally, they were major players in the emergence of new organizations operating on a global scale to expedite their operations there and in the rest of the world.

Notes

1. Lyman C. White, *International Non-Governmental Organizations*. Rutgers University Press, New Brunswick, New Jersey, 1951, p. vii.
2. Akira Iriye, *Global Community, The Role of International Organizations in the Making of the Contemporary World*. University of California Press, Berkeley, California, 2002, p. 1.
3. Joseph C. Kiger, "Foundations and International Affairs," *Foundation News*. Vol. VI, No. 4, July, 1965, p. 67.
4. F. Emerson Andrews, *Foundation Watcher.* Franklin and Marshall College, Lancaster, Pennsylvania, 1973, p. 202.
5. Joseph C. Kiger, "Foundations and International Affairs," *Foundation News*. Vol. VI, No. 4, July, 1965, p. 68.
6. Ibid., p. 67.
7. Carnegie Corporation of New York, *Annual Report,* 1983, p. 5.
8. Ibid., p. 10.
9. For a brief history of this foundation at the time of its inception, see Joseph C. Kiger (ed.), "International Foundation for the Survival and Development of Humanity," *International Encyclopedia of Foundations,* Greenwood Press, Westport, Connecticut, 1990, pp. 237-238.
10. Information Pamphlet, *The International Foundation for the Survival and Development of Humanity.*
11. The Gorbachev Foundation's web site http://www.gorby.ri/ provides information in Russian and English about its history, Gorbachev's relationship to it, and its programs and activities since its founding.
12. Carnegie Corporation of New York, *Annual Report.* 1990, p. 77.
13. Carnegie Corporation of New York, *Annual Report,* 1996, p. 23.
14. Carnegie Corporation of New York, *Annual Report,* 1999.
15. Anne Ellen, (ed.), *Search for Security: The ACCESS guide to Foundations in Peace, Security, and International Relations.* ACCESS, Washington, D.C., 1989, pp. 11, 38, 51, 81.
16. Ford Foundation, *Annual Report,* 1951, p. 12.
17. Oona Sullivan, "The Ford Foundation," in Keele and Kiger, (eds.) *Foundations.* Greenwood Press, Westport, Connecticut, 1984, p. 129.
18. Ibid., pp. 129-135.
19. Ford Foundation, *Annual Report,* 1988, p. 143.
20. Joseph C. Kiger, *Philanthropic Foundations in the Twentieth Century,* p. 138.
21. John D. and Catherine T. MacArthur Foundation, *Annual Reports,* 1983, p. 3; 1984, p. 4; 1985, p. 4; 1986, pp. 12-14; 1987, p. 5; 1993, p. 6.
22. Rockefeller Brothers Fund, *Annual Report,* 1982, p. 7.
23. Rockefeller Brothers Fund, *Annual Report,* 1991, p. 7. For a detailed account of the Fund and other foundation aid for the region and its effect, see Daniel Siegel and Jenny Yancey, *The Rebirth of Civil Society: The Development of the Non profit Sector in East Central Europe and the Role of Western Assistance.* Rockefeller Brothers Fund, New York, 1992.
24. Rockefeller Brothers Fund, *Annual Report,* 1993, p. 15.
25. Andrew W. Mellon Foundation, *Annual Report.* p. 17.
26. Andrew W. Mellon Foundation, *Annual Reports,* 1983, p. 17; 1987, p. 37; 1989, p. 19; 1993, p. 8; 1993, pp. 17-33; 1994, p. 13; 1995, p. 14; 1996, p. 23.
27. Pew Charitable Trusts, *Annual Report,* 1988, p. 14.
28. Pew Charitable Trusts, *Annual Report,* 1994, p. 27.

29. Joel R. Gardner, *Sustaining the Legacy: A History of the Pew Charitable Trusts,*
     Pew Charitable Trusts, Philadelphia, Pennsylvania, 2001.
30. Charles Stewart Mott Foundation, *Annual Reports,* 1981, p. 9; 1982, p. 9; 1984,
     p. 3; 1989, p. 9; 1990, p. 9; 1994, p. 44;
31. George Soros, *Underwriting Democracy,* The Free Press, New York, 1991, vi.
32. Ibid., pp. 64-65.
33. Soros Foundation Network, *1996 Report,* 1996, p. 14.
34. For brief histories of organizations of this type located in Central and Eastern
     Europe, see Joseph C. Kiger (ed.), *International Encyclopedia of Learned Societies
     and Academies,* Greenwood Press, Westport, Connecticut, 1993.
35. For brief histories of organizations of this type located in the United States, see
     Joseph C. Kiger, *Research Institutions and Learned Societies,* Greenwood Press,
     Westport, Connecticut, 1982.
36. See Aryeh Neier, "Foundations Under Attack," *Open Society News,* Open Society
     Institute, New York, Fall 1995/Winter 1996, pp. 14-15.
37. Michael T. Kaufman, *Soros,* pp. 298-299.
38. Steven Myers, " Kremlin Pushes Measure to Curb Private Groups," *New York
     Times,* November 24, 2005.
39. Loren Renz, Josefina Atienza, et.al. , *International Grantmaking: A Report on U.S.
     Foundations Trends.* Foundation Center, New York, 1997. Loren Renz, Josefina
     Atienza, et.al., *International Grantmaking II : An Update on U.S. Foundation
     Trends.* Foundation Center, New York, 2000, See also, Loren Renz, " International
     Grant Making by U.S. Foundations: Issues and Directions in the 1990s," *Nonprofit
     and Voluntary Sector Quarterly,* 27, no.4 (December 1998), pp. 507-521.
40. Frances Pinter "The Role of Foundations in the Transformation Process of Central
     and Eastern Europe," in Andreas Schluter, Volker Then, and Peter Walkenhorst
     (eds.), *Foundations in Europe: Society, Management , and La .* Directory of Social
     Change, London, 2001, pp. 316-317.
41. David A. Hamburg, *No More Killing Fields; Preventing Deadly Conflicts.* 2nd
     edition. Rowman @Littlefield Publishers, Inc., Lanham, Maryland, 2004, p. 88.
42. For a detailed discussion of foreign/international foundation organizations, see
     Joseph C. Kiger, *Philanthropic Foundations in the Twentieth Century,* pp. 145-
     165.
43. For a more detailed history of the earlier years of CAF, see Joseph C. Kiger
     (ed.), "Charities Aid Foundation," *International Encyclopedia of Foundations,"*
     Greenwood Press, Westport, Connecticut, 1990, pp. 248-250.
44. Cathy Pharoah, Michael Brophy, and Paddy Ross, "Promoting International
     Philanthropy through Foundations," in Andreas Schluter, Volker Then, and Peter
     Walkenhorst (eds.), *Foundations in Europe: Society, Management, and Law.*
     Directory of Social Change, London, 2001, pp. 587-601.
45. The founding members of EFC were: Charities Aid Foundation (United Kingdom),
     European Cultural Fund, (Netherlands), Fondation de France (France), Fundacao
     Oriente (Portugal), Juliana Weizijn Fonds (Netherlands), King Baudouin Founda-
     tion (Belgium), and Stifterverband fur die Deutsche Wissenschaft (Germany).
46. *Philanthropy International,* INTERPHIL, Geneva Switzerland, April 1994, p. 8.
47. "What is INTERPHIL?" INTERPHIL, Geneva, Switzerland, October, 1994, p. 1.
48. Stephen G. Greene, "Interphil Group Eyed as Potential Leader of World Philan-
     thropy," *The Chronicle of Philanthropy,* January 8, 1990, p. 5.

7

Conclusion

From the Civil War to the present, the twenty-four philanthropists who amassed the wealth forming the basis for the some fifty larger foundations they, or in some cases succeeding family members, established have been discussed historically and biographically in Chapters 1, 2, 4, and 5. Also discussed therein have been the initial purpose and activities of these foundations established during that period, counting as well the approximately fifty set up by George Soros under one Open Society Institute cognomen. With the exception of the previously noted Russell Sage Foundation, which restricted its operations to domestic giving, these fifty foundations comprise our larger foundations that, at their inception or since, have engaged in global grantmaking and activities.

As was stated in the Preface, Chapter 6 was written to give historical accounts of the international activity of a few of these foundations in a particular region in a specific time period and the accomplishments accruing therefrom. It provides revealing examples of when and how some of these foundations' trustees and staff became interested and willing to embark upon a 180-degree change in their scope and areas of operation in a relatively short period of time in response to rapidly changing international political and economic conditions.

Chronicled in Chapter 3 are the some twenty major private and public studies and investigations, domestic and foreign, carried on during the period; ranging from those involving one or a few individuals to those involving hundreds. They probably provide a unique reflective public position on overseas spending by U.S. foundations. There follows an analysis derived from this section that forms the basis for the resulting conclusion made in this chapter.

Depending upon one's classification of a foundation and depending upon what constitutes foreign activity, there appear to be about as many foundations with assets comparable to those studied herein that confine a large portion of their grantmaking to programs in the United States. Large and well known examples are the Lilly Endowment, recent assets about $11 billion, that limits just over half of its grants to the state of Indiana; the Duke Endowment, recent assets about $2.3 billion, that makes the preponderance of its grants in North and South Carolina; and the Robert Wood Johnson Foundation, recent assets about $8 billion, that focuses its grants on health issues in the United States.

Most of the fifty foundations studied were established by men. Some of these men were immigrants, some were not; some were short, some were tall; some were happily married, some were unhappily married or not at all. Such comparisons, of a physical or social nature, become endless if one really starts drawing them. Approaching the matter from another way, there are only a few instances where such differences cannot be drawn. The assets, which made possible their founding and operation, were initially acquired by white males, except for Mrs. Sage, in the nineteenth and twentieth centuries. With a few exceptions, they were of North European descent and Protestant religious background. A few were basically self-taught, Andrew Carnegie being the outstanding example; the remainder had some solid secondary or technical educational grounding or in many cases they attended and in some cases graduated from higher educational institutions.

Some exceptions to founders having acquired their own fortunes, as in the case of five familial foundation principals, Sage, Harkness, Mellon, Tinker, Pew, and the second and succeeding generation Rockefellers, who established foundations based on inherited wealth. To this number the second and third generation Fords can be added. The rest, again with the exception of Mrs. Sage, were founded by the men who made the money. The primary economic/business endeavors, spanning some dozen different means, that produced the wealth which formed the corpus for the foundations they established included:

- Banking: Peabody, Mellon
- General Business and Real Estate: Sage, Tinker
- Iron and Steel Manufacture: Carnegie
- Oil and Gas: Rockefeller, Harkness, Jones, Pew
- Mining: Guggenheim: Markle
- Automotive: Mott, Ford
- Food: Kellogg
- Gambling and Entertainment: Kerkorian
- Insurance: Starr, MacArthur
- Computers: Packard, Hewlett, Gates

- Currency Trading: Soros
- Stock Trading: Templeton
- Journalism and Advertising: Luce, Turner

From the Civil War to the present, the increasing globalization of transportation, communication, and education impinged on all business activity. With a few possible exceptions, such as Markle and Kerkorian, it is clear that, beginning with Peabody and extending on down to Gates, most of these men made a significant part of their fortunes as the result of international dealings in a variety of business endeavors. Prominent early examples include Rockefeller in petroleum and Carnegie in steel; more recent ones are Hewlett, Packard and Gates in computers.

The geographical base of most of our larger earlier foundations was the northeast section of the United States. Today, however, the later ones are widely dispersed in other sections of the country. Similarly, our twenty-four philanthropists and the approximately fifty foundations they, or their heirs, established show a more diverse geographical base particularly since World War II. The outstanding example of this change is the present day location of the computer business behemoth, Microsoft, created by Bill Gates and his establishment of the Bill and Melinda Gates Foundation, the U.S. foundation with the largest assets (over $28 billion) in the United States and the world, in the far western state of Washington.

Consideration of the initial members of the boards of trustees and staff of these foundations shows that in the main they consisted of the donor, members of his family, and friends and business associates. Exceptions were those founded and located abroad, such as the ones founded earlier by Carnegie, later ones by Harkness and Mellon in the United Kingdom, and some by George Soros. With the passage of time, most of the foundations saw a gradual increase in the number of non-family members serving on the boards of trustees, though in many cases, family members still constituted a controlling majority. In some few instances, for example the David and Lucile Packard Foundation, provisions were installed in pertinent legal instruments to ensure such family continuance of control. On the other hand, John D. MacArthur's pithy remarks, "I made the money, you fellows (trustees) will have to decide how to spend it," made in connection with his founding of the John D. and Catherine T. MacArthur Foundation, imply that he was steering control away from family members.

Only a few of the approximately fifty foundations did not engage in significant foreign activity at their beginnings. In the case of the John Simon Guggenheim Memorial Foundation and the Rockefeller Brothers Fund such activity was inaugurated soon after they were founded and was engineered by the philanthropic donors themselves. In the case of the Ford Foundation, established primarily by a second generation Ford in the 1930s, such a change was wrought by third generation Henry Ford II following World War II. The Charles Stewart Mott Foundation, Pew Charitable Trusts, and W. Alton Jones Foundation were launched internationally by the heirs of the original philanthropists serving later in various capacities on the boards of trustees of these three foundations. The dramatic change to an international agenda on the part of the first two has been described in some detail in Chapter 6. The heirs controlling the W. Alton Jones Foundation have recently trifurcated it into different foundations and now one of them appears to be confining its activities to the United States. John and Mary R. Markle established the foundation bearing their name and died in the early 1930s without heirs. Their foundation became active in the foreign area by the action of succeeding trustees and staff. The death in 1978 of the founder of the John D. and Catherine T. MacArthur Foundation was followed in a few years by the death of his wife and son. Similarly, succeeding trustees and staff of this foundation ushered in its foreign programs. Regardless of when such foreign activity was launched, it invariably resulted in an initial and continuing surge in the number of staff members employed by a foundation.

The foregoing analysis brings us to the question as to what motivated these philanthropists to establish these foundations, and subsequently their heirs to continue on the path charted at their founding or to change their course. Associated with the answer to this question one encounters individual and group criticism of U.S. foundations. Implicit or in some cases explicit in such criticism is the belief that the founders had other motives in creating them than the beneficent ones usually claimed by them. Such critical views of philanthropists and their foundations by individuals appear to be, when boiled down, that the foundations criticized should expend their funds on projects the critics deem worthy. In other words, if we were in charge of your giving we would do thus ... rather than what was decided upon by the philanthropist and trustees and staff of the foundations. Examples range from the individual earlier criticisms of William Lloyd Garrison and Bishop Warren A. Candler to the later ones of Pablo Eisenberg and Henry Ford II. More serious charges are that foundations have been used as devices by those who establish and control them to siphon off foundation tax-exempt funds for their benefit rather than the charitable purposes for which they were established. Such charges have been periodically leveled by journalists. Damaging examples of the latter are the recent exposes of the *Boston Globe* wherein individuals made lavish expenditures for their own benefit from the funds of foundations they controlled. A serious example charged that Paul C. Cabot, Jr., the head of the Cabot Foundation, had among other alleged irregularities, financed the $300,000 costs of his daughter's wedding with salary increases for himself paid to him by his foundation.[1] Such revelations have led many informed observers to believe that the U.S Internal Revenue Service, charged with the major governmental oversight of foundations, has been both inattentive and weak in carrying out its duties. They also believe that, because of financial and structural impediments, it has and will prove impossible to rectify the workings of the IRS in this regard. They have advocated the adoption of English practices in the philanthropic area. In particular, they have urged the creation of a supervisory agency, similar to England's Charity Commission. In the 1970s deliberations of the Filer Commission, such views were considered and favored by a minority but ultimately rejected by a majority of the members of the Commission.

Over the years individuals and participants in a number of other organized studies and investigations, presented in Chapter 3, have advanced more specific and selfish motives and reasons for their establishment and operation. The transfer of economic power to descendants was advanced as a major reason for their creation. Doubtless the economic protection of descendants, as a universal desire, has played a role in many cases. As this writer wrote years ago, however, to ascribe such motives to those establishing foundations one must visualize them:

> as the Machiavellian creation of far-sighted men attempting to pass or transfer economic and concomitant political and social power. The question arises: to whom were they attempting to transfer it and for what purpose? Certainly, some of the children of donors are still included among Boards of Trustees, but that is not a satisfactory answer since many had no [or a very few] children.... To ascribe a desire to mold the future in a conservative or liberal shape, as a reason for creation [of foundations] gets one off on a tortuous road that can end where one wills.[2]

Closely aligned with this line of reasoning are the criticisms advanced by those accepting, to a greater or lesser degree, Antonio Gramsci's Marxist interpretations referred to in the Preface. Doctrinarily, the larger foundations operating domestically are instruments of capitalistic exploitation; operating internationally they are doing the same thing abroad. A reverse of this approach was the one advanced at the birth of the Cox Committee but rejected in its 1953 final report, but then subsequently embraced in large measure by that of the 1954 Reece Committee. In this interpretation, the larger foundations at their inception, or more likely under the later influence of leftist trustees and staff, have engaged domestically and internationally in the undermining of the Western capitalistic economic/political system, i.e., working to change it to a Communist/socialist one. The final report of the Cox Committee in its refutation stated:

> It seems paradoxical that in a previous congressional investigation in 1915 the fear most frequently expressed was that the foundations would prove the instruments of wealth, privilege, and reaction, while today the fear most frequently expressed is that they have become the enemy of the capitalistic system. In our opinion neither of these fears is justified.[3]

The Cox Committee concluded, in its review of foreign activities by U.S. foundations, that "The committee believes that these international activities and foreign expenditures of the foundations are motivated chiefly by consideration of the welfare of the American people and as such are entirely praiseworthy."[4] The Reece Committee stated: "*Foreign Use of Foundation Funds.* In this area the Committee has not been able to do sufficient study to come to a final evaluation." It followed this with the "suggestion tentatively and subject to further investigation" of a ten-percent limit on foreign expenditures by foundations but then followed with a vague statement that exceptions might be made in the case of religious or other organizations.[5]

Turning back to the earlier (1915) work of the Walsh Commission and later (1961-1972) Patman Committees, in both cases criticism of motivations for the establishment of foundations is couched in economic rather than ideological terms. In both instances objections were raised to the use of foundation funds for foreign activities. In testimony provided the Walsh Commission, several labor leaders were the strongest opponents of such giving. They expressed the view that such foundation funds were siphoned off from the workers who had produced the excess. In other words, increased wages should rightfully have been afforded the workers rather than such moneys being expended abroad. Congressman Wright Patman's major criticism was that foundations were instruments used to evade taxes and gave their creators unfair advantages in the business arena. Regarding foreign giving by foundations, Congressman Patman simply advanced the belief that foundation funds were better spent domestically rather than abroad. No recommendations were made by either the Walsh Commission or the Patman Committees, however, that restrictions be placed on such giving. Subsequently the revisions made in the U.S. tax legislation in 1969, although tightening the laws under which foundations operate, carried no penalty or restrictions directed solely at U.S. foundations' foreign operations.

The foregoing analysis and the biographic/historical accounts presented herein provide ample evidence that a very wide array and mixture of motives, other than the dynastic, the left or right politico/social interpretive ones, or the nefarious economic ones alleged, were at work in the minds of philanthropists creating these foundations. An overriding motive on the disposition of many appears to be the amelioration of the effects of and prevention of war. But there are many others: medical and health advances, religious motives, memorialization, native son interest, efficiency in giving, taxation, among other reasons. Various of these same motives appear to have been present at the initial or later globalization projects of these foundations. Some of them, as has been related, were set up with specific titles and spelled out purposes embodying such motives; for example the Carnegie Endowment for International Peace. In this connection, often clearly stated as in the case of Carnegie, aid provided during the prosecution of a war, relief following a war, and the drive for a peaceful world, are three interrelated and major motives. The first two are generally charitable in nature and the last, generally philanthropic. These threefold and intertwined motives are clearly apparent at the time of the creation of many of our larger foundations from the late nineteenth and early twentieth centuries and persist and assume even more importance with those created or revamped since that time up to the present. The movement of some of our foundations into Central and Eastern Europe, as discussed in Chapter 6, is a telling example of this process.

Carrying out the initial or later mandates, it comes as no surprise that foundation officials engaged in global activity have uniformly advanced beneficent reasons for it. For example, then president of the Ford Foundation, Henry T. Heald, in 1963 gave one of the best succinct justifications for its global activities:

> First, that the resolution of our domestic problems would be a hollow victory if two-thirds of the world continued to be racked by deprivation and unrest.
>
> Second, that the Foundation has sufficient resources to make a significant contribution to overseas development. (The overwhelming majority of American founda-

tions confine their activities to the United States and in most cases lack the funds for meaningful assistance overseas.)

Third, as a private institution the Foundation has certain advantages of independence, flexibility, selectivity, and perseverance in its assistance abroad.[6]

On balance, this writer concludes that the overriding term that can be used to describe both the philanthropists and their heirs together with the globally active foundations they established is: *diversity*. This includes the fact that those considered here, and indeed most of the larger foundations in the United States, as individual units, have consciously and successfully diversified the present day makeup of their boards of trustees and staff.[7] Though not with diversity as a goal, foundations operating globally have diversified their physical operating locations and the staff direction of their varied projects. Overall they are so diverse in all respects that they present an infeasible target for their critics, informed or not, of whatever persuasion. Such critics have certainly not been able to convince the regulatory authorities with their arguments. The persuasive conclusion is, therefore, that it is this *diversity* on almost all counts that has been the key to their beneficial operations, nationally and internationally, and also accounts for the continued absence of punitive measures directed at them toward the curtailing or restricting of their freedom of action on the global stage. It is probably one of the most important factors in their emergence today as a most respected institution, both in this country and globally.

Notes

1. "Some officers of charities steer assets to selves," *Boston Globe*, October 9, 2003, p. 1, A42; see also, November 9, 2003, pp. A26-A27.
2. Joseph C. Kiger, *Operating Principles of the Larger Foundations*, Russell Sage Foundation, New York, 1954.
3. *Final Report of the Select Committee to Investigate Foundations and Other Organizations*, p. 10.
4. Ibid., p. 12.
5. *Report of the Special Committee to Investigate Foundations and Comparable Organizations,* p. 220.
6. Ford Foundation, *Annual Report,* 1963. pp. 2-3.
7. For a detailed discussion of this change, see Joseph C. Kiger, *Philanthropic Foundations in the Twentieth Century.* Chapter V, "Personnel Diversification," pp. 83-100.

Index